Edvard Munch

Between the Clock and the Bed

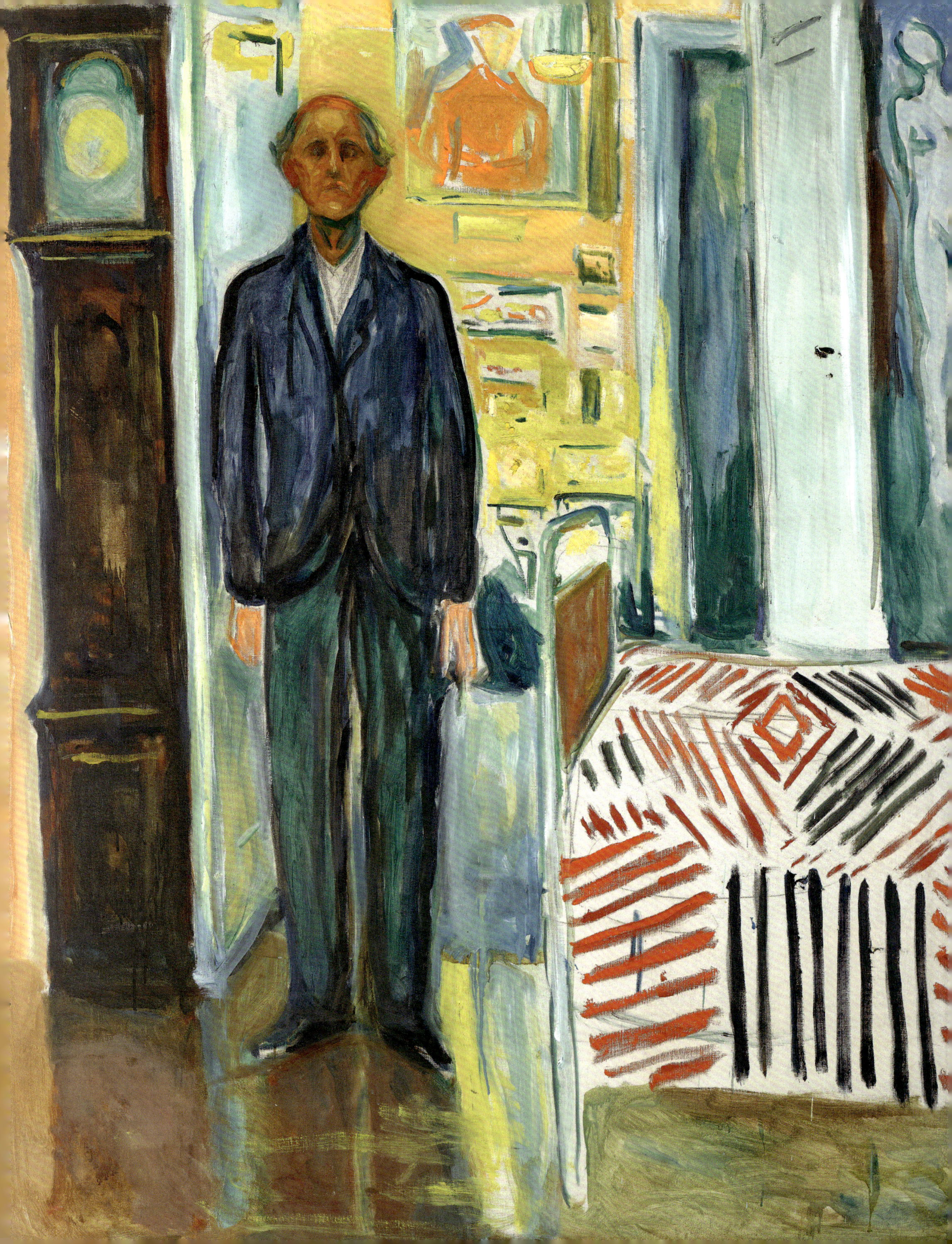

EDITED BY

Gary Garrels, Jon-Ove Steihaug,
and Sheena Wagstaff

PREFACE BY

Karl Ove Knausgaard

ESSAYS BY

Patricia G. Berman, Allison Morehead,
Richard Shiff, and Mille Stein

Edvard Munch

Between the Clock and the Bed

THE MET

The Metropolitan Museum of Art, New York
Distributed by Yale University Press, New Haven and London

This catalogue is published in conjunction with "Edvard Munch: Between the Clock and the Bed," on view at the San Francisco Museum of Modern Art from June 24 through October 9, 2017; The Metropolitan Museum of Art, New York, from November 14, 2017, through February 4, 2018; and the Munch Museum, Oslo, from May 12 through September 9, 2018.

At the San Francisco Museum of Modern Art, the exhibition is made possible by Charles Schwab & Co., Inc., The Bernard Osher Foundation, Jacqueline Evans, Linda and Jon Gruber, Franklin and Catherine Johnson, Christine and Pierre Lamond, Diana Nelson and John Atwater, Shannon and Dennis Wong, the Norwegian-American Cultural Foundation, and the Federal Council on the Arts and the Humanities.

At The Met, the exhibition is made possible by Leonard A. Lauder.

At the Munch Museum, the exhibition is made possible by Idemitsu Petroleum Norge and Viking Cruises.

The exhibition is organized by the San Francisco Museum of Modern Art, The Metropolitan Museum of Art, and the Munch Museum.

This publication is made possible by The Andrew W. Mellon Foundation.

Published by The Metropolitan Museum of Art, New York
Mark Polizzotti, Publisher and Editor in Chief
Gwen Roginsky, Associate Publisher and General Manager of Publications
Peter Antony, Chief Production Manager
Michael Sittenfeld, Senior Managing Editor

Edited by Margaret Donovan
Production by Paul Booth
Designed by Roy Brooks
Bibliography edited by Ellen Hurst
Image acquisitions and permissions by Josephine Rodriguez-Massop
Translation of Knausgaard Preface: Kari Dickson

Typeset in Bodoni and Vendetta
Printed on 150 gsm Perigord
Separations by Professional Graphics, Inc., Rockford, Illinois
Printed and bound by Conti Tipocolor, S.p.A., Florence, Italy

Cover illustrations: front: Edvard Munch, *Self-Portrait: Between the Clock and the Bed*, 1940–43, Munch Museum, Oslo (pl. 51, detail); back: Edvard Munch, *Self-Portrait with Cigarette*, 1895, Nasjonalmuseet for Kunst, Arkitektur og Design, Oslo (pl. 16, detail)

Frontispiece: Edvard Munch, *Self-Portrait: Between the Clock and the Bed*, 1940–43, Munch Museum, Oslo (pl. 51, detail)

First printing

The Metropolitan Museum of Art
1000 Fifth Avenue
New York, New York 10028
metmuseum.org

Distributed by Yale University Press, New Haven and London
yalebooks.com/art | yalebooks.co.uk

Library of Congress Cataloging-in-Publication Data
Names: Garrels, Gary, editor. | Steihaug, Jon-Ove, editor. | Wagstaff, Sheena, editor. | Knausgaard, Karl Ove, 1968- writer of preface. | Berman, Patricia G., writer of supplementary textual content. | Morehead, Allison, writer of supplementary textual content. | Shiff, Richard, writer of supplementary textual content. | Stein, Mille, writer of supplementary textual content. | Munch, Edvard, 1863-1944. Paintings. Selections. | San Francisco Museum of Modern Art, host institution. | Metropolitan Museum of Art (New York, N.Y.), host institution, issuing body. | Munch-museet (Oslo, Norway), host institution.
Title: Edvard Munch : Between the clock and the bed / edited by Gary Garrels, Jon-Ove Steihaug, and Sheena Wagstaff ; preface by Karl Ove Knausgaard; essays by Patricia G. Berman, Allison Morehead, Richard Shiff, and Mille Stein.
Other titles: Edvard Munch (2017)
Description: New York : Metropolitan Museum of Art, [2017] | This catalogue is published in conjunction with "Edvard Munch: Between the Clock and the Bed," on view at the San Francisco Museum of Modern Art from June 24 through October 9, 2017; the Metropolitan Museum of Art, New York, from November 14, 2017, through February 4, 2018; and the Munch Museum, Oslo, from May 12 through September 9, 2018. | Includes bibliographical references and index.
Identifiers: LCCN 2017012250 | ISBN 9781588396235 (hardcover)
Subjects: LCSH: Munch, Edvard, 1863-1944—Themes, motives—Exhibitions. | Munch, Edvard, 1863-1944. Self-portrait between the clock and the bed—Exhibitions. | Art and mental illness—Exhibitions.
Classification: LCC ND773.M8 A4 2017 | DDC 759.81—dc23
LC record available at https://lccn.loc.gov/2017012250

Contents

Directors' Foreword

The Norwegian artist Edvard Munch, whose work explores themes of love, death, social isolation, and psychic pain, is so closely associated with the artistic revolutions of the symbolist era that the latter part of his career is often overlooked. This exhibition began as a conversation between Gary Garrels, Elise S. Haas Senior Curator of Painting and Sculpture at the San Francisco Museum of Art (SFMOMA), and Sheena Wagstaff, Leonard A. Lauder Chairman of the Department of Modern and Contemporary Art at The Metropolitan Museum of Art, about the importance of Munch's late career and his continuing influence on many contemporary artists. They presented their proposal for an exhibition to Jon-Ove Steihaug, Director of Exhibitions and Collections at the Munch Museum, who embraced it enthusiastically and, along with Caitlin Haskell, Associate Curator of Painting and Sculpture at SFMOMA, and Sabine Rewald, Jacques and Natasha Gelman Curator for Modern Art at The Metropolitan Museum of Art, became a partner in developing this idea into an exhibition.

The point of departure for this fresh examination of Munch's work is his last significant self-portrait (1940–43), a powerful meditation on art, mortality, and the ravages of time. As the authors of this catalogue demonstrate, Munch was an astonishingly accomplished painter who grappled with themes of enduring importance to modernity. *Edvard Munch: Between the Clock and the Bed* addresses the myths surrounding the artist by bringing together early and late works and showing that he returned to earlier motifs with renewed intensity throughout his career, all the while inventing new ways of painting into the 1910s, 1920s, and 1930s. For the loan of these extraordinary artworks, many of them treasures from their home institutions and from private homes, we are profoundly grateful.

One of the pleasures of leading a museum is the opportunity to collaborate with esteemed cultural institutions. *Edvard Munch: Between the Clock and the Bed* is organized by SFMOMA, The Metropolitan Museum of Art, and the Munch Museum, Oslo.

We are also grateful to all our colleagues — from Oslo to New York to San Francisco — for enabling us to bring Munch's work to new audiences and for their fruitful partnership in creating this beautiful catalogue.

We acknowledge the generosity of our sponsors at all three venues: At SFMOMA, we extend our gratitude to Charles Schwab & Co., Inc., The Bernard Osher Foundation, Jacqueline Evans, Linda and Jon Gruber, Franklin and Catherine Johnson, Christine and Pierre Lamond, Diana Nelson and John Atwater, Shannon and Dennis Wong, and the Norwegian-American Cultural Foundation for their commitment to the exhibition in San Francisco. We also thank the Federal Council on the Arts and the Humanities for its vital indemnity support and the Royal Norwegian Consulate General in San Francisco for underwriting Richard Shiff's travel to Oslo for research. At The Metropolitan Museum of Art, we send our deepest thanks to Leonard A. Lauder for his leadership support in realizing this remarkable project and for his long-standing commitment to the Museum's modern and contemporary art program. At the Munch Museum, we thank sponsors Idemitsu Petroleum Norge and Viking Cruises for their vital role in making possible the exhibition in Oslo. We also applaud The Andrew W. Mellon Foundation for its essential support of the catalogue.

Neal Benezra
Helen and Charles Schwab Director
San Francisco Museum of Modern Art

Thomas P. Campbell
Director
The Metropolitan Museum of Art, New York

Stein Olav Henrichsen
Director
Munch Museum, Oslo

Acknowledgments

Edvard Munch: Between the Clock and the Bed is the result of close collaboration between our three institutions. For their unwavering support and enthusiasm, we are most grateful to Neal Benezra, Helen and Charles Schwab Director of the San Francisco Museum of Modern Art (SFMOMA); Thomas P. Campbell, Director of The Metropolitan Museum of Art; and Stein Olav Henrichsen, Director of the Munch Museum.

Our project was largely made possible by the generosity of the Munch Museum, which has provided more than half the paintings in the exhibition, many of them deeply personal works from the artist's own collection. Jon-Ove Steihaug, Director of Exhibitions and Collections at the Munch Museum, offered countless varieties of help and advice.

We are grateful for the support of colleagues at several distinguished national and international institutions. First and foremost, our thanks goes out to many kind friends in Norway, including Audun Eckhoff and Nils Ohlsen at the Nasjonalmuseet for Kunst, Arkitektur og Design, Oslo; and Karin Hindsbo, Line Daatland, and Knut Ormhaug at the KODE Kunstmuseene i Bergen. We also owe a debt of gratitude for the support of Patrik Steorn, Director of the Thielska Galleriet, Stockholm, which launches an expanded international loans program with this exhibition. Our thanks are due as well to Isabella Nilsson and Eva Nygårds at the Göteborgs Konst-museum; Mikkel Bogh and Kasper Monrad at the Statens Museum for Kunst, Copenhagen; Gerhard Finckh at the Von der Heydt-Museum, Wuppertal; and Nicholas Serota and Frances Morris at Tate Modern, London, for their superb loans. Outside of Europe, Glenn D. Lowry and Ann Temkin at the Museum of Modern Art, New York; and James D. Clifton, at the Sarah Campbell Blaffer Foundation, Houston, deserve special recognition for their generosity. Heartfelt personal thanks also go out to Catherine Woodard and Nelson Blitz, Jr., as well as to several other private collectors who wish to remain anonymous.

We extend our sincere thanks to catalogue contributors Karl Ove Knausgaard; Patricia G. Berman, Theodora L. and Stanley H. Feldberg Professor of Art, Wellesley College; Allison Morehead, Associate Professor, Queen's University Department of Art History and Art Conservation; Richard Shiff, Effie Marie Cain Regents Chair in Art and Director of the Center for the Study of Modernism, The University of Texas at Austin; and Mille Stein, Paintings Conservator and Senior Researcher Emerita, Norwegian Institute for Cultural Heritage Research (NIKU).

At SFMOMA, our efforts benefited immeasur-ably from the oversight of Ruth Berson, Deputy Museum Director for Curatorial Affairs. Under her guidance, Gary Garrels, Elise S. Haas Senior Curator of Painting and Sculpture, and Caitlin Haskell, Associate Curator of Painting and Sculpture, led an accomplished team, ably assisted by Gabriella Moreno. For additional research and administrative support, we also relied upon Craig Corpora and the dedicated members of SFMOMA's library and archives staff.

For her tireless commitment, we extend our gratitude to Emily Lewis, Co-Director of Exhibitions. In the day-to-day management of this project, Emily was assisted by Clarissa Morales and Jillian Aubrey. In our registration department, Olga Charyshyn and Eliza Chiasson provided their typically excellent support in managing the loan logistics and, together with Elizabeth Waller and Misty Youmans, expertly carried out the application for USGI indemnity. We also extend special thanks to Tina Garfinkel, Head Registrar, for her insights, and General Counsel Adine Varah, for valuable legal support.

Conservator Paula De Cristofaro was, as always, an indispensable member of our team. Along with Installation Manager Brandon Larson and Senior Museum Preparator Rico Solinas, she ensured that the paintings looked their best and that the gallery experience was free of distractions. We thank also our colleagues Kent Roberts and Sarah Choi in

Exhibitions for their assistance during the planning phases of the show.

The efforts of our Content Strategy and Digital Engagement team were led by Chad Coerver. Bosco Hernández was responsible for developing the show's graphic identity, while the exhibition was given a striking online presence by Keir Winesmith and Sarah Bailey Hogarty. Thanks go to Stephanie Pau for the compelling audio guide. Amanda Glesmann and Lucy Medrich in Publications adeptly shepherded the gallery texts through various revisions.

Caroline Stevens, Associate Director of Major Gifts, was a champion of this exhibition in every sense. Very many thanks are owed to the marketing and communications team, particularly Jennifer Northrop, Jill Lynch, Tracy Wada, Chris Pacheco, and Dana Goldberg. For their counsel on image rights and reproductions, we are grateful as well to Layna White and Sriba Kwadjovie.

Finally, we would like to thank Janet Alberti, Deputy Director for Administration and Finance, and Nan Keeton, Deputy Museum Director for External Affairs, who do so much to help SFMOMA realize its potential in all its endeavors.

At The Metropolitan Museum of Art, many colleagues were instrumental in the successful realization of the project. Under the leadership of Sheena Wagstaff, Leonard A. Lauder Chairman of the Department of Modern and Contemporary Art, the day-to-day management of the exhibition was supervised by Sabine Rewald, Jacques and Natasha Gelman Curator for Modern Art, who was assisted with administrative details by Michèle Wijegoonaratna. Pari Stave advised on the contents of the catalogue. Quincy Houghton gave expert advice, as did Martha Deese. Amy Desmond Lamberti provided legal counsel and was assisted by Nicole Sussmane and Rachel Ferrante. Isabelle Duvernois provided conservation for the paintings. The task of designing the exhibition and its accompanying graphics was creatively handled by Michael Langley, Chelsea Amato, and Anna Rieger. We thank Clyde B. Jones III, Senior Vice President for Institutional Advancement, for his efforts. Cynthia Iavarone, Rebecca R. Kusovitsky, and Sara K. McBride in the Department of Modern and Contemporary Art were unfailingly helpful. At The Met Breuer, Katy Uravitch administered the budget and schedule, while Allison E. Barone oversaw transportation and insurance arrangements with patience and expertise.

The invaluable guidance of Mark Polizzotti, Publisher and Editor in Chief, throughout this project was greatly appreciated, as was the wise counsel of Michael Sittenfeld and Anne Rebecca Blood. Margaret Donovan proved to be a diligent and sensitive editor. Ellen Hurst edited the bibliographic material with close attention to detail. Under Peter Antony's expert supervision, Paul Booth skillfully saw the book through all phases of production. Josephine Rodriguez-Massop worked conscientiously to acquire the images and rights for reproduction. The striking catalogue design is the work of Roy Brooks.

At the Munch Museum, numerous staff members made valuable contributions to the exhibition, for which we are extremely grateful. Under the direction of Cecilie Krokeide, Head of the Projects and Plans Department, Project Manager Knut Listerud smoothly coordinated every aspect of the endeavor, including the mounting of the exhibition; he was assisted in this task by Registrar Tiril Krabbesund. Paintings Conservator Inger Grimstad and Paper Conservator Magdalena Godzimirska, led by Pedro Gaspar, Head of the Conservation Department, oversaw the meticulous conservation of the Munch Museum loans featured in the exhibition. Gitte Skilbred, Head of Marketing and Communications, and her staff coordinated the press and communications responsibilities, while Head of Security Trygve Lauritzen handled security concerns, both during the exhibition and in connection with the shipment of the artworks.

Gary Garrels, Elise S. Haas Senior Curator of Painting and Sculpture, San Francisco Museum of Modern Art

Jon-Ove Steihaug, Director of Exhibitions and Collections, Munch Museum

Sheena Wagstaff, Leonard A. Lauder Chairman of the Department of Modern and Contemporary Art, The Metropolitan Museum of Art

Lenders to the Exhibition

Denmark
Statens Museum for Kunst, Copenhagen

Germany
Von der Heydt-Museum, Wuppertal

Norway
KODE Kunstmuseene i Bergen
Munch Museum, Oslo
Nasjonalmuseet for Kunst, Arkitektur og Design, Oslo

Sweden
Götesborgs Konstmuseum
Thielska Galleriet, Stockholm

United Kingdom
Tate Modern, London

United States
The Museum of Modern Art, New York
Sarah Campbell Blaffer Foundation, Houston

Private collections
Collection of Catherine Woodard and Nelson Blitz, Jr.
Anonymous lenders

Preface: On Edvard Munch

Karl Ove Knausgaard

My art has been an act of confession." So said Edvard Munch at the end of his life. I believe that anyone who has seen Munch's paintings will understand this remark. Not only because he painted so many self-portraits, or because so many of the stock scenes he returned to again and again have clearly autobiographical elements, but because it's as if something is revealed in everything he painted, even the landscapes without people, a field covered in snow, a jetty by the shore, a pine forest in the gloam. This is the essence of Munch's art. But also what we can say least about. In fact, the question is rather whether it is possible to say anything about the essence of Munch's paintings at all. The paintings are wordless, they are silent and unmoving. They are made up of colors and shapes and they touch us in a way that words never can, they reach places in us where words have no access.

So much in our culture is rational, so much is reason and logic. The apparatus we use to understand ourselves and the world we are part of is enormous and sophisticated; it seems we have a language for everything, from the components of the atom and their movements to the destruction of the soul through schizophrenia. But we have no words for the simplest of things — for example, the way in which a person is present in the room, that person's essence, it's not something we understand, but something we feel and know with our emotions. He is like this, she is like that. If I were to ask you to think about your mother, you would all have a clear picture of who she was, a feeling of your mother's personality, presence, soul. You would just know it. She is like this, or she was like that. But if you were then to communicate this snapshot to someone else, by writing a description of her, for example, you would never be able to fully communicate the image of her that only you have, what you feel, what it is that makes her *her* for you. Even if you were to write a thousand pages, it wouldn't work. Because what I am talking about here is her presence.

And this is true not only of people. It is also true of trees. Every tree has its own expression, its own way of standing in the world. A beach. A forest. A field. A house. A living room. When I say it like that, it sounds like any beach, any forest, any field. But there is no such thing as any field. There are only specific fields in the world, with a definite presence. And this presence is not determined by the field alone, just as your mother's presence in your world is not determined by her alone. Equally important is the way in which we perceive the field or our mother, who we are, what our accomplishments and experiences are, what mood we are in when we see them or think about them.

In other words, reality is not something that exists beforehand, it is something we create, something that manifests in each encounter. The world is constantly in the making. It is always moving, it is fundamentally unpredictable and chaotic. It is, of course, impossible to live in such a world, one that is created every time we open our eyes in the morning. It is impossible to live with such unpredictability and chaos, the fact that we never know what is waiting behind the next house or around the next corner. To process the profusion of details that every encounter entails is also impossible. Which is why we have developed all our categories and concepts and systems. And why culture is organized around repetitions and rituals, and our daily lives are so ruled by habits and routines, traditions and fixed behavioral patterns.

We never look for what is new, we look for what is the same in the new. It's a coping mechanism, a survival strategy. And it's effective. We no longer sit around a fire in the wilderness and listen in fear to all the sounds out there in the dark, we sit in our homes and watch documentaries about predators while we drink coffee from the same cup that we always drink coffee from. Imagine for a moment that you were to get up and go to the bathroom, and when you came back, there was a man you had never seen before sitting on the sofa. How would you react? Presumably with horror, fear, or anger. And I can guarantee that you would remember that man's face for many years to come, what he said, the way in which he said it. And if you were then to go into town the next day, you would be surrounded by strangers, you would see hundreds of faces that you had never seen

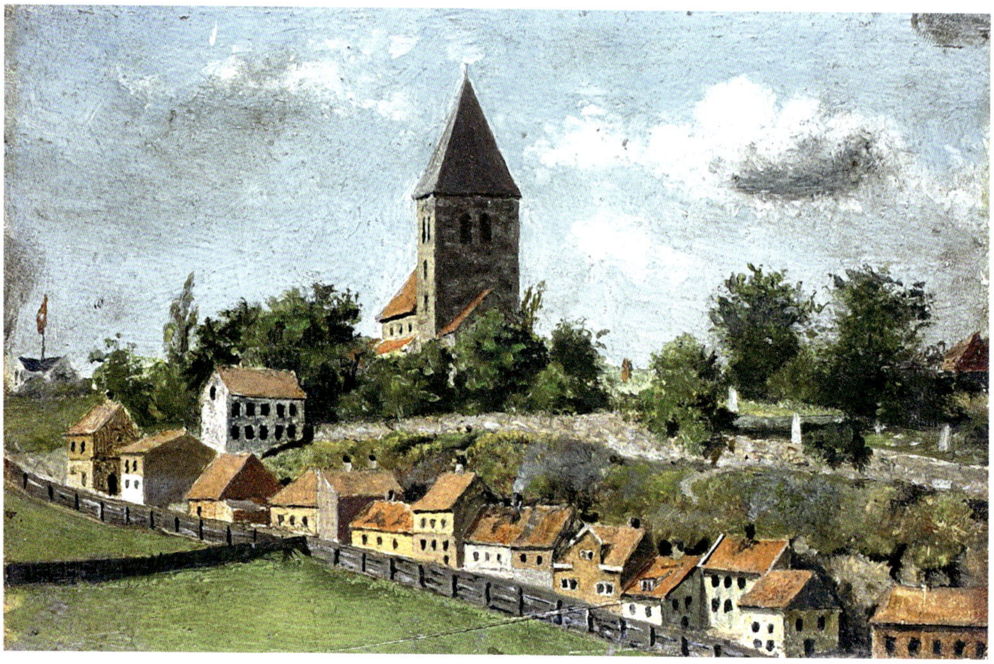

Fig. 1
Edvard Munch, *Telthusbakken with Gamle Aker Church*, 1880. Oil on cardboard, 4¾ × 7⅛ in. (12 × 18 cm). Location unknown

before, but they would not fill you with horror, fear, or anger, and you would not remember them later when you got back home. Because that is how we work, we always have our guard up, it protects us against all these impressions, which become visible only when our guard is down, and then the world can touch us suddenly and with great intensity.

There are people who are so sensitive and aware that they have no such guard, no protection against reality. We often say that they are too sensitive, not thick-skinned enough or overemotional. This always implies a form of functional incompetence, as these overemotional people are dependent on greater stability, constancy, and predictability than others. Traveling, for example, becomes impossible. Because then everything is new, the impressions build into a storm that is impossible to navigate. It's hard not to think about the Norwegian author Tor Ulven in this context, who, in the final years of his life, never left the house, he simply couldn't do it, he was too scared. He took his own life, and people do that only when they are so tormented that life becomes unbearable. What was it that tormented him? I don't know, but I assume that it was not anything specific, rather something more general, a feeling of pain for no reason. But what Tor Ulven did, as he sat there captive to his own emotions, was write. And he wrote with such feeling, with an almost limitless sensitivity, that we can read about a glass of water, a breadboard, and some crumbs as part of the universe without big words, which make everything invisible, ever being used.

What Tor Ulven did is exactly what painters through the ages have done — I'm thinking, for example, about the Dutch seventeenth-century masters, how they painted their still lifes of everyday

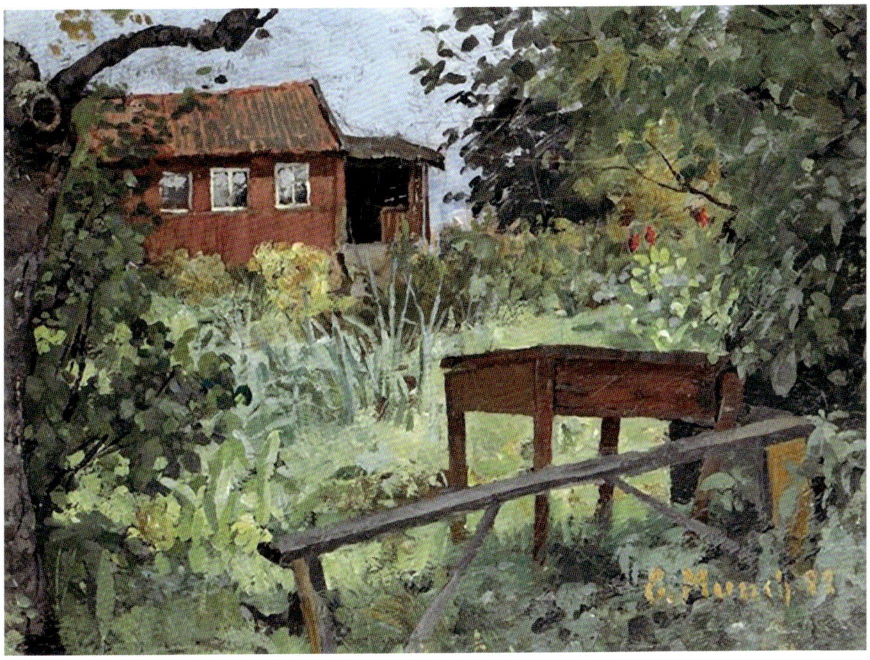

Fig. 2
Edvard Munch, *Garden with Red House*, 1882. Oil on cardboard, 9 × 12 in. (23 × 30.5 cm). Private collection

objects and made them radiate with such a presence that a sense of belonging was sparked in anyone who saw them: this is where we are, this is what we really are. But belonging is treacherous, because it invites intimacy, and intimacy pulls reality into what is familiar, which then in turn becomes part of our guard, part of what stands between us and the world. I don't think Edvard Munch knew that, but I think he felt it. He did his first oil paintings when he was sixteen, and even though the very first painting, which depicts the view toward Telthusbakken in Kristiania (fig. 1), as Oslo was then called, is perhaps a little stiff and lacks elegance, as though painted with great effort, he developed incredibly quickly. Only a few months later, his painting was of a very high standard, and as a nineteen-year-old, he produced small masterpieces. From the outset, his sense of color, his sense of light, his sense of composition, and his sense of mood are striking. It is hard to get enough of many of these pictures, for example, the one called *Garden with Red House*, which he painted when he was eighteen (fig. 2), or the fantastic self-portrait he did when he was nineteen (fig. 5).

If Edvard Munch had, for one reason or another, stopped painting when he was twenty-two, that is to say, with his masterpiece *The Sick Child* (fig. 3), we would perhaps not have celebrated the one hundred and fiftieth anniversary of his birth, but he would still be remembered: Edvard Munch, one of our great young dead, lost his mother when he was five, grew up with an introverted, religious father, showed great talent at an early age, was taken under the wing of Christian Krohg and the Kristiania Bohemians, and his last painting, the famous and iconic *Sick Child*, provoked both admiration and disgust when it was shown at the autumn exhibition in 1886.

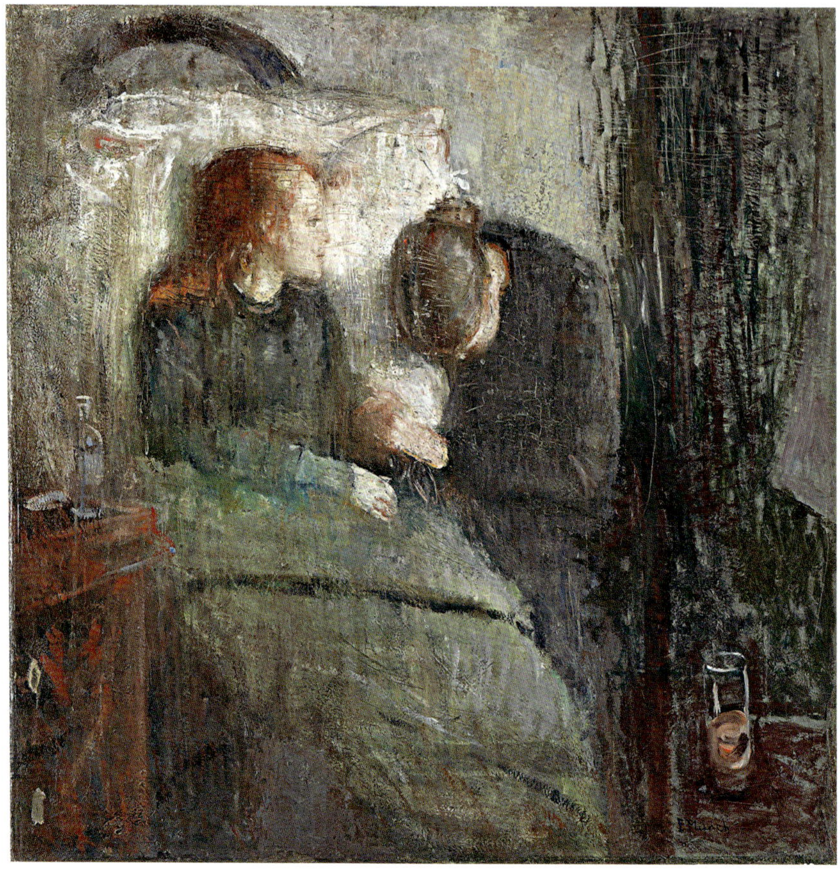

Fig. 3
Edvard Munch, *The Sick Child*, 1885–86. Oil on canvas, 47 ¼ × 46 ⅝ in. (120 × 118.5 cm). Nasjonalmuseet for Kunst, Arkitektur og Design, Oslo (NG.M.00839)

But that is not what happened, Edvard Munch lived until he was eighty, and he painted almost every day for the rest of his life, and more or less in isolation for the final thirty years. The most incredible thing about Edvard Munch is the fact that he produced such a phenomenal amount of work, and that he did it on his own. He had no children, and apart from a few difficult relationships in his youth, he had no wife or lovers, and he kept the few friends he did have at a distance. The only thing he did was paint. And his paintings, they were constantly changing, from day to day and period to period. This is where I believe Munch's uniqueness lies, in this great fluidity, because what he left behind is a record of his encounters with the world, just as he was, in the form of his paintings, where it's as if the world is renewed every time, under ever-changing circumstances, so that he meets the world with all his experience, everything he has lived, and in this encounter the paintings are created, an experience in itself, which is then thrown back to him, and in turn to the pictures in a continuous, sixty-four-year-long process.

It is in this context that the word "confession" comes into its own right, because in these pictures he stands naked, with his guard down, even in his landscape paintings. There is nothing between him and the world, and it is this unguarded encounter that we see, not just once in one picture, but again and again, in hundreds of paintings. Naturally, not all of them are masterpieces, not all of them are of the same high quality, but Munch didn't care about quality, and he didn't care about creating masterpieces. No artist worth mentioning does, because quality, that's something that is already there, it's the protection, it is the wood fence that holds reality at bay. And a masterpiece, that's something we can no longer truly see, it has become an icon, something rigid and unchangeable, a brand. *The Scream* by Munch (fig. 8, pls. 15 and 31) is just such a masterpiece, we don't see it anymore. But there are more than seventeen hundred other paintings, and one of them, which he painted just before *The Scream*, has the same flaming red background, the same bridge, but instead of the iconic skull-like face, there is a man in a hat standing in profile in the foreground (pl. 4). When I saw it, a shudder ran through me, because *here* was emotion, *here* was the abyss, *here* was the angst.

It's hard to think of anything less exclusive and more human than emotions. Everyone feels joy, happiness, pain, sorrow. But we cannot live with the strongest emotions, because sorrow and being in love become unbearable in the end, we have to wear them down in order to carry on living. What is so special about Edvard Munch is that he never managed to wear down these emotions, which is also true of many. I know several hypersensitive people. In the old days, they were said to be suffering from "nerves," so perhaps what is so special about him is that he was so extremely artistic and talented that he was able to give these nerves shape, and in the simplest way as time went on. That was what he was striving for. Which is why his pictures are so often unfinished, often more like sketches. They are not meant to represent reality, a door should not look like a door, but rather like a painted door, that's to say, as a door should be felt, or experienced.

Munch was a painter in the extreme: the painting was an object, a thing in itself to be pursued, and therefore he was able to go where only a painting can go, to that which is beyond words, but which is still part of our reality. And this is why reproductions never do Munch's paintings justice. Just as a mother, a tree, or a field exudes something unique, a soul if you like, Munch's paintings do the same. Which is why he sometimes left them out in the wind and rain. It didn't matter if they were damaged, it was not only what they portrayed that was meaningful, but also what they were, in and of themselves, as objects. And if you have ever stood in a room in front of a painting by Munch, or Van Gogh or Rembrandt for that matter, you will know that part of the painting's magic is that it brings together its time and yours, its place and yours, and there is comfort in that, because even the distance that is inherent in loneliness is suspended in that moment.

Introduction

Gary Garrels, Jon-Ove Steihaug, and Sheena Wagstaff

This study of the art of Edvard Munch actually begins at the end, with *Self-Portrait: Between the Clock and the Bed* (1940–43; pl. 51), the artist's last major self-portrait. Though often interpreted as a meditation on Munch's impending death (which occurred a year after its completion), the canvas holds more complex meanings that provide a lens through which to view his entire oeuvre and reassess certain long-held myths surrounding him. Among these is the assumption that, after his nervous breakdown in 1908–9, the quality of his work declined and he was no longer a conscious, active protagonist in the European modernist narrative.

Between the Clock and the Bed is a remarkable painting, conveying a powerful sense of place, yet with a symbolic and spatial ambiguity that complicates and transcends the binaries of time and eternity, birth and death, past and present. The compositional space defies logical mapping: the tight framing of the room not only highlights the inherently theatrical nature of an artist's studio but also evokes a stage set, a concentrated area in which dramatic and consequential events occur. Munch was well acquainted with the construction of such spaces, having in 1906 designed the sets for the Berlin productions of Henrik Ibsen's *Ghosts* and *Hedda Gabler*. Years later, as he was painting *Between the Clock and the Bed* in the early 1940s, he admitted to identifying with the protagonist of Ibsen's eponymous play, *The Master Builder*.[1]

The portrayal of an artist's studio has a long tradition in art, and it is evident that Munch was influenced by this history and by more contemporary examples, such as Henri Matisse's *L'Atelier rose* (1911; Pushkin State Museum of Fine Arts, Moscow), in which the contents of the artist's studio, including a number of previous works, are arranged in a frieze-like array in an impossibly flat space. But Munch chose to place his portrait in a more complex setting, with a door that leads into an undefined room beyond the studio and a suggestion of a window in the reflection in the shiny floor that stretches before his feet.

Many pictures cover the walls in *Between the Clock and the Bed*, but only two are clearly legible — the half-length portrait hanging on the yellow wall and the long, blue female nude that hovers above the bed, a representation of Munch's painting *Krotkaja* (1927; Munch Museum, Oslo). As Elizabeth Prelinger has written, Munch named this woman after a suicidal character in Fyodor Dostoyevsky's short story "A Gentle Spirit" (1876). Suggesting a darker relationship between Munch and his model, the painting also reflects "the central role of Eros in Munch's life and art."[2] Numerous Munch self-portraits inspired by the traditional artist-and-model genre imply a similarly complicated, often vexed connection in which two personas become intertwined (pls. 36 and 37).

As we look more closely at the painting, particularly at the grandfather clock, we see that the work stands outside of measurable time. Lacking a face or hands, the clock stands vertically, in poignant relationship to the bed, in which the span of a human being's life takes place. It is impossible to discern the artist's emotions — his stance is detached, his undefined facial features deter any reading of emotion, and the tension between the clenched fist and the loose hand is impossible to resolve. Is the visitor to the studio (or the viewer of the painting) being shunned or welcomed? The painting is a reflection of Munch's state of mind, a self-examination by an artist aware of his legacy as he stands like a sentinel in the liminal space between his bedroom and studio, between the clock and the bed, each charged with powerful symbolic meaning.

Munch painted self-portraits throughout his career, but with increased intensity and frequency after 1900. These "self-scrutinies," as he called them, provide insight into his perceptions of his role as an artist, as a man in society, and as a protagonist in his relationships with others, especially women. Not simply functioning as visual autobiography, the self-portraits are occasions for painterly experimentation in which his techniques ranged from the thick application of paint to the employment of thin washes to the scraping of canvas. Using himself as subject but always allowing technique to influence effect, Munch was able to powerfully investigate the interplay between depicting external reality and meditating on painterly means.

Munch's obsessive absorption with painting's medium and method is another key focus of this book, and one of the primary reasons for selecting *Between the Clock and the Bed* as the entry point for our discussion. The simple bed with its coverlet appears unfinished, or semicomplete. It is a remarkable comment on painting, calling attention to facture and technique with pencil lines visible beneath the bold, clearly delineated brushstrokes that create the abstract pattern of the bedspread. Here, the basic, elemental nature of painting comes to the fore, revealing the work to be not only a self-portrait but a comment on the act of painting itself.

As a painting about painting, *Between the Clock and the Bed* dispels the myth of a decline in the quality of Munch's work as he aged. Instead, we can trace a sustained and intense preoccupation with the physical aspects of painting practice, also evident, for example, in the six variants of *The Sick Child*, of which we illustrate three in these pages (fig. 3, pls. 20 and 29). Fascinated with the painterly qualities of his subject, Munch allowed the paint to run down the canvas, dissolved it with solvent, or scraped it away in a destructive act of creation. Similarly, for the last and definitive version of *The Death of Marat* (1907; pl. 28), Munch emphasizes form over content with characteristically long horizontal, vertical, and diagonal brushstrokes that almost push the image toward a gestural abstraction. "The idea," he later wrote of this work, "was to break through the surface and get to the depths — It was a kind of cubism."[3] *The Death of Marat*, but also *Jealousy* (ca. 1907; pl. 30) and *Death Struggle* (1915; pl. 34), certainly show that Munch was ahead of his time, and as such they serve as a paradigm of a new twentieth-century style.

Although Munch occupies his own rung on the narrative ladder of modernism, it has always been a deterministic one, drawing heavily on both the late nineteenth-century notion of the artist as a social outsider and the belief that his mental pathologies contributed to his genius. Munch's breakdown of 1908–9, driven by exhaustion and acute alcoholism, is typically viewed as a watershed moment. Before that experience and his subsequent stay at Dr. Daniel Jacobson's clinic in Copenhagen, Munch had lived a cosmopolitan and itinerant life, drifting between Norway, Germany, and France for nearly twenty years. After the termination of his treatment, he settled relatively permanently in Norway and lived a more peaceful, secluded existence during which he came to reconcile his enthusiasm for the international avant-garde with an occasional embrace of nationalistic subject matter, including farming scenes and landscapes. Prevailing narratives present Munch as having been cured of his illness and his nervous disposition, after which his work diminished in potency. The problem with this normalizing view is that it privileges the narrative of abuse and excess that is an intrinsic part of the romantic myth of the artist and encourages a view of Munch's later works as being subordinate to those initially recognized as evidence of his mature style in the 1890s. By presenting a full selection of the late paintings here, we aim to counteract that view, which has emphasized Munch's private experience and public image at the expense of a more nuanced and complete appreciation of his art.

When Munch retreated to Ekely in Norway after his illness, he experimented with technique with renewed vigor, and his canvases were drenched in bright, expressionistic color. Often, he revisited earlier subject matter, such as in the two versions of *Starry Night*, from 1893 and 1922–24 (pls. 9 and 43). Repetition enabled Munch to dispel the charged aura surrounding his subject matter and allowed him to explore and invent, keeping content stable while radically experimenting with form. This is particularly true of his self-portraits.

The widespread tendency to see Munch's early work (from the 1880s and 1890s) as more important than what came later sidesteps the enormous inspiration that these later paintings have provided to a long line of artists, among them the Danish modernist painters Asger Jorn and Per Kirkeby and, more recently, Peter Doig, Marlene Dumas, Tracey

Emin, and Steven Shearer. More important, this tendency ignores the spontaneous painterly execution and intensified use of color found in the late Munch and its impact on subsequent artists. When, for example, Jasper Johns chose, around 1980–82, to cite Munch's *Self-Portrait: Between the Clock and the Bed* as the grand finale for his decade-long work on the crosshatch motif, it was arguably the unconventional painterly style that inspired him as much as the theme.[4] This volume has also been inspired by the same masterwork, which reflects Munch's intense engagement with the physical qualities of paint and canvas even as he plumbed the depths of his psyche.

In his preface to this volume, the Norwegian novelist Karl Ove Knausgaard has likenened Munch's paintings to confessions, noting that his emotions remained undiminished throughout his career. He was able, writes Knausgaard, "to go where only a painting can go, to that which is beyond words, but which is still part of our reality."

In the following pages, conservator Mille Stein provides an analysis of Munch's painting techniques and the materiality of his paintings, from his early self-portrait of 1886 (pl. 2) to *Between the Clock and the Bed.* She traces his development as a painter and his constant adjustments, analyzing the way his style and technique gradually changed yet retained a unique fidelity.

The other authors, noted art historians, critically review Munch's art and career through multiple perspectives. Allison Morehead focuses on the importance of self-portraits to the artist's oeuvre, examining the role of such works in European painting and questioning whether Munch's works in that genre provide a way to structure his "inventive, repetitive, and inconsistent" career. Patricia Berman queries and dismantles Munch's public image — cultivated by him throughout his lifetime — as the alienated artist who opposed commoditization. Instead, she finds him to be a master not only of painting but also of career building, who used his self-portraits constructively, as a crucial element of self-fashioning that became a cornerstone of his reception.

Finally, Richard Shiff, like Knausgaard, grapples with the essence of Munch's painting. Shiff finds that Munch did not maintain an absolute distinction between thinking and feeling, choosing instead to paint feeling where it converges with thinking and might itself be regarded as an active aspect of thought. Munch developed a "radical sense of materiality within representational painting." As a result, scholars and theorists of modern art have sometimes dismissed his work as lacking an avant-garde purity, but it has increasingly been recognized for its importance, including by major contemporary painters from Bridget Riley to Georg Baselitz.

All the authors analyze the artist's accomplishments across the expanse of a career lasting more than sixty years and focus on the continuities that link his work from its beginnings to its end. In establishing the complexity of Munch's art and career, they illuminate why his work remains a touchstone for modern painting and continues to grow in importance.

The Untimely Face of Munch

Allison Morehead

Late in life, probably in the early 1930s, Edvard Munch reproduced a drawing as a hectograph that addressed in a joking, almost gimmicky way the importance of self-portraiture to his oeuvre and to the projection of himself as the ultimate self-portraying artist (fig. 4).[1] The drawing shows an image of the artist, bearded, spectacled, and in profile, holding up with comically small hands another, framed image of the artist, also bearded and spectacled but seen from the front looking directly out, whether from a mirror, a canvas, or some other support is left unclear. The simultaneous presence of the profile and frontal views recalls the conventions, in place since the late nineteenth century, of the police mug shot, in which both views together constituted the standard for criminal identification.[2] In part in this way, the double self-portrait undermines the notion that any one self-portrait might offer some physiognomic or indeed psychological truth about the artist.[3] While the avuncular profile betrays a hint of a smile crinkling the eyes and the sides of the mouth, the head-on self-portrait, with its staring round eyes framed by round glasses, deep crease extending from arched eyebrows, and crosshatched shadowing on one side of the face, comes off as slightly menacing. The frontal image might promise a more complete view of the face and one more in keeping with the stereotype of Munch as the psychologically intense genius. And yet, it is being held up by another self-portrait, and is thus presented as further removed from the artist's self than the benign profile, as the picture in the frame, the self-portrait *in* the self-portrait.

The European traditions of self-portraiture, rooted in the Renaissance and specifically in constructions of male artistic genius, are dominated by heads torqued in relation to bodies, a convention with particular temporal implications. As in Munch's earliest painted self-portraits of the 1880s (fig. 5 and pl. 2), a head rotated from the body, even ever so slightly, suggests that the artist has momentarily looked away from the task at hand, perhaps to consult his own reflection in a mirror and to acknowledge the

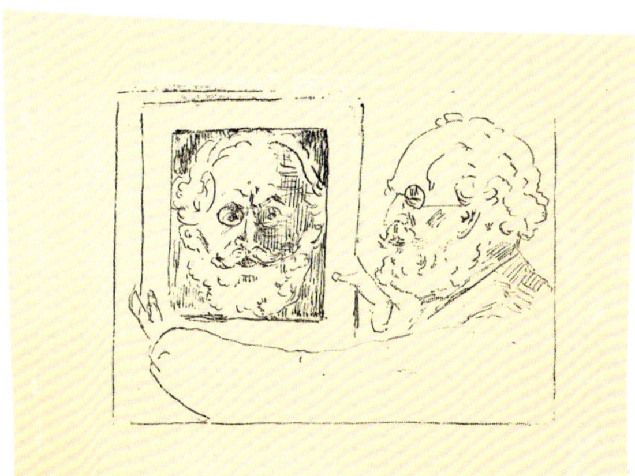

Fig. 4
Edvard Munch, *Self-Portrait in Self-Portrait*, 1933(?). Hectograph, 7 ½ × 10 ⅜ in. (19.2 × 26.2 cm). Munch Museum, Oslo (MM G 782-02)

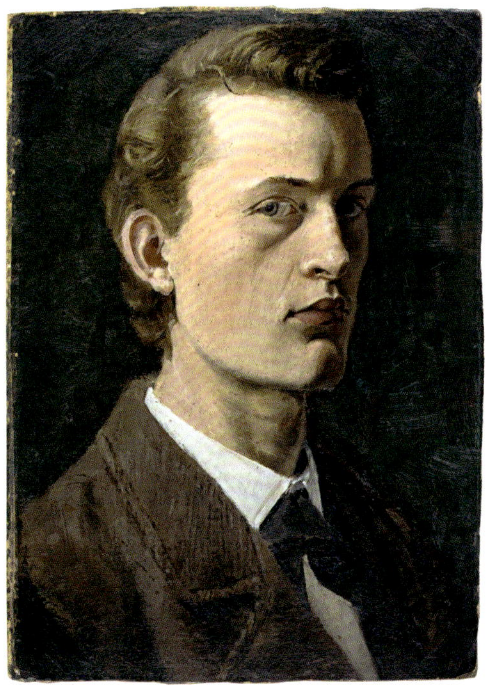

Fig. 5
Edvard Munch, *Self-Portrait*, 1882. Oil on paper mounted on cardboard, 10 ¼ × 7 ½ in. (26 × 19 cm). Munch Museum, Oslo (MM M 1049)

presence of a viewer, who is also implied to be the artist looking back at himself.[4] A common conceit of self-portraiture, sometimes heightened by the inclusion of an easel, canvas, or palette, is that the task at hand is the artwork in front of him and now in front of us.[5] Torqued heads, no less so than in Munch's highly unconventional self-portraiture, thus tend to telescope time, signaling not only a moment in the making of the work but also the moment in which we as viewers encounter the artist in the work, as if one of us has traveled backward or forward in time. This momentariness, or "occasionality" in Hans-Georg Gadamer's term,[6] is often emphasized by the artist's expression, usually a fleeting one: a hint of a smile, a mouth slightly parted as if about to speak, an arched eyebrow animating the moment.

The frontal self-portrait, however, in which the head is in neutral and both body and face are oriented toward the viewer and parallel to the picture plane, as in Munch's so-called *Self-Portrait under the Mask of a Woman* (pl. 8), and much more famously in Albrecht Dürer's *Self-Portrait in Fur Cloak* of 1500 (fig. 6),[7] affords a different kind of encounter. In seeking to present what one writer calls "maximum frontage," Munch's and Dürer's self-portraits are by definition confrontational, but paradoxically less revealing,[8] especially given the artists' impassive expressions and the way that the painted eyes narrowly avoid meeting the viewer's gaze. While promising (but spectacularly failing) to reveal all, they downplay any moment-in-timeness in favor of a temporal protraction through which the image reaches iconicity: the artist is not about to turn his head back to neutral and back to his task, but might remain still and staring out of the picture forever. This radical frontality thus invokes not so much time travel on the part of the artist or the viewer, but the anachronistic potential of the object itself. It shifts attention away from the moment that the work originated to its ongoing existence in time.

Munch probably completed this particular self-portrait with a red background in 1893, after what seems to have been a lull in painting self-portraits of at least five years, a lifetime in the context of his early, rapid-fire artistic development. Executed on one of the largest wood panels he ever used,[9] the painting was probably never exhibited in Munch's lifetime,[10] but it has since become a staple in large showings of his work, a cultlike object now encased in a frame that provides its own climate-controlled microenvironment. Munch himself gave it no title. The so-called female mask at the top, which most likely connotes an exaggerated architectural element known as a *masqueron* taken from the Neo-baroque interiors of the casino at Monte Carlo, where Munch spent extensive time in 1891–92,[11] more than anything else draws attention to the provocations of the work. Those provocations are most obviously found in the frontal view, but also, more disturbingly, in the violence visited upon the face (fig. 7). For at some point after Munch painted a relatively naturalistic image of himself, clean-shaven, with a prominent cleft chin and pillowy lips, the cheeks, forehead, and other areas of the work were abraded, large areas of paint removed from the face, the wood even gouged into, in what appears to be an act of self-desecration.[12]

The striking combination of what remains of the naturalistically depicted face and the ambiguous symbolist background — broad black arabesques on red suggestive of damask and the exaggerated *masqueron* — has fueled debates about when the work was made, debates that are not at all unusual in the art-historical literature on Munch.[13] Does the painting date from 1891 or 1892, when the artist was still working in a more naturalistic mode?[14] Or does it date from 1893, after Munch's arrival in Berlin, where, with works such as *The Scream* (fig. 8), he self-consciously shifted to more symbolist visual practices and, the argument goes, a more pessimistic view of women influenced by his new milieu?[15] Or, as Reinhold Heller has more plausibly suggested, does it straddle this key moment of "Munch becoming 'Munch,'" with the more naturalistic face predating the more symbolist background?[16]

Each of these arguments, in its own way, invokes a familiar chronological unfolding of art history, in which ideas change in logical ways, one style follows another, and art historians such as

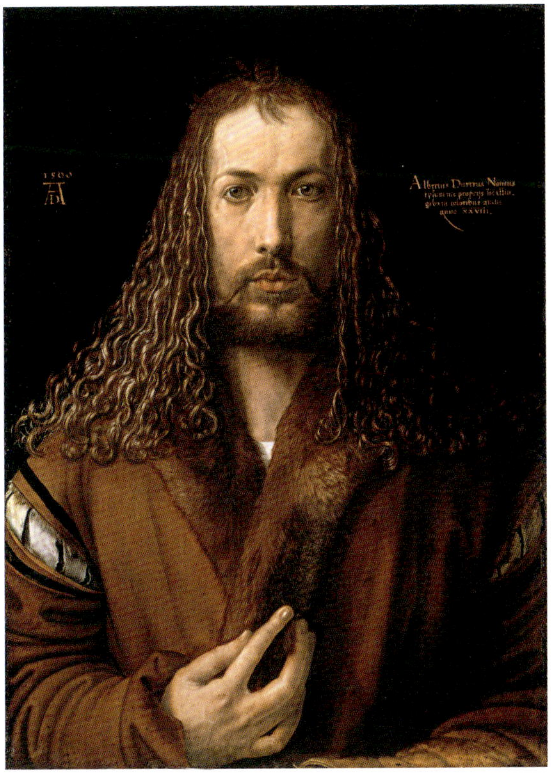

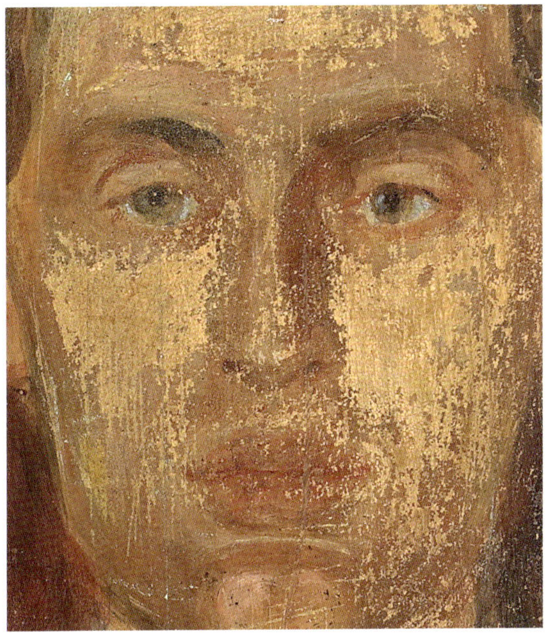

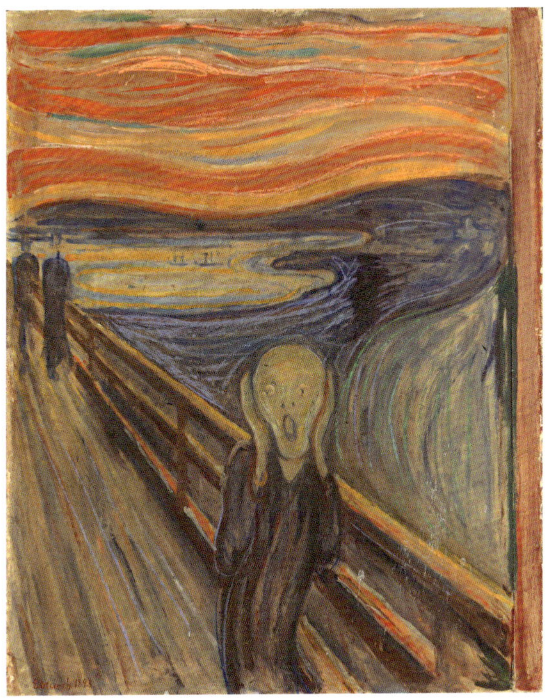

Fig. 6

Albrecht Dürer, *Self-Portrait in Fur Cloak*, 1500. Oil on limewood panel, 26 3/8 × 19 1/4 in. (67.1 × 48.9 cm). Alte Pinakothek, Bayerische Staatsgemäldesammlungen, Munich (537)

Fig. 7

Edvard Munch, *Self-Portrait under the Mask of a Woman*, 1893 (pl. 8, detail)

Fig. 8

Edvard Munch, *The Scream*, 1893. Tempera and crayon on unprimed cardboard, 35 7/8 × 29 in. (91 × 73.5 cm). Nasjonalmuseet for Kunst, Arkitektur og Design, Oslo (NG.M.00939) myself deploy visual acumen to discern the finer details of style in order to, among other things, assess the temporal origins, the dating, of an individual work of art.[17] Especially in the age of mechanical reproduction, the opportunity to assess lifelikeness in a self-portrait seems to hold out additional hope for resolving thorny dating problems inherent in constructing an oeuvre. The argument for this self-portrait's being completed before Munch went to Berlin in no small part hinges on photographs from the Berlin period that show him sporting a mustache.[18]

Despite the hope implicit in these debates, that knowing the temporal origins of this particular self-portrait will help unlock Munch's thought on the eve of painting *The Scream* and thus bring us into more intimate contact with Munch himself at what is undoubtedly an extraordinary moment in his career, there has been a strange reluctance — I am tempted to call it a classic case of displacement — to pay much attention to how Munch depicted himself in the painting. Instead, scholars have focused almost entirely on the fearful form of the head at the top of the panel and its possible significance (mask, Medusa, and so on) for Munch's complex views on women. In Dürer's day, as the inscription on his self-portrait of 1500 intimates, twenty-eight was considered the age at which men reached their physical prime.[19] The face of Munch in his twenty-eighth, twenty-ninth, or thirtieth year is nearly symmetrical and, with its sensually painted lips, conventionally beautiful. But it is also abraded and inscrutable. Defacement coupled with inaccessibility at the site of our desire, the face of Munch, in a work that refuses to settle down temporally and stylistically seems to be more than we as art historians can bear.

"Can one make anachronism a paradigm for historical inquiry?" asks Georges Didi-Huberman.[20] Answering in the affirmative, he nominates art history, with its defining objects of inquiry being powerful images that already in their iconicity have the potential for anachronism, as a leading contender for such an approach, an irritant that might provoke more critical historical reflection. If we were to emphasize the anachronisms of Munch's self-portrait against a red background rather than its origins in the early 1890s, we would highlight its ongoing existence, its presence, well beyond the moment of its making and the continuing fascination it seems to hold for scholars (myself included) as an iconic image-object.[21] Embracing anachronism would also lead us to interrogate those very oddities in the work itself that seem to evidence different moments of origin, not only the disparate naturalist and antinaturalist elements but also the willful stylistic mixing: the naturalist origins — the casino — of a background exaggerated for antinaturalist effect and the antinaturalist abrasion of the naturalist surface. To take this thought experiment to its limits is to imagine that Munch may have produced anachronistic style in successive moments, alternating between adding to the naturalism of the face and subtracting from it, touching up one ear perhaps while abrading the other, painting the icon while engaging in acts of iconoclasm.

The idea of anachronism as a starting point for a different kind of history is not as alien to Munch as one might imagine. Its genealogy, as Didi-Huberman points out, includes Michel Foucault's writing on Friedrich Nietzsche, whose philosophy was critical to Munch's Berlin circle of the early 1890s, which is to say well before Munch took up a commission to paint a posthumous image of the philosopher in 1905 (fig. 9).[22] A genealogical model derived from Nietzsche underpinned the histories of modern art published later by Julius Meier-Graefe, a critic, dealer, and historian who was a member of Munch's circle in Berlin. As Patricia Berman has argued, Meier-Graefe's "elaborate genealogies of genius" drew on Nietzsche to claim common ground between past and present masters such as El Greco and Cézanne, who were thereby "removed from their national and temporal contexts and relocated to a transhistorical realm in which they were not restricted to membership in any particular culture or normative category."[23]

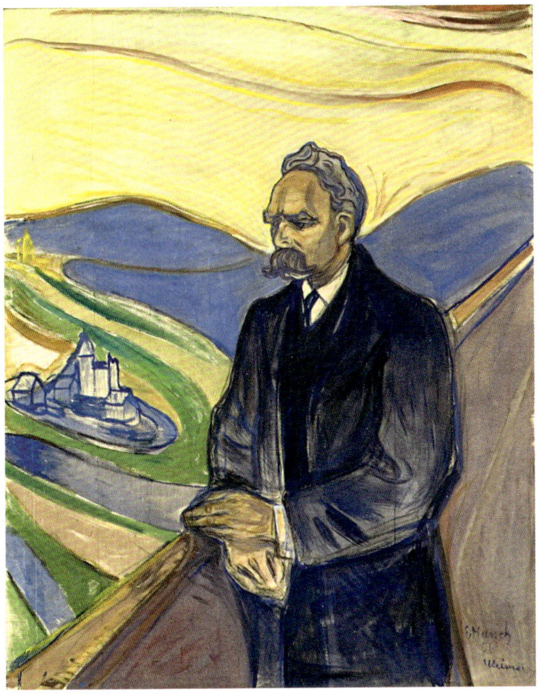

Fig. 9

Edvard Munch, *Friedrich Nietzsche*, 1906.
Oil on canvas, 79 ⅛ × 63 in. (201 × 160 cm).
Thielska Galleriet, Stockholm

But Meier-Graefe went only so far along this Nietzschean path, and his inability or reluctance or perhaps conscious decision not to fully insert Munch into his genealogy of modern art, still conceived of as a "developmental" history,[24] defined the very limits of his project. For Munch, Meier-Graefe implied, escaped the history he was writing because the artist — "unconsciously," Meier-Graefe took pains to emphasize — was deeply anachronistic and his works fundamentally without style:

> What he had to say did not admit of the application of a traditional form; indeed it may be doubted whether form concerns him at all.... Sometimes he gives us glimpses of the past.... At such moments one almost believes that Norway lies in a region quite different from the rest of the world, in which things move according to strange yet profound laws, and men have other and more wonderful thoughts than ourselves. One has almost a physical feeling as of the impact of a foreign body, and one's longing to grasp the strange thing more closely impels one to the conquest of a new form of beauty.[25]

Lack of form or consistent style made Munch the anti-Cézanne and thus largely disqualified him from Meier-Graefe's history, which was essentially a history of form. Yet, knowing Munch's work intimately,[26] Meier-Graefe seems to have suspected, and in his brief comments on the artist allowed his readers to glimpse, the possibility that other kinds of history might still be written.

Munch's anachronisms, as I conceive them, would comprise his stylistic anomalies, including his periodic and often strategic returns to naturalism,[27] as well as the frequent recurrences in his oeuvre, sometimes at great intervals, of both style and motif.[28] Anachronistic works, such as the abraded self-portrait against a red background or the later painted version of *The Scream* (pl. 31), itself the subject of protracted debates over dating,[29] are outliers and problems no doubt, but they are also the very works that, if we let them, turn our attention away from temporal origins, that is to say away from the logical, developmental structure of an oeuvre, and away from history itself.[30]

"He is not attached to any school or any direction," wrote the Norwegian critic and art historian Jappe Nilssen in 1916, "because he himself is one of those who advances and creates his own school and forges his own direction."[31] Surely with Munch's complicity, Nilssen described his friend as both stereotypical avant-garde outsider and chronological anomaly, as an art history unto himself, his own school, his own doctrine, and his own teleology. Perhaps then it is little wonder that Munch made so many self-portraits from the beginning to the end of his career, regularly depicting himself in paintings, prints, drawings, and photographs, and also little wonder that art historians have found them so preoccupying.[32] If Dürer's self-portrait unleashed the very modern conflation of man and oeuvre, then self-portraiture, especially the kind that leaves little doubt that it deserves to be called self-portraiture,[33] would seem to offer a way to structure an oeuvre, especially an oeuvre such as Munch's that is so inventive, repetitive, and inconsistent.

The year 1916 would not be the last time that Nilssen described Munch as a man heroically outside of temporal constraints. "With his fifty-five years," Nilssen wrote two years later, on the occasion of another important solo exhibition in Munch's home country, "he is still the youngest among our painters.... Munch possesses a sense of self-renewal and the strength of self-rejuvenation."[34] The Nietzschean tone is unmistakable. In his claim for Munch's eternal youth, self-generated power, and strength alongside the argument for the artist's out-of-timeness, Nilssen echoed a Nietzschean vision of an individual for whom action and therefore life demanded a counterintuitive relationship to history: "No painter will paint his picture," Nietzsche wrote in his "untimely meditation" on history, "without having first desired and striven for it in an unhistorical condition." For Nietzsche, the "unhistorical condition" involved putting "the power of forgetting" into action in the interest of constant renewal. Along with the "suprahistorical," or the eternal, these were the "natural antidotes" to the "malady of history" plaguing modern man.[35]

Munch benefited enormously from and actively contributed to the historicization of his work, energetically organizing solo exhibitions (including his earliest in 1889, in which he offered an audacious survey of his artistic development up to that point) and collaborating with cataloguers and biographers who sought to bring order and logic to the oeuvre and the life.[36] But undoubtedly he would also have diagnosed himself and his art as suffering from a "malady of history," for an oeuvre with no one signature stroke to fetishize, in which form was always subservient to meaning, was not so easily incorporated into the emerging histories of modernism. This, perhaps, was one of the hazards of being, as one of his earliest supporters publicly claimed, an "artist of the future."[37]

Dürer's self-portrait was both an icon and an index of what the artist, divinely inspired, Christlike even, could do, and it thus identified the artist with the products of his own making in a way that was not only new but also modern.[38] Munch, who called his work his "lifeblood,"[39] seems to have been thoroughly committed to blurring the lines between his art and his life, between his oeuvre and his self. Nevertheless, a simultaneous commitment to certain Nietzschean ideals also appears to have led him to counter the conflation of artist and work. *The Scream* gives visual form to a text that Munch wrote in the first person and often included with versions of the work, "I was walking along the road with two friends.... And I felt a loud, unending scream piercing nature,"[40] and the motif is more often than not regarded as a form of autobiographical statement. That being said, however, it is also painted and treated as if it were radically anonymous, alien to the rest of Munch's oeuvre and indeed to Munch himself.[41] In other words, at the same time that it fulfills the ideal of Dürer's self-portrait, it also affords the means to undo it.

Munch's self-portraiture might have offered a solution to the difficulties of historicizing a stylistically inconsistent oeuvre by anchoring the artist and his production at particular moments in time, thereby giving shape to the body of work, signposting periods of change, of special continuity perhaps, or breakthrough. In fact, this was my initial assumption in approaching the self-portraits, and since all writing about self-portraiture involves the writer's trying to commune with the artistic self on display, it seems only fair to acknowledge what occurs to me now as a rather obvious starting point. But I now suspect that Munch had what the American critic James Huneker accused him of in 1901, a "Nietzsche-like contempt for ... the obvious,"[42] including this all too obvious historical use of self-portraiture. While the art historian and philosopher Malcolm Bull recommends reading Nietzsche tactically "like a loser," in order to avoid identifying with the strong

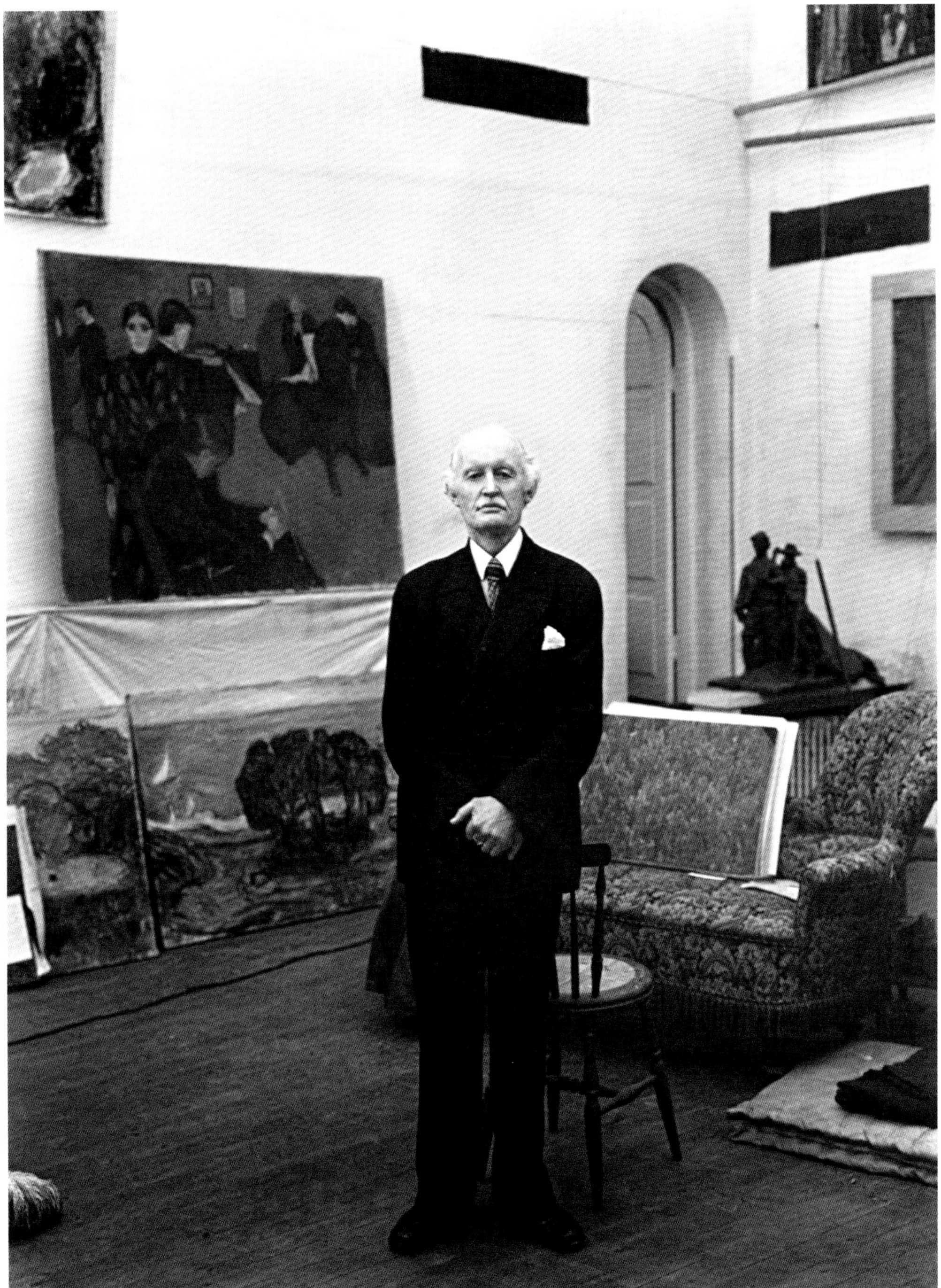

Fig. 10

Edvard Munch in the winter studio at Ekely, November or December 1938. Munch Museum Archives, Oslo at the expense of the weak,[43] I think it likely that Munch more often than not envisioned himself as a "winner." Nevertheless, I would prefer to feel like a loser when I meet Munch's contemptuous gaze from his early self-portraits (see fig. 5 and pl. 2) rather than imagine that they are addressing someone other than myself. This is largely because, on a feminist basis, I want to categorically reject the desire for and even the possibility of becoming Nietzsche's profoundly gendered "genuine historian," the great authority who "must possess the power to remit the universally known into something never heard of before, and to express the universal so simply and profoundly that the simplicity is lost in the profundity and the profundity in the simplicity."[44]

Like the little hectograph with which I started, which simultaneously signaled the importance of self-portraiture for Munch's oeuvre and afforded the means to criticize the desire for physiognomic and psychological truth invited by that genre, the abraded self-portrait against a red background and no doubt other works by Munch function, at times via anachronism, as their own critiques. Thus, in Nietzschean terms, they make a claim for the oeuvre as a living, actionable entity rather than a finished, dead thing. Munch, like Nietzsche, would surely have hoped that the study of his work would be untimely, by which Nietzsche meant "acting counter to our time and thereby acting on our time and, let us hope, for the benefit of a time to come."[45]

Munch confronts the viewer directly again in two untimely images made toward the end of his life, the first taken by a professional photographer in the artist's winter studio at his home in Ekely to mark Munch's seventy-fifth birthday in December 1938 (fig. 10), and the second the painting from which this volume takes its title, *Self-Portrait: Between the Clock and the Bed* (pl. 51). Heller has recently argued that the photograph and two others taken on the same occasion represent Munch as the collector and guardian of his art for future generations, as the constitutor and protector of an oeuvre that itself was a work of art, endlessly generative, to be donated to the city of Oslo for perpetual consideration, study, and enjoyment.[46] In the photograph, Munch looks directly and blankly out at us. No turn or tilt of the

Fig. 11
Munch's bedspread, seen in *Self-Portrait: Between the Clock and the Bed* (pl. 51). Munch Museum, Oslo (MM I 316)

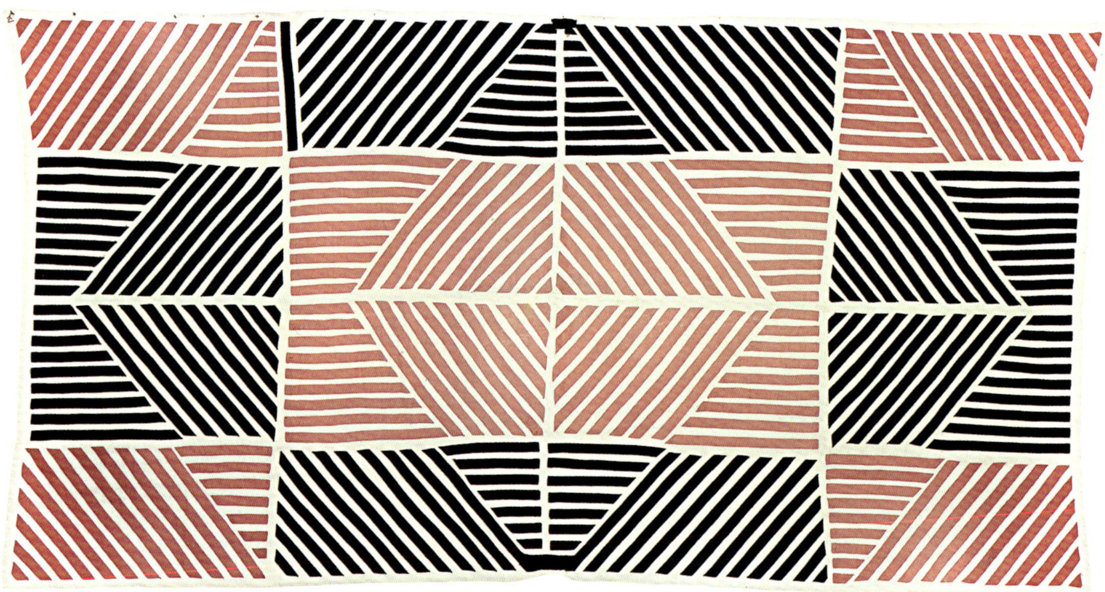

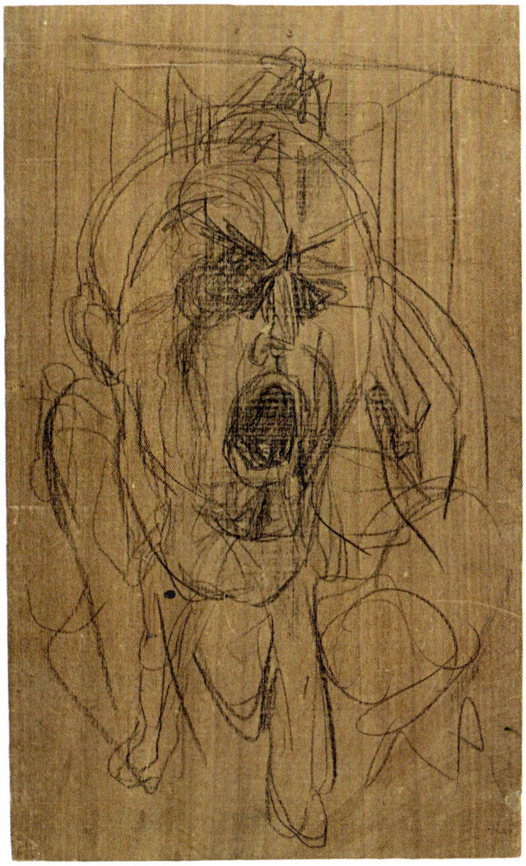

Fig. 12
Edvard Munch, *Self-Portrait with Open Mouth*, 1920s(?)–(?)1930s. Charcoal on cherry woodblock, 22 ¼ × 13 ¾ in. (56.6 × 34.9 cm). Munch Museum, Oslo (MM P 470)

head breaks the temporal spell under which he might stand there forever. No hint of an expression predetermines the nature of our encounter with him. Like the self-portrait against a red background, the photograph challenges future viewers to confront the man and his oeuvre head-on, to forget what we might think we know about Munch, and to look at his work again and again — in short, to approach his work and indeed art history unhistorically.

Munch strikes the same signpost pose in *Self-Portrait: Between the Clock and the Bed*. Squeezed between the vertical clock and the horizontal bed, between an object that keeps time and an object in which time is lost, the figure again confronts the viewer, although with eyes open or closed I cannot be sure. Arms hanging by his sides, feet splayed, the figure is fully in neutral, meditative, perhaps even asleep on its feet. Like the abraded self-portrait, it too offers a mingling of naturalist and antinaturalist elements: the bedspread, with its abstract patterning, is based on Munch's own, still in the collection of the Munch Museum (fig. 11), but it also dialogues with mid-twentieth-century abstractions, asserting today an uncanny relationship with the work of Jasper Johns.[47] Undoubtedly a meditation on the artist's present (old age and impending death),[48] it also seems designed for future presence — among other things, a warning not to relegate Munch to a figurative past.

This essay began with an obscure hectograph and ends with an even more obscure work, an apparent self-portrait sketched in charcoal on a cherry woodblock that was never cut or printed (fig. 12). On the one hand, this little oddity seems to confirm what we might be led to believe about Munch's art and life, in particular that *The Scream* is a form of self-portraiture, a projection or a performance of the artist's self, and an invitation to confront that self in extremis. But it also presents the artist as *The Scream*, performing his own iconic work almost as a form of self-parody. In the same moment that it confirms that the man and the oeuvre are one, it makes us as viewers conscious of the very conventionality of that idea. In other words, in the name of Nietzschean regeneration through destruction, Munch's oeuvre might contain within it the means to critique and undo itself, no less — perhaps above all — in the realm of self-portraiture, precisely where we might once have hoped to find some stable, fixable Munch. As in the desecrated self-portrait against the red background, Munch gives us the face we want only to strip it away, modeling a process of creating and destroying in one untimely instant.

Patterns in Munch's Painting Technique

Mille Stein

Picture Edvard Munch in 1941, sitting at his desk in Ekely and composing one of his rare comments on his way of painting. A successful painter in his late seventies, acknowledged by colleagues, art lovers, and art collectors at home and internationally, he still smarts from having been criticized fifteen years before, when the murals of the Festival Hall (Aula) at the University of Kristiania had to be cleaned only a decade after their unveiling. Defending his artistic methods, he writes:

> I have used the same technique as Cézanne — In cases when some of the canvas remains I, and most likely Cézanne too, have anticipated that it would produce a somewhat deeper tone without damage — When I use turpentine and have experimented with it as with oil paints and more it's not what they call contemptible turpentine painting —.[1]

Picture him again, at the same desk, about the same age, surrounded by his paintings, palettes, paint tubes, and brushes, again feeling he has to defend himself, but this time for being compared with Renoir:

> I have heard this comparison often but have not understood it — Now I have finally figured it out — Renoir rubs the paint and painting medium into the canvas so that the support shines through — Thereby becoming a kind of glaze — I have since my twenties frequently done the same — Anyone can convince themselves of this by studying my pictures from the earliest years — For example: The Portrait of Jensen Hjell, the portrait of Ludvig Meyer, —[2]

And, finally, picture him protesting again, when he felt he was accused of imitating Cézanne, Van Gogh, and Renoir, simply because they all were, according to Munch, related in time.[3]

What can we learn from these imaginings? First, like Cézanne, Munch would occasionally leave the white preparatory layer, or ground, exposed as part of the composition. Second, he would thin his oil paint with turpentine, and he would sometimes (as in the murals of the Festival Hall) use so much that he called the result a "turpentine painting," one resembling a watercolor more than an oil. Third, he would make his oil paint more transparent by first adding a mixture of stand oil and turpentine or Dammar varnish and linseed oil and then applying it to the white ground with a fairly dry brush, thus producing a glaze with a visible, open brushwork. He had experimented with this technique as early as 1885, when painting the portrait of the painter Karl Jensen-Hjell (Nasjonalmuseet for Kunst, Arkitektur og Design, Oslo). Finally, even though he was acutely aware of contemporary influences, he still saw himself as a unique artist, painting in his own style.

Was Munch describing his painting career accurately? Are these characteristics widespread in his paintings? If so, are there other aspects of his painting technique that recur throughout his career and others that appear for only a short time? Let us look more closely at how Munch made use of his painting tools to create his own style.[4]

Self-Portrait: Between the Clock and the Bed versus *Self-Portrait* of 1886

Self-Portrait: Between the Clock and the Bed (1940–43; pl. 51), one of Munch's last paintings, employs strong, contrasting colors. The forceful brushwork and rough application of paint suggest an artist painting quickly and self-assuredly. While he undoubtedly worked fast, Munch was also well prepared, having started by sketching the main elements of the composition on paper.[5] Then, on the ground of the large canvas, measuring nearly five feet high, he drew black lines (probably in charcoal) that traced the outlines of the body, the head, and the front of the shirt, adding a few to indicate the placement of the bed. The underdrawing is easily detected, especially in the shirt, where it serves as an active descriptive element in the composition (fig. 13).

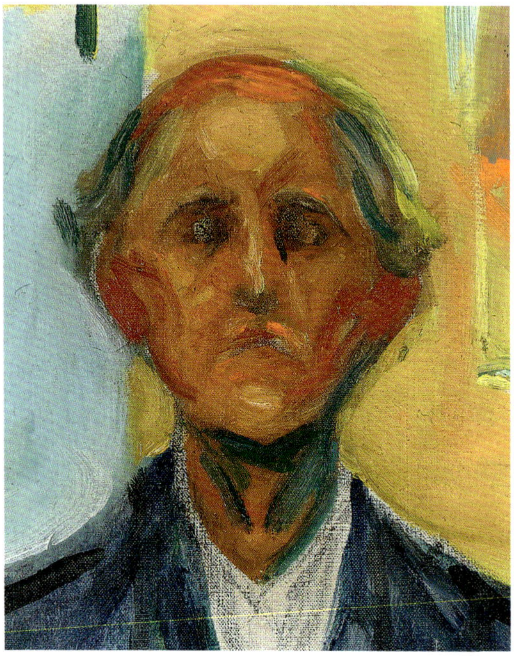

Fig. 13
Edvard Munch, *Self-Portrait: Between the Clock and the Bed*, 1940–43 (pl. 51, detail)

Then Munch started to paint, most likely with the face and body, where he used a fairly turpentine-diluted oil paint and flat, wide, stiff brushes for the jacket and the trousers and a heavier, less diluted paint for the flesh.[6] He may have continued with the clock and then added the various other elements of the composition, painting them next to each other with no overlap. He left quite a lot of the white ground on the canvas exposed, as an active element in the color scheme; the whites of the bedspread, the shirt, and even the minor highlights on the shoes all derive from the ground. Munch must have set the canvas aside for a while, leaving the paint to dry, before adding the final touches, such as the outlines of the jacket, some small paintings on the wall, and the blue areas to the left of the bed.

The way in which Munch varied the consistency of the oil paint is notable here. In most areas, he applied the turpentine-diluted paint in differing thicknesses with a fairly dry brush, but in a few others he diluted the paint to such an extent that it ran down the surface. And for some of the minor details, including the lemon-yellow pictures on the wall and the crimson-red stripes of the bedspread, he employed a heavier paint. Because he wanted the colors to remain clear, he took great care to work with absolutely clean brushes and not to blend the various colors.

Between the Clock and the Bed was painted about the same time as Munch's previously quoted remarks on Cézanne. It may be seen as the artist's status report on himself as an old man: he is telling us that his time is running out and that his career, symbolized by the paintings on the wall, soon will be history. His approach when painting his self-portrait in 1886 (pl. 2), fifty-five years before, was very different. In this small painting he zooms in on his own face, studying the play of light and shadow across it: he is addressing himself, not the viewer. This is a young, self-conscious man with the future ahead of him. Nevertheless, his flesh seems to disintegrate, his collar is not a collar, just some greenish-white patches, his ear, his hair, and his shoulder are melting into a foggy background. Munch scraped away dry paint on the neck to expose the texture of the canvas; he used murky, dark colors, except for the face; and he scratched into the still-wet flesh paint in order to blur it.

It is difficult to get a clear idea of how Munch painted the 1886 self-portrait.[7] Look at the face, where there are so many layers of paint and such varied brushwork, executed in a sketchy manner, especially in the neck and ear. Puzzling dark spots in flaked areas on the forehead indicate that another image lies underneath; the eyes of this image, a (self?-)portrait, are still slightly visible below the eyebrows of the painting we see today (fig. 14a). The overpainted portrait was probably a finished work, since it is signed, in the lower right corner; the signature is visible under ultraviolet light. For reasons unknown, Munch rejected this first portrait, scraped away some of its paint, and reused the canvas for his *Self-Portrait* of 1886.[8]

To leave a painting like the *Self-Portrait* in such an imprecise and "damaged" condition was unheard of at the time.[9] One wonders whether the scratches and scraping on its surface were intended as an artistic effect or whether they express Munch's frustration over a failed painting. The 1886 self-portrait is not the only Munch painting with an intentionally despoiled surface. The first version of *The Sick Child* (fig. 3), from the same period, displays a similar technique: thick layers of paint, hasty and abrupt brushwork, and scratches in the paint surface. Even though *The Sick Child* was positively reviewed by some art critics and colleagues, it was still extremely provocative because of the way it was painted.[10] Munch himself explained, "The picture was painted over many times — in the course of the year I scraped away at it countless times — I wanted to regain the first impression."[11] This description suggests that the scratches in *The Sick Child*, as well as its thick paint layers, resulted from Munch's inability to achieve his intentions; they reflected his struggle with the canvas and were not the result of deliberation. When years later he copied the motif, when he knew how to paint the subject, he may have retained the scratches as a reminder of the first version, but they do not have the same effect. Having lost their original context, they are reduced to surface patterns (pls. 20 and 29).

Munch also scraped his face in *Self-Portrait under the Mask of a Woman*, painted in 1893 (pl. 8 and fig. 7), but there he scratched through the dried paint down to a lighter support, and the scratches are therefore very noticeable. Since Munch never exhibited or sold this painting, these scratches might indicate that he had given up working on it. As for the self-portrait of 1886, Munch must have at least accepted the scratches as an integral part of the painting, both because he signed it and because, when the painting was restored in 1905, Munch (or the owner at that time) did not have these extraordinary irregularities retouched.[12]

When Munch painted *Self-Portrait: Between the Clock and the Bed*, he made a preparatory sketch on paper. For the *Self-Portrait* of 1886, there is also a contemporaneous drawing on paper representing the same subject (fig. 14b). Whether Munch created the drawing or the painting first cannot be determined, although it may be significant that the drawing is a carefully conducted study of light and shadow, without the scratches seen in the painting. The works are so similar in both design and size that the composition must have been transferred from one support to the other (fig. 14c).[13]

Between the two very differently executed self-portraits of 1886 and 1940–43, there are approximately 1,630 paintings. What ties them together technically and what divides them?

Munch Teaches Himself to Paint

Educational opportunities for art students in Kristiania were scarce in Munch's youth. For a few months in 1881–82, he attended the Royal School of Design, where he received lessons in life drawing, his only formal art education. In the early 1880s, he was also occasionally tutored by recognized Norwegian painters who were inspired by French naturalism and the nonacademic approach to art education. From 1885, grants enabled Munch to study abroad, mainly in France. Although enrolled in Léon Bonnat's classes in Paris in 1889, he rarely attended, preferring to visit museums and galleries by himself to learn from the old masters at the Louvre and from the pioneers of modernism, like Van Gogh, Seurat, and Toulouse-Lautrec.

Observing and experimenting with styles and techniques throughout the first half of the 1890s, Munch established his own way of painting. He tried to make the painting process visible by employing forceful brushstrokes, heavily diluted and dripping paint, and a subjective color scheme. For the rest of his career, he would repeatedly return to and modify these methods. They would make him a forerunner of modern painting, but — an individualist at heart — he never joined any school of painters and kept mostly to himself.

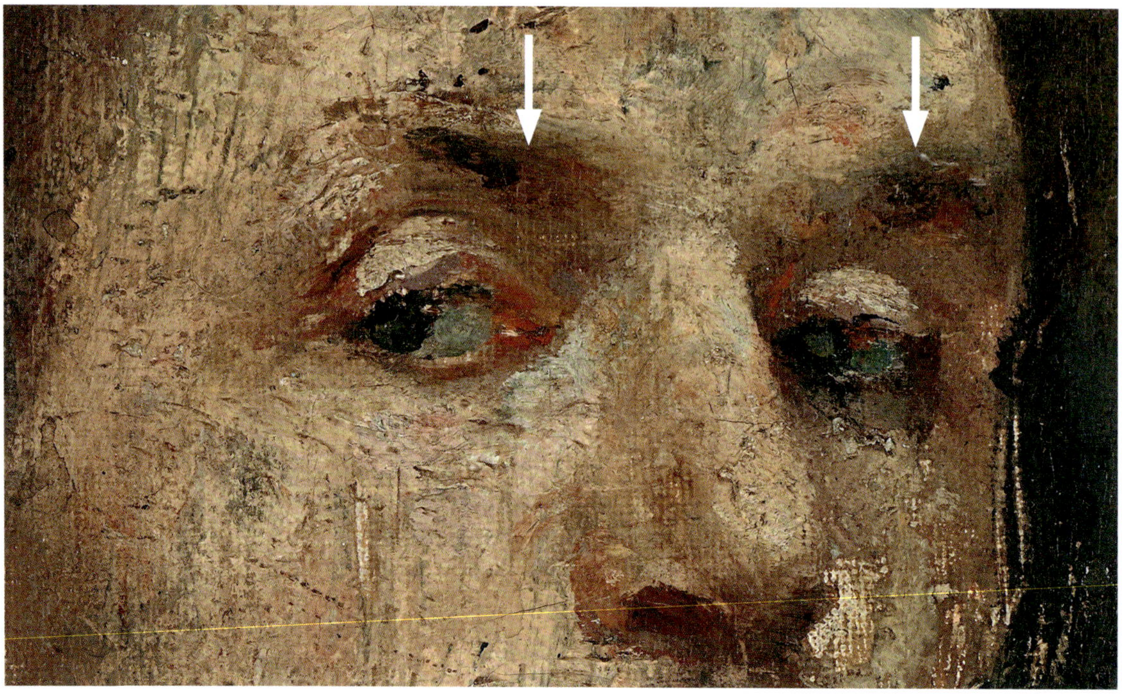

a

Fig. 14a–c

(a) Edvard Munch, *Self-Portrait,* 1886 (pl. 2, detail). (b) Edvard Munch, *Self-Portrait*, 1886. Charcoal on paper, 13 ⅛ × 9 ⅝ in. (33.4 × 24.5 cm). Munch Museum, Oslo, Rolf E. Stenersen Collection (RES.A.00220). (c) Transparent sheet, upon which the main features of the painted self-portrait are traced, is placed on top of the drawing to show their similarities.

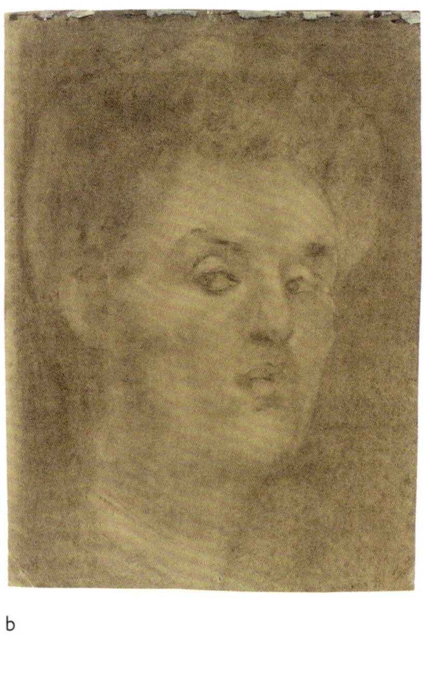

b

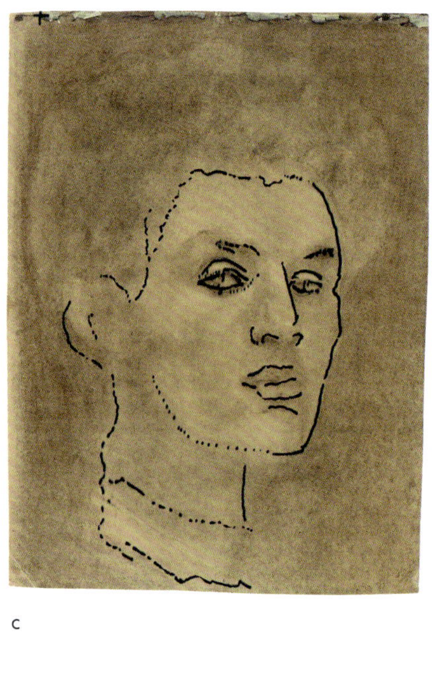

c

Experimenting with Painterly Means: *Puberty*

In 1894 Munch began *Puberty* (pl. 13), an important painting that reflects many of his characteristic artistic effects. On a finely woven, pale, and unprimed canvas, he made the initial underdrawing, which is easily visible in an infrared reflectogram (fig. 15b).[14] He then adjusted the drawing, moving the girl's body more to the center, shortening her right arm so that the hand came closer to the knees, and playing with the position of the bedpost. When filling in the sketch with oil paint,[15] he most probably started on the main subject, as he so often did.[16] He applied the paint thickly in several layers of highlights in the girl's skin, which stand out as whitish areas in the X-radiograph of the painting (fig. 15a). The darker parts of the body, applied in a paint that is less X-ray absorbing, are placed alongside the lighter ones and are therefore visible as dark gray and black areas on the X-radiograph.

When painting, Munch did not follow the underdrawing exactly, but instead left a narrow gap along the outlines. Later he filled these "reserved" areas with a blue contour along the body and arms. Because the synthetic ultramarine blue he used for the contour is less X-ray absorbing than the lead and zinc white employed for the flesh,[17] the contour is visible as dark lines on the X-radiograph. Munch used this reserve method even for certain tiny details, such as the eyebrows and some fingers of the left hand, again seen as dark lines on the X-ray image. To give a warmer tone to certain areas of the skin, he applied a local yellow-tinted glaze based on a natural varnish,

Fig. 15a–c
(a) X-radiograph of Munch's *Puberty*, 1894 (pl. 13, detail). (b) Infrared reflectogram of detail of *Puberty*. (c) Detail of *Puberty*

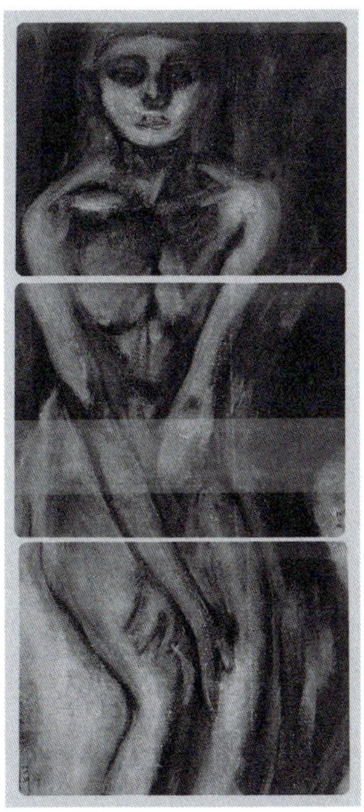

a

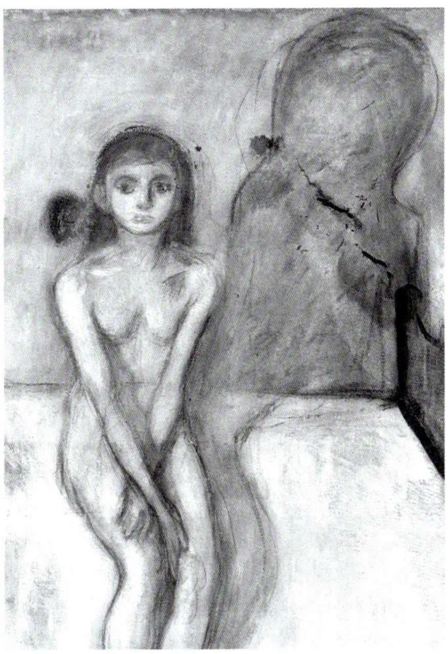

b

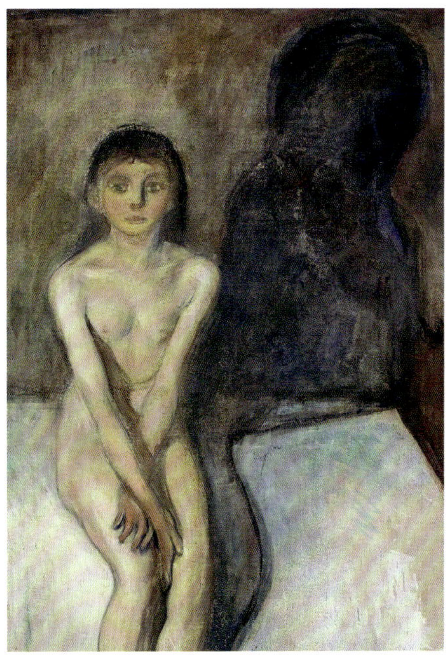

c

most notably on the cheeks, forehead, and left thigh (fig. 15c).[18]

Munch continued with the background and the floor, using thin, translucent washes of paint applied in a range of consistencies and rubbed into the absorbent canvas. The effect is one of a turbulent play of colors behind the girl and a menacing darkness under the bed. The shadow behind the girl became larger and more overwhelming than in the underdrawing; the upper part of the bedpost, as seen in the underdrawing, was overpainted in the final work. The white of the bedspread derives mainly from the exposed color of the light canvas, while its volumes and folds are painted with open brushwork in shades of off-white and light blue. Finally, using his brush, Munch spattered a light blue paint on the bedspread in order to blur the transition between it and the shadow of the girl.

Puberty looks different today from when it was newly painted.[19] Its colors are less vivid and not as sharply contrasted because of the accumulation of surface dirt and the degradation of materials. Natural aging of the resin in the glaze may have caused it to yellow further, resulting in a warmer and darker flesh tone than it had originally.[20] And, last but not least, the painting is somewhat less clear as a result of numerous small losses, especially in the girl's hair.[21] Yet even in its altered state, many characteristics of Munch's experiments with technique are apparent: the bare, absorbent canvas; the combination of turpentine-diluted and more heavily applied paint; the visible, forceful brushwork; the dripping paint; the fine paint spatter; the reserve technique; the use of two different painting mediums (oil and varnish) in one work; and the employment of various surface effects.[22] In later instances of the reserve technique seen in this volume — including *At the Deathbed*, *Self-Portrait with Cigarette*, *Death Struggle*, the 1925 version of *The Dance of Life*, and *Self-Portrait: Between the Clock and the Bed* (pls. 14, 16, 34, and 47) — Munch would leave the ground exposed as white lines or patches.

Experimenting with Paint Consistency: *Self-Portrait with Cigarette*

By the next year, when he painted *Self-Portrait with Cigarette* (pl. 16), Munch had further developed his painterly means.[23] At first glance, the work might recall what Harold Rosenberg termed Action Painting in 1952, with its noticeably dynamic, splashing brushstrokes and dripping paint. But the composition is well organized, and the painting technique is not as spontaneous as one might think. Some of the paint is applied wet on wet, as at the bottom of the painting, where the dripping violet paint has blended into the dark blue farther down (fig. 16). When applying other colors, like those in the smoke, the green stroke under the arm, and some of the white splashes in the lower right corner, Munch first set the painting aside to dry so that the colors would not blend into each other.

Munch placed the image of himself on the vertical mid-axis of the painting, with his hand at the center.[24] As usual, he started painting the figure and then moved on to the background, which partly overlaps the outlines of the head and the upper body. He painted the flesh wet on wet, blending the colors on the palette and on the canvas. The reserve technique here is very delicate: he left the white ground exposed as slender white lines around the eyes and mouth and on the jaw. Munch shaded the flesh, mustache, and eyebrows in a light blue color, while using a similar color on the hair. He blurred the flesh and shirt with bluish paint, most likely by simply spattering it with his finger and a short, stiff brush, as he had in *Puberty*.

For the dematerialized background and suit, Munch used a wide, flat brush to sparingly apply blue and violet oil paint, highly diluted with turpentine, onto the canvas. In this way, he created a translucent paint layer that would allow the ground to act as an essential component of the color scheme and would also let the fine texture of the canvas become part of the painted surface. This way of applying paint was a further development of the technique he had used when painting the backgrounds for the

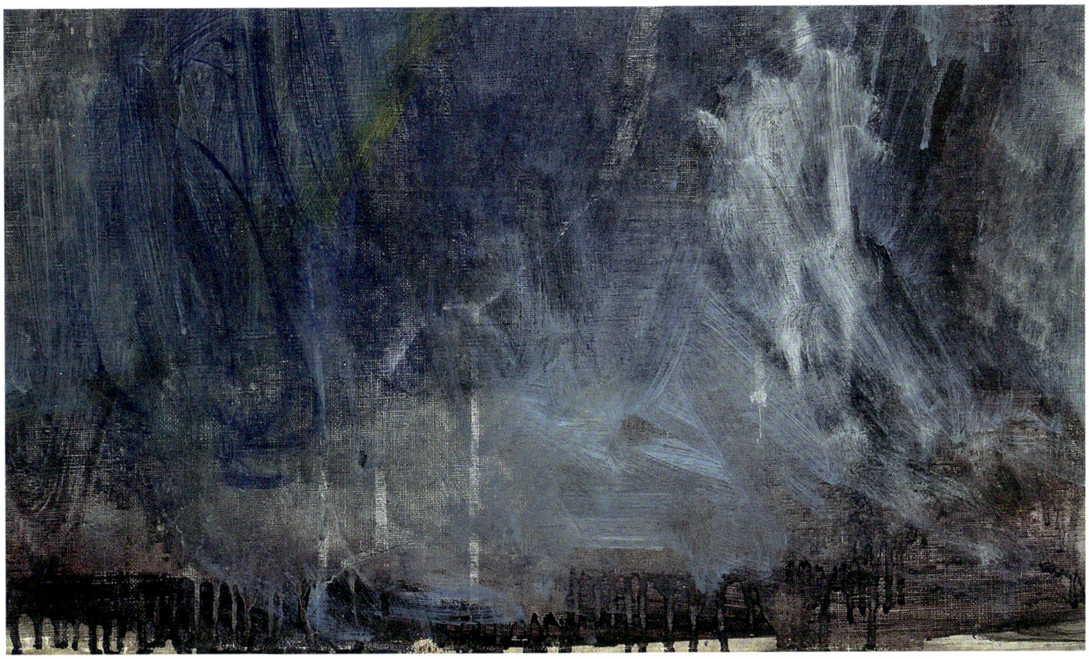

Fig. 16
Edvard Munch, *Self-Portrait with Cigarette,* 1895 (pl. 16, detail)

Jensen-Hjell portrait and *Lady in Black (Olga Buhre)* (pl. 3). It was not a typical oil painting method in the 1880s and 1890s, but was in fact closer to a watercolor technique, in which the white of the paper, instead of white paint, is employed to brighten the colors.

Munch completed the work by painting the smoky foreground. To imitate the smoke from the cigarette and the light from below, he covered the initial, translucent paint layer with a semiopaque paint, but subsequently lightened the blue paint with white. In some areas, the paint was so diluted that it ran down the surface. This way of handling diluted paint may be seen as an early instance of what Munch would call "turpentine painting." Later in his career, in 1906, after Munch had painted two portraits of his patron Max Linde, the two engaged in a discussion about this technique in which Linde asked the artist why he "painted so thinly and used so much turpentine."[25]

Self-Portrait with Cigarette, Night in Saint-Cloud (pl. 7), and *Self-Portrait in Hell* (pl. 25) are all examples of Munch's experimentation with turpentine.

Variations and Repetitions

Throughout his life, Munch painted multiple versions of many of his works, both the lesser-known ones, such as *The Death of Marat* (pl. 28), and the famous, such as *The Sick Child* (fig. 3, pls. 20 and 29), *The Scream* (fig. 8, pls. 15 and 31), *Madonna* (pls. 12, 18, and 19), and *Puberty*. Some of these were done more or less contemporaneously, like the 1894–95 versions of *Puberty* and *Madonna*, others, including *The Sick Child* reworkings, at greater intervals. Some looked

Fig. 17a–c

(a) Edvard Munch, *By the Deathbed: Fever,* 1893. Pastel, 14 × 18¾ in. (35.4 × 47.5 cm). Munch Museum, Oslo (MM M 121). (b) Edvard Munch, *At the Deathbed,* 1895 (pl. 14). (c) Edvard Munch, *Death Struggle,* 1915 (pl. 34)

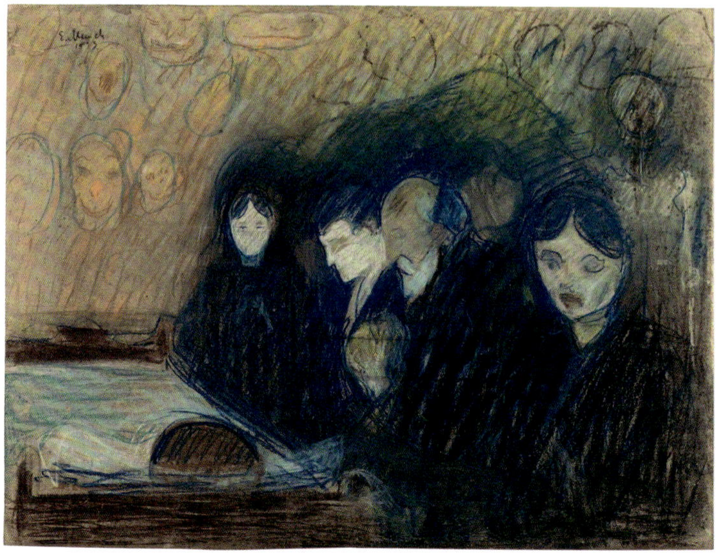

a

fairly similar, despite gaps in time, like *The Dance of Life*, while others are very different, including *At the Deathbed* (pl. 14) and *Death Struggle* (pl. 34). Scholars have discussed why Munch repeated himself in this manner more often than how he did it.[26]

At the Deathbed versus *Death Struggle*

Plagued by poor health in his childhood, Munch would later write in a diary entry dated February 5, 1890, about a crisis in which he recovered from a serious illness: "And he [his father] folded his hands upon the bed and prayed . . . and around the bed all of the others some red in the face from weeping others white — ."[27] Three years later, he made a pastel, titled *By the Deathbed: Fever,* that is like a visualization of his diary note (fig. 17a). He is in bed, surrounded by his desperate, praying family. In his fever fantasy, he sees ghostly faces flickering on the walls and glimpses Death in the form of a skeleton-like body in the background to the right. The same subject later gave rise to three paintings: *At the Deathbed* of 1895 and two versions of *Death Struggle* made in 1915, varying in size but fairly alike in composition.[28]

At the Deathbed (fig. 17b) has a matte finish, with colors that are murky and symbolic. The faces are reduced to masks, the eyes to black dots, the shadow behind the family is as dark as their clothes, and the dense, opaque colors suggest an airless room. The dull surface is due to the absorbent support Munch chose — a canvas sparingly primed with a whitish ground,[29] as seen in the face of the young man in profile — and to the highly diluted paint he adopted for the blood-colored walls and bed, the family's clothes, and the threatening, nearly black shadow behind them. He later added thicker layers of paint for the whitish bedsheets and some of the faces. Finally, Munch drew (probably with a pointed brush) the facial contours, the hands, and the figure of the body under the duvet; he made minor adjustments with a pencil on the duvet and with crayon on the face of the woman to the right. Note how the woman's face resembles that of the girl in *Puberty* in the X-radiograph (fig. 15a): the eye sockets are dark

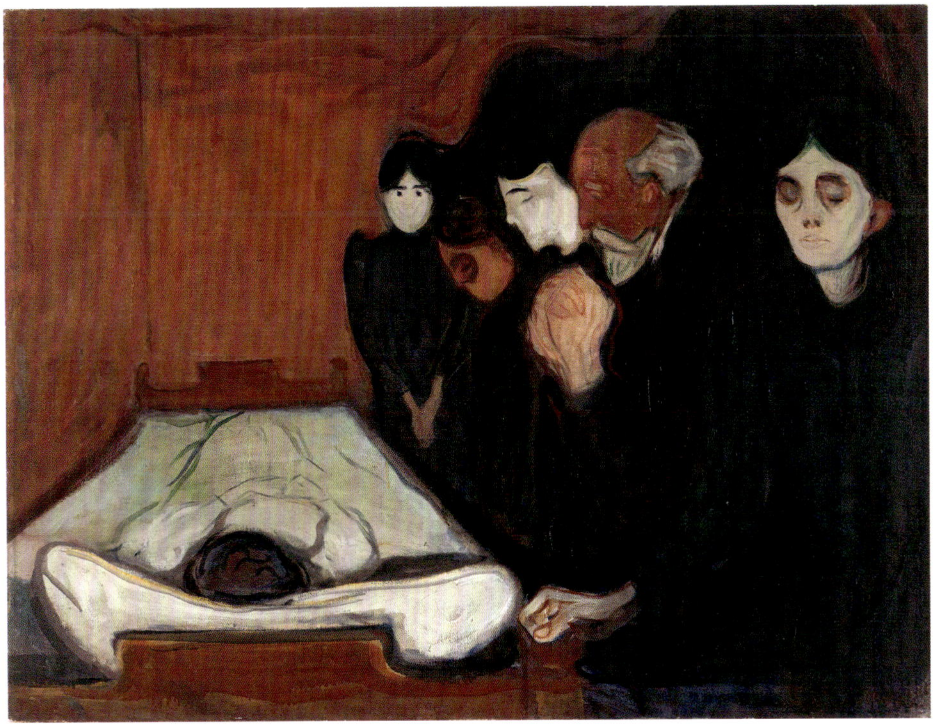

b

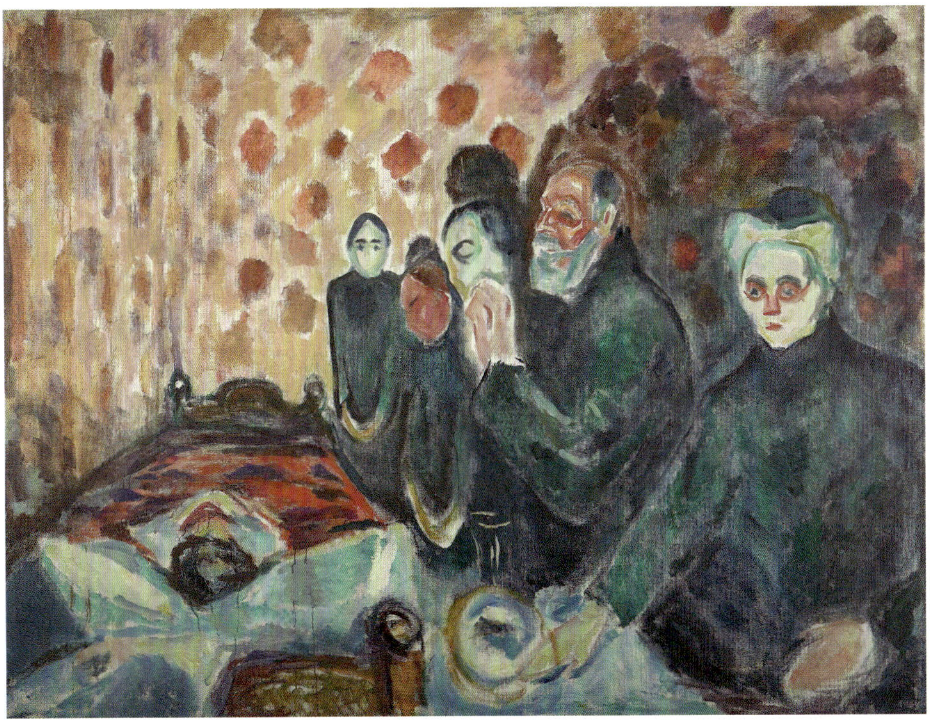

c

wells surrounded by a contrasting corona painted with light, opaque colors.

When painting *At the Deathbed,* Munch most certainly consulted the earlier pastel, but he omitted the macabre faces and skeleton-like body. Returning in 1915 to the same subject in *Death Struggle,* he must have again looked to the pastel as a model, since *At the Deathbed* had already been sold. This time he did not omit the ghostlike faces, but instead reduced them to reddish and yellowish globes, depicted as a continuation of the patterned wallpaper and melting into the shadows behind the family.

It is likely that Munch painted the smaller version of *Death Struggle*, now in the Statens Museum for Kunst, Copenhagen, first and then placed it next to his easel for reference when painting the larger one (fig. 17c). This theory is based on the fact that the smaller work has an underdrawing to guide in the painting process,[30] as well as on the larger's simplified approach, in terms of both composition and paint application.[31] For the larger version, Munch apparently first used fairly wide brushes, loaded with paint to boldly draw the faces, the outlines of the clothes, and the bed on the preprimed canvas. He then filled in most of the open spaces, this time with so little paint on the brush that if he did not rub it into the surface it just covered the crowns of the canvas weave. By working in this manner, he left the white ground either totally exposed or simply reflecting through the thinly applied paint; it is visible in all the areas that are left unpainted, including the father's face, around his hands, and on the walls. When it came to the head of the invalid, however, Munch again returned to the turpentine-diluted paint. As the highly diluted paint began to run down the canvas, he simply painted over the drips he considered incongruous for the composition and kept the rest as they were. Here, as elsewhere, he intentionally left his painting process visible.

Death Struggle is painted very differently from *At the Deathbed*. Its colors are brighter and more translucent, the exposed white ground imparts more air to the room, the visible texture of the canvas suggests that the family members tremble with fear, and the irregular, tilted patterns on the walls create the impression that the room is spinning. Not only do the painting techniques differ in the two works, but so do the styles — Expressionism has given way to modernism.

The Dance of Life: 1899–1900 versus 1925

In 1925 Munch went to the National Gallery in Oslo to copy some of his works, including *The Dance of Life* (fig. 18a), which was painted in 1899–1900 and acquired by the museum in 1910. At first glance, the original and the copy (fig. 18b) display obvious similarities: a dance on the beach in the Nordic summer night, the full moon reflected in the sea, the joyous dancers in the background, the lust in the face of the man to the right, the resistant body of the girl he is dancing with, the innocent, red-cheeked young girl in white to the left, the older, cheerless woman in black to the right. And in the center, the dancing couple, completely engrossed in each other. But look again, and the differences are nearly as obvious. Most noticeable among these are the colors. The duller, more opaque palette of the 1899–1900 painting appears to suggest that its scene occurs later at night. Yet the purplish-blue sky in the 1925 painting seems more threatening; the spiky red hair of the woman to the right and the repeated outlines around the four people in the foreground set the whole composition in motion.

Munch has clearly treated the same image in two different styles: the sharp, flat forms and meandering lines of the original version recall Art Nouveau, while the seminaturalistic later version is more modernist. The differences also arise from the ways in which the works were painted. The earlier version seems to have been executed on a support so thinly primed that the canvas itself is visible — as in the folds of the red dress, for instance. It is also likely that Munch drew the main outlines of the composition on this ground, probably in charcoal; some of these can be seen in the lower part of the white dress of the woman dancing at the right, on her left arm (fig. 18c), and in the clasped hands of the couple in the center.

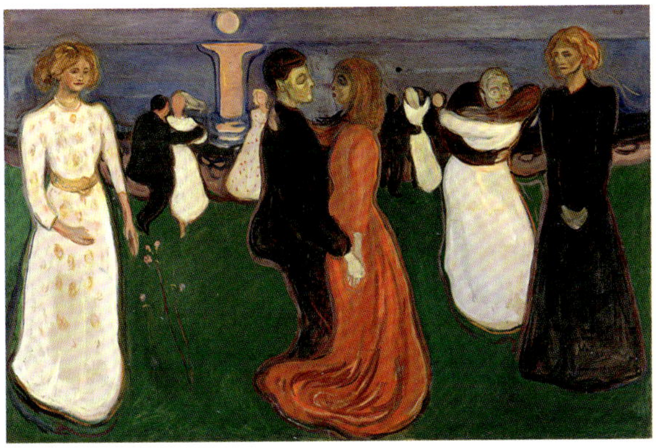

a

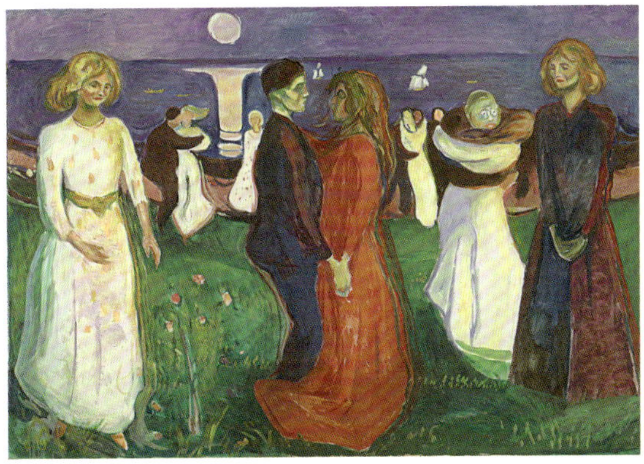

b

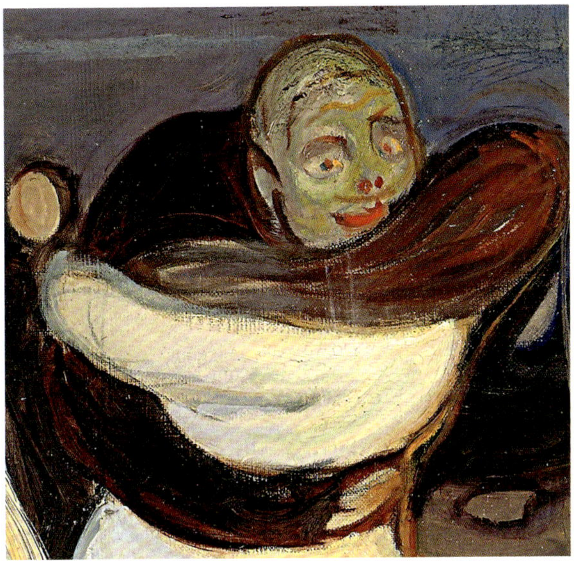

c

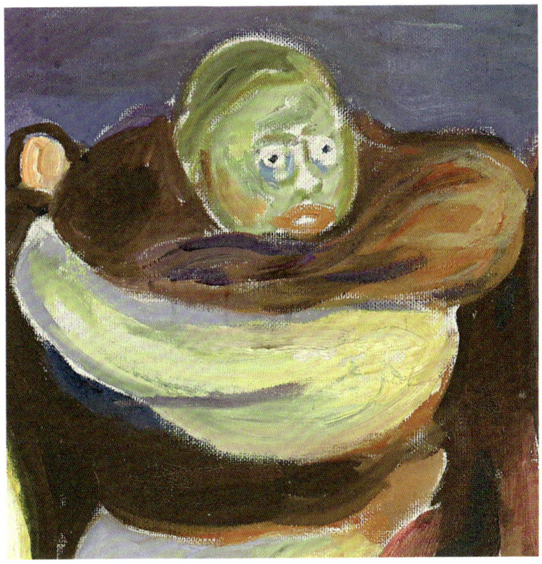

d

Fig. 18a–d

(a) Edvard Munch, *The Dance of Life*, 1899–1900. Oil and crayon on canvas, 49 ¼ × 75 ¼ in. (125 × 191 cm). Nasjonalmuseet for Kunst, Arkitektur og Design, Oslo (NG.M.00941). (b) Edvard Munch, *The Dance of Life*, 1925 (pl. 47). (c) Detail of the 1899–1900 version. (d) Detail of the 1925 version

Munch then applied oil paint of varying thicknesses within the underdrawn lines. The fact that the brushstrokes can be traced around the figures confirms that he painted them first, before the landscape. When the oil paint was dry enough to be painted over, he added the contours and outlines of the people in the foreground and perhaps some final details. The painting is signed and dated twice: (18)99 and 1900. It may have been at the later date that Munch adjusted with crayons the color of the sea around the head of the woman to the right and the hair of the girl in the center. At that time as well, he may have applied the glazes to two of the white dresses, yellow on the one to the right and brownish on the dress with the red dots.

When painting the 1925 version in the museum, Munch most likely would have placed the preprimed canvas (just a bit larger than the original) on an easel next to the earlier version. No underdrawing is visible on the surface of the second version, so he might have drawn the composition directly on the canvas with paint-loaded brushes, using the earlier version as a guide. This time, however, his oil paint was generally more diluted and translucent so that it allowed the white ground to reflect through. And while the original version exposes very little of the support, the white here often derives mainly from the ground; it is even visible in the reserved space around the head of the dancing man to the right. A comparison of the way the face of this man was painted in the two versions clearly demonstrates the different approaches (fig. 18c and d).

The complex brushwork and colors in the original *Dance of Life* contrast strikingly with the simplified painterly means Munch employed for the same subject twenty-five years later. However, whether the 1925 version should be regarded as essentially a copy of the earlier painting is open to discussion. In my opinion, the differences in style and execution reflect Munch's particular view of himself as an artist — that is, as one who painted experimentally, with the aim of always reaching new heights. Accordingly, the second version of *The Dance of Life* is not merely a copy, it is a new work of art.

Technical Characteristics of Munch's Paintings

The eight paintings described here cannot, of course, give a complete picture of how Munch painted. This small selection does not include the earliest pictures, paintings made on board, wood, or bare canvas, monumental works such as the murals for the Festival Hall, and paintings with so-called weather marks.[32] Nevertheless, the works discussed here do display many significant technical patterns that regularly appear in Munch's oeuvre.

Munch generally concentrated on what he considered important to convey. He therefore started by painting the most significant elements in a composition, omitting details that were not meaningful for him, and he finished by painting the background. From very early on, he seems to have favored rapid, visible brushwork, a subjective rendering of his theme, and an expressive palette at the expense of one that faithfully reproduced reality. Consequently, he had little use for small, pointed brushes, but preferred rounded or flat hog examples, as seen in *Self-Portrait with Brushes* (pl. 26). The outlines of the eyes in *Self-Portrait with Cigarette* are a rare example of fine brushwork executed with a pointed brush.

Normally but not always, Munch used oil paints, more often diluted than not, that were applied using a reserve technique, as in *Death Struggle*. Sometimes he "painted" by squeezing the paint directly from the tube, as in *The Death of the Bohemian* (1915–20; Munch Museum, Oslo), sometimes with pastels and crayons in combination with oils, as in two versions of *The Scream* (fig. 8 and pl. 15)[33] and the 1899–1900 version of *The Dance of Life*. He experimented with combining tempera with oil paint, as in *Self-Portrait under the Mask of a Woman* (pl. 8), or with casein, as in *The Reinhardt Frieze* (1906–7; Neue Nationalgalerie, Staatliche Museen zu Berlin). And he used glazes made from tinted varnish, as in *Puberty*. These often unconventional ways of combining different mediums were perhaps the result of his search for varied surface effects and may also have led him to avoid varnishing his paintings overall.[34]

When working with colors, Munch adopted a number of techniques to achieve his ends. His colors seldom imitated what he saw while painting but instead reflected his mood while seeing it: "I painted the colors and the lines I had seen in an emotional state — and I was thus able to create the quivering emotional atmosphere once more —."[35] Also, his palette changed over time, as demonstrated by the differences between his earlier palettes found in his summer house at Åsgårdstrand and some of the later ones from his estate.[36] Equally important is how Munch applied the colors. In the turpentine paintings, the light seems to come from inside the works because it is reflected off the white ground, seen through the translucent paint. In works employing the reserve technique, in which the ground is so often totally exposed, the ground frequently seems to stand in for the pure white color. And while Munch employed the turpentine painting technique less extensively in his sixties and seventies, his use of the exposed ground became increasingly important over the years.

A comparison of Munch's early and late paintings reveals that the artist's style and technique evolved over time. His palette became brighter and his application of paint simpler, but there were no sudden breaks in his process. It was a slow evolution, with several returns to his earlier means. When he settled in Norway in 1909, Munch's life became easier because of his improved finances, more stable living arrangements, and better health. These factors allowed him to enter the competition for the university murals, which involved executing hundreds of square feet of studies and paintings during the ensuing years; they may also have influenced his choice of subject matter, which increasingly focused on the present rather than on the past.

Thus, as he sat down to write in his study, the elderly Munch seems to have been fairly accurate in his assessments. He had used the same technique as Cézanne, when he let the primed support be visible.[37] And yes, he had experimented with the consistency of the oil paint by diluting it with turpentine and had done this so extensively that he could rightly call some of his works "turpentine paintings." Furthermore, he often rubbed the paint into the canvas — whether inspired or not by Renoir is difficult to prove. And finally, although he was aware of the influence of certain contemporaries, Munch had always been faithful to his own unique style.[38]

The Business of Being Edvard Munch

Patricia G. Berman

Ours is a time of markets — a time of bazaars.... Contemporary art is under the thumb of the worst band of capitalists — the bourgeoisie.... Is art influenced by too much business?

— Edvard Munch, undated notation[1]

Now I have an intense demand for my prints. I must soon raise my prices.... *Voilà l'homme de commerce.*

— Edvard Munch, 1913[2]

In the winter of 1913–14, Norway's new (and only) art journal, *Kunst og Kultur*, dedicated a special issue to Edvard Munch on the occasion of his fiftieth birthday. Jappe Nilssen, the art reviewer for the liberal newspaper *Dagbladet*, Norway's most prominent professional art critic, and Munch's close friend, contributed a career overview: "Munch emerged as an artist in the midst of the most ardent period of struggle in Norway... [at that time] older artists had the public, the press, and opinion all to themselves."[3] Into the midst of the generational battle had stepped the youthful Munch with a series of scandals involving his mode of painting and, in the spring of 1889, an audacious one-person exhibition at the University Students' Association in Kristiania. Later that year, as Nilssen recounted, when Munch exhibited works at the annual Autumn Exhibition to negative critical opinion, Erik Werenskiold, one of the young leaders of Norway's 1880s "breakthrough" generation, quickly purchased the painting *Summer Night: Inger on the Beach* (fig. 19)[4] "as a protest against the merciless and stupid criticism put forward by both the press and the public at large."[5] This is the generally accepted story, one of the passing of a torch of radicalism.

Werenskiold later recalled a different circumstance, one in which Munch was not the hapless victim of critical contempt, but an ambitious self-promoter. Munch had confronted him in 1889 and begged him to buy the same painting:

> "Are you crazy?" said Werenskiold. "Do you think I have the money to buy paintings?"

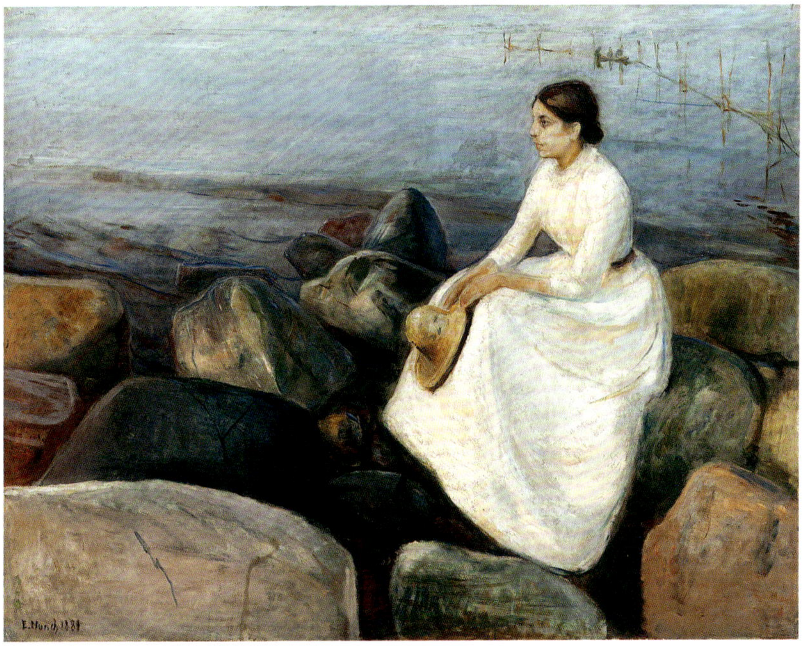

Fig. 19
Edvard Munch, *Summer Night: Inger on the Beach,* 1889. Oil on canvas, 49 ¾ × 63 ⅝ in. (126.5 × 161.5 cm). KODE Kunstmuseene i Bergen, Rasmus Meyers Samlinger (RMS.M.240)

> "But I will sell it to you for a good price," [Munch] answered. "What do you mean by a good price?" I said. "One hundred kroner," he answered. "I refuse. That is a ridiculous price..." "Then do me a huge favor," [Munch] said, "borrow the painting so I can list your name as the owner."[6]

In addition to this reminiscence, in which the savvy young Munch sought instant credibility for his work, Werenskiold recalled the ways in which a network of admirers mobilized around the artist. In 1909, shortly after Munch's longtime champion Jens Thiis became the first professional director of Norway's National Gallery, Thiis had proposed purchasing five significant paintings for the museum, for the sum of ten thousand kroner, which he and Munch had agreed upon. The sum exceeded the museum's overall acquisition budget of nine thousand kroner. That, and the fact that Thiis had approached Parliament for the funds without consulting the museum's newly appointed steering committee, occasioned a scandal in the local press. Werenskiold, who served on the committee, attempted to block the purchase because of what he later characterized as price-fixing:

> Jappe Nilssen and another friend had strategized how to approach the Parliament, which was to allocate the purchasing funds. To that end, they had set complete "fantasy prices," then slashed them in half so that they would appear extremely cheap, while in reality they were inflated over Munch's normal prices.[7]

In the end, in the spring of 1909, the museum purchased the five paintings for the price it had originally stipulated.

Werenskiold's memories may or may not have been accurate, but their contours are consistent with Munch's activities on behalf of his business. By "business," I mean the labor — numerous interwoven types of labor, one kind prompting another — that is normative in any successful artist's career. Productive and inspired work in the studio is the visible labor, while exhibition logistics, networking with patrons and buyers, strategies of promotion, and the management of a studio are invisible but necessary labor. In Munch's case, the business of "business" seems anathema: the public image of the artist was, during his lifetime and in his well-crafted legacy, so strongly associated with an alienated, pained, and oppositional figure who eschewed commoditization. As early as 1895, the art critic, dealer, and historian Julius Meier-Graefe helped to shape such an image:

> If I had not been aware of Munch's complete lack of economic insight, I would have thought that his most recent interest, making engravings, was an instance of well-timed cunning... compared to [such a person as Munch], Buddha is a ridiculous materialist.[8]

As several scholars have recently demonstrated, however, Munch as an image and Munch as an actor in the management of his business and reputation were parallel concepts, one masking the other to such an extent that the very notion of the manager became anathema to any understanding of the artist.[9] This condition is what Robert Jensen has termed the "paradox of avant-gardism," a metaphorical binarism in which "avant-gardism takes its identity from opposing that which it most relies on: the trade in art."[10] Munch had a long and active career, producing approximately seventeen hundred paintings and, by his own estimation, thirty thousand prints.[11] He also sent his work to well over three hundred exhibitions. Yet he was represented by commercial galleries for only three of those years. The Berlin art dealer Bruno Cassirer offered Munch an exclusive contract to represent the artist's prints beginning in the spring of 1904. At the same time, the artist entered into a contractual agreement with Galerie Commeter in Hamburg to represent his paintings in Germany and Austria. Gerd Woll notes that Cassirer's 33.3 percent commission, and his pledge to arrange for the exhibition, promotion, and sale of Munch's work, did not relieve the artist of the burden of managing his career, but instead merely interfered with his control and income. In 1907 Munch bought his way out of the Cassirer contract for a thousand marks, the sum provided by the collector Ernest Thiel in Stockholm in exchange for a number of his graphic works.[12] He also terminated the contract with Commeter through the agency of Hamburg collector Gustav Schiefler.[13] Thus, between 1877, when he published his first drawings, and his death in early 1944, Munch was essentially a free agent.

Munch did not traverse the distance between his status as an unknown provincial artist and as an internationally renowned star through his works alone, but through the strategic use of exhibitions, networks, travel, and a range of mechanisms central to the expanding art market of his time. As noted by Michael FitzGerald:

> The market was not peripheral to the development of modernism but central to it. It was the crucible in which individual artists' reputations were forged as critics, collectors, and curators joined with artists and dealers to define and confer artistic standing.[14]

Munch's matrix of promotional activities was as pathbreaking as his studio production.[15] Woll notes that the multiplication of his motifs, via printmaking and revised painted versions, and their repetition through exhibitions and public projects "were central aspects of his artistic project."[16] To examine Munch's "business" is not to undermine the power or authenticity of his work, or to invalidate his efforts to communicate an unfathomable depth of sensation to his audiences. Rather, it is because of the very strength of his work, the elaborate textual and practical apparatus surrounding it, and the artist's active participation in his own market (as demonstrated by the scholars Tina Yarborough and Jay Clarke) that Munch's modernity can be understood. This essay examines the development of his commercial strategies.

Munch as *"Homme de Commerce"*

Munch learned the importance of promotion early on, when he curated, installed, prepared the catalogue for, and advertised his show at the University Students' Association, one of the first large-scale solo exhibitions ever held in Norway.[17] The year before, in 1888, he had been declined for a government stipend to study in Paris, and Woll surmises that he organized this show in part to garner attention from the grants committee.[18] He charged admission to the exhibition and was assisted in the newspaper promotion by the fact that the University Students' Association had recently installed electric lighting at its venue.[19] There were few models for solo exhibitions in Norway and, with a hundred works — among them *Morning* (pl. 1), *Self-Portrait* (pl. 2), and the first version of *The Sick Child* (fig. 3) — none at all on Munch's scale.[20] Although admiring the work, the critic Andreas Aubert chastised the "young, immature artist [who] must possess great impudence and a total lack of modesty to appear like this especially when he is obviously not at all finished with his training."[21]

A decade later, Munch was also among the first artists in Norway to create his own exhibition posters. Groups of artists had already advertised their exhibitions through the new medium of poster art, including the Vienna Secession, the Munich Secession, Les Vingt in Brussels, and in Kristiania, as early as 1885, the Statens Kunstutstilling.[22] A solo show, however, advertised by the exhibiting artist, represented an innovation in publicity. Munch's first poster, an advertisement for his 1897 exhibition at Dioramalokalet, a former Kristiania diorama repurposed as an exhibition venue, used a mirror image of his 1896 woodcut *Man's Head in Woman's Hair* (fig. 20). With its green motif and gold details vibrating against a red background, the poster was distinctive both in its design and in its dual identity as artistic work and ephemeral advertisement. It also bore the same motif that graced the covers of prototypes for a print portfolio that Munch had intended for sale.[23] Moreover, although the poster advertised a "painting

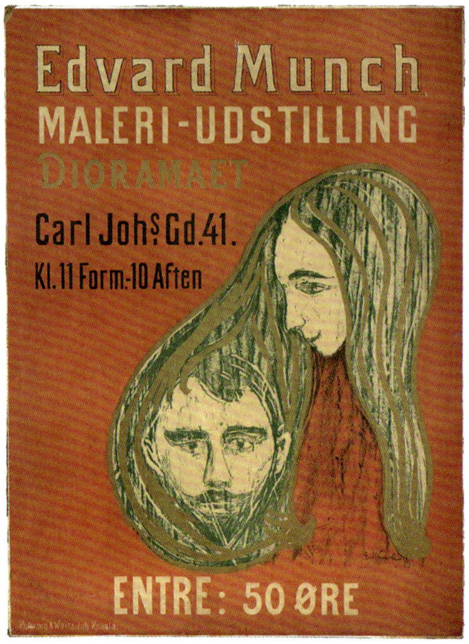

Fig. 20

Edvard Munch, *Man's Head in Woman's Hair*, poster printed by Petersen & Waitz, Kristiania, 1897. Lithographic crayon and tusche on paper, 27⅝ × 20⅝ in. (70.2 × 52.3 cm). Munch Museum, Oslo (MM G 820)

exhibition" (*maleri-udstilling*), the signal motif clearly represented the materiality of a woodcut. Thus, the poster simultaneously advertised the exhibition, became a branding device for the projected portfolio, and subtly asserted graphic art to be equal to painting.[24] The "impudent" Munch exploited the potential of every artistic and commercial medium he encountered, whether painting, graphic art, public display, or promotion.

The expanding world of newspaper criticism and advertising also offered Munch a platform for promotion. When, in 1892, Munch's exhibition with the Verein Berliner Künstler was forced to close by a vote of the organization's membership, the artist became a cause célèbre in the popular press.[25] "This entire event has been great advertising —," he wrote to his family, "... soon some magazine will want to plaster a picture of me on its pages. And next, they'll want my entire life history."[26] His aunt, Karen Bjølstad, in turn reported that the family was collecting the press clippings: "You can forward the criticism that you want to be published in our newspapers. Andreas [Munch's brother] will translate them and Ludvig [cousin Ludvig Ravensberg] will deliver them."[27] Shortly thereafter, a translated and much-edited section of an article from Berlin's *National Zeitung* appeared in the Kristiania newspaper *Aftenposten*.[28] Munch also intended to address the Norwegian press directly:

> The Press hated it ... but that doesn't worry me since attendance continues to be good and chances are, the show will probably make some money. I have written to a number of critics and expect one [letter] will soon be published in *Dagbladet*. I hope Inger [Munch's sister] arranged for me to be published in *Morgenbladet*.[29]

Munch monitored his reviews attentively. After the turn of the century, he and his family began to subscribe to press clipping services. Norsk Argus, Norway's first such business, as well as a number of German and French services, permitted the archival systematization of criticism and reviews, therefore facilitating an artist's ability to resurrect an older piece of writing for reissue.[30] For example, in exhibition catalogues in Stockholm in 1894, at Dioramalokalet in 1897, and at Kristiania's leading art gallery, Blomqvist, in 1903, Munch reprinted earlier reviews of his work. Notably, in 1903, he selected two previously published negative reviews from *Aftenposten* that, as Nils Messel has demonstrated, allowed him to rescript his own career as one of struggle and critical misunderstanding.[31] One, entitled "Vi gjør Strike!" (We should strike!) proclaimed, "This is not art. This is a mess. This is filth";[32] the other warned the public about such "slapdash" work.[33] In the same catalogue, Munch also published positive opinions by Schiefler from Hamburg and from Marius Ary Leblond (the pen name for the writers George Athénas and Aimé Merlo) in Paris, along with an invitation from the painter Carl Moll to exhibit with the Vienna Secession. Taken together, these texts emphasized the presumed sophistication and receptivity of the rest of Europe in contrast to the uncomprehending and small-minded Norwegians.[34] The demonstration of such a gulf between "cultured Europe" and "backward" Norway would be a theme that ran throughout Munch's self-narration.

As a further promotional tool, Munch also assembled stock books, catalogues of black-and-white photographs of his graphic work, for buyers to use as a reference.[35] From a 1913 exhibition at the Salon Joël in Stockholm, for example, he compiled a catalogue of photographs of 188 graphic works, shot in clusters while installed on the gallery walls and accompanied by a separately published price list. In it, the graphic portfolio Alpha and Omega is offered at two different price points, depending on the paper type; *The Sick Child,* printed in four or seven colors, ranged from four hundred to two thousand kroner per print.[36] Such a book, a portable exhibition in miniature that reduced Munch's prints to thumbnail references (obviating any opportunity to note surface or color), offered maximum sales opportunities through its capacity for easy circulation.

As Tina Yarborough has demonstrated, Munch devised his exhibitions with a canny eye toward meeting and shaping the tastes and desires of his audience, and he utilized the medium of the exhibition itself as a means of staking a market position.[37] Munch's self-portraits served as cornerstones of his reception.[38] Looking into his studio mirror, he recorded himself, but on the other side of that mirror stood his audience. When exhibited, his self-portraits often signaled transformations in the artist's identity that, in turn, refracted back throughout the works on display. After Munch's *Self-Portrait with Cigarette* (pl. 16) had been enlisted as "evidence" of his and his family's perceived degeneration by a medical student when it was exhibited in Kristiania in 1895, it is hard to imagine that Munch did not have the reception of his self-portraits in mind, both at their moment of genesis and upon his decision to exhibit them. The audience beyond the mirror was present in the studio as he fashioned his self-representations.[39]

The new commercial gallery context at the turn of the century prompted this "cult of the self" by celebrating an artist's singularity and authenticity as measured by his or her distance from the surrounding culture.[40] *Self-Portrait in the Clinic* (fig. 21) is a work that functions as such a public disclosure. Painted while Munch was in widely publicized treatment for a nervous disorder in the clinic of Dr. Daniel Jacobson in Copenhagen, it was exhibited at Blomqvist under the title *Self-Portrait*. Signed and dated "E. Munch Kjøbenhavn –1909–," it is among the few of Munch's paintings to identify the location of production.[41] In reviewing the exhibition, Munch's friend Hans Dedikem read the work as an acknowledgment of psychic pain and endurance, since Munch still resided at the Copenhagen clinic while the painting was on display:

> Among the most important works is the self-portrait by Munch, painted this year. . . . This is a man whose life has been touched by tragedy. The sides of his mouth are drawn with pain, and yet he exudes pride and power.[42]

At a 1912 exhibition at the Kunstnerforbundet (the gallery of the newly established Artists' Association) in Kristiania, Munch included a self-portrait reminiscent in pose and some strategic details of Vincent van Gogh's *Portrait of Dr. Gachet* (figs. 22 and 23), which had entered the collection of Harry Graf Kessler in 1904 via Paul Cassirer's gallery.[43] His inclusion of his self-portraits reminded Munch's audience of his presence in and behind his images, as well as signaling subtle changes in his identity. A reviewer in the newspaper *Verdens Gang*, identified only as "A.S.," remarked:

> I found myself in front of an exhausted man, his eyes staring dreamily back at me. His mouth is weak, trembling despondently. As my eyes drift across the art I ask myself: "How it is possible that this dreamer of a man has actually painted these powerful, gloomy, almost brutal images?"[44]

Fig. 21

Edvard Munch, *Self-Portrait in the Clinic*, 1909. Oil on canvas, 39 3/8 × 43 1/4 in. (100 × 110 cm). KODE Kunstmuseene i Bergen, Rasmus Meyers Samlinger (RMS.M.262)

Fig. 22

Edvard Munch, *Self-Portrait with Hand under Cheek*, 1911 (pl. 32)

Fig. 23

Vincent van Gogh, *Portrait of Dr. Gachet*, 1890. Oil on canvas, 26 3/8 × 22 in. (67 × 56 cm). Private collection

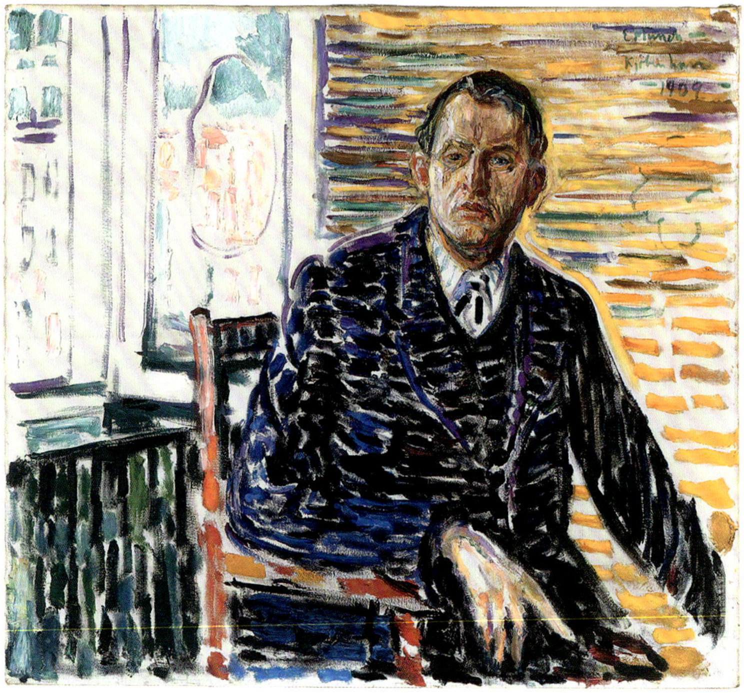

Munch's active and at times frenetic exhibition schedule required elaborate materials and logistics for framing and crating the works as well as coordinating and paying the costs of travel and delivery throughout Europe. Consequently, mobility was important to Munch's "business." With rental spaces and fire insurance to pay, and property to organize, he had a very elaborate, if invisible, career as a manager.[45] When disaster struck, such as when a shipment of works bound for Rasmus Meyer in Bergen sank, or when a crate of prints and matrices for woodcuts went temporarily astray, Munch would have to deal with all aspects of the consequences, repainting the motifs or carving fresh matrices[46] and, behind the scenes, processing paperwork. It is no wonder that a series of letters in 1912 from the artist to his supporter Albert Kollmann reported the following: Munch suggests that "it might be good to hold a small exhibition now [at Cassirer]" (November 11); he is surprised that Kollmann was able to arrange the exhibition so quickly and orders it delayed (November 27); Munch determines not to exhibit so much and to "live for his art" (December 20[?]).[47] Munch's collector and patron Eberhard Grisebach sympathized with his situation as a "free agent," promoting his own work:

> You have no use for these small salon exhibitions, the art dealers use them merely to attract new customers, and you will have great difficulties. People will storm you from all sides. Keep calm and remain indifferent to the cries from the market![48]

At various times, Munch organized as many as six exhibitions simultaneously in different countries.[49] In this regard, international transit via railway and steamship was a crucial tool for his promotional activities in that it enabled him to install, de-install, and move his works from site to site with great facility. Stephen Kern has analyzed the phenomenological and conceptual effects of the railroad, among other

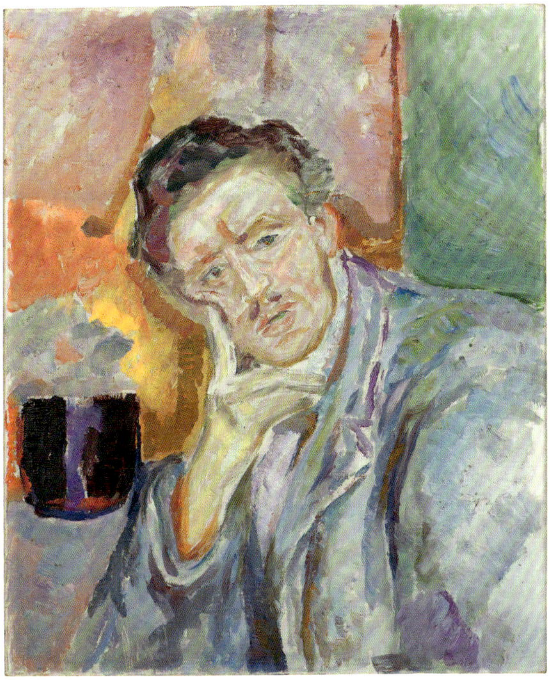

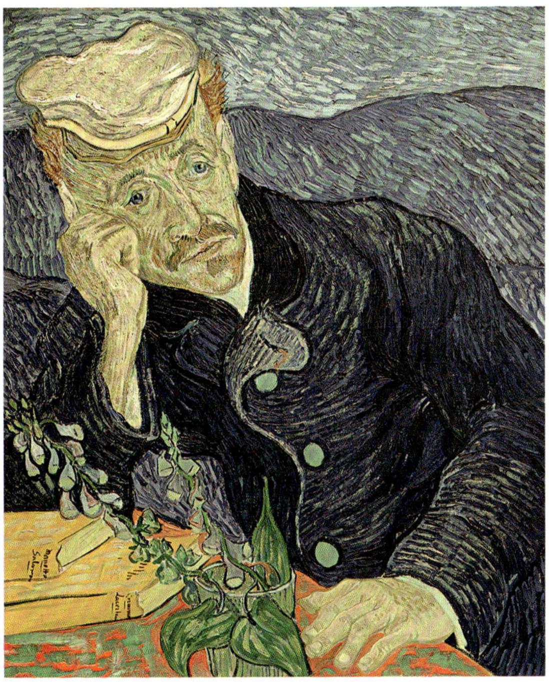

technologies, on cultural practices in the very years that Munch emerged as a working artist.[50] We forget now how easily Europe could be traversed at that time via railway, whose dense networks enabled rapid and even spontaneous mobility (fig. 24).[51] Munch also built and consolidated his networks through travel. Not only did he receive a hero's welcome in Prague when he exhibited at the Manes Association of Fine Arts in 1905,[52] but the younger artists likened Munch's visit to the times when "Donatello went to Padua, Rembrandt to Amsterdam, Michelangelo appeared in Florence, or when Caravaggio worked in Rome."[53] In an era in which a cult of personality was central to art history and criticism, direct association with the renowned artist by his younger admirers offered support to their self-definition as members of an avant-garde.[54]

Munch's Networks

Munch seems to have had a gravitational field within which circulated the important art historians, critics, gallerists, museum directors, facilitators, and interpreters committed to promoting his work.[55] He and his networks can be understood as interleaving their objectives: building their institutions, demonstrating their prescience, sharing mutually reflected glory, and (most especially for Munch) chasing sales. In 1892 Munch had settled in Berlin, where he became enmeshed in a literary and intellectual circle that congregated at the wine bar Zum Schwarzen Ferkel.[56] Within that group of German and émigré intellectuals, he began to amass his network of admirers and actors in the building of his reputation. It was there that he began the close alliances with writers that would continue throughout his life. The Polish writer and critic Stanisław Przybyszewski published the first monograph on Munch, *Das Werk des Edvard Munch: Vier Beiträge* (*Edvard Munch: Four Contributions*), a book of essays coauthored by the eminent writers Franz Servaes and Willy Pastor and the up-and-coming art historian Julius Meier-Graefe, all intimates within Munch's Berlin circle. Appearing in 1894, the

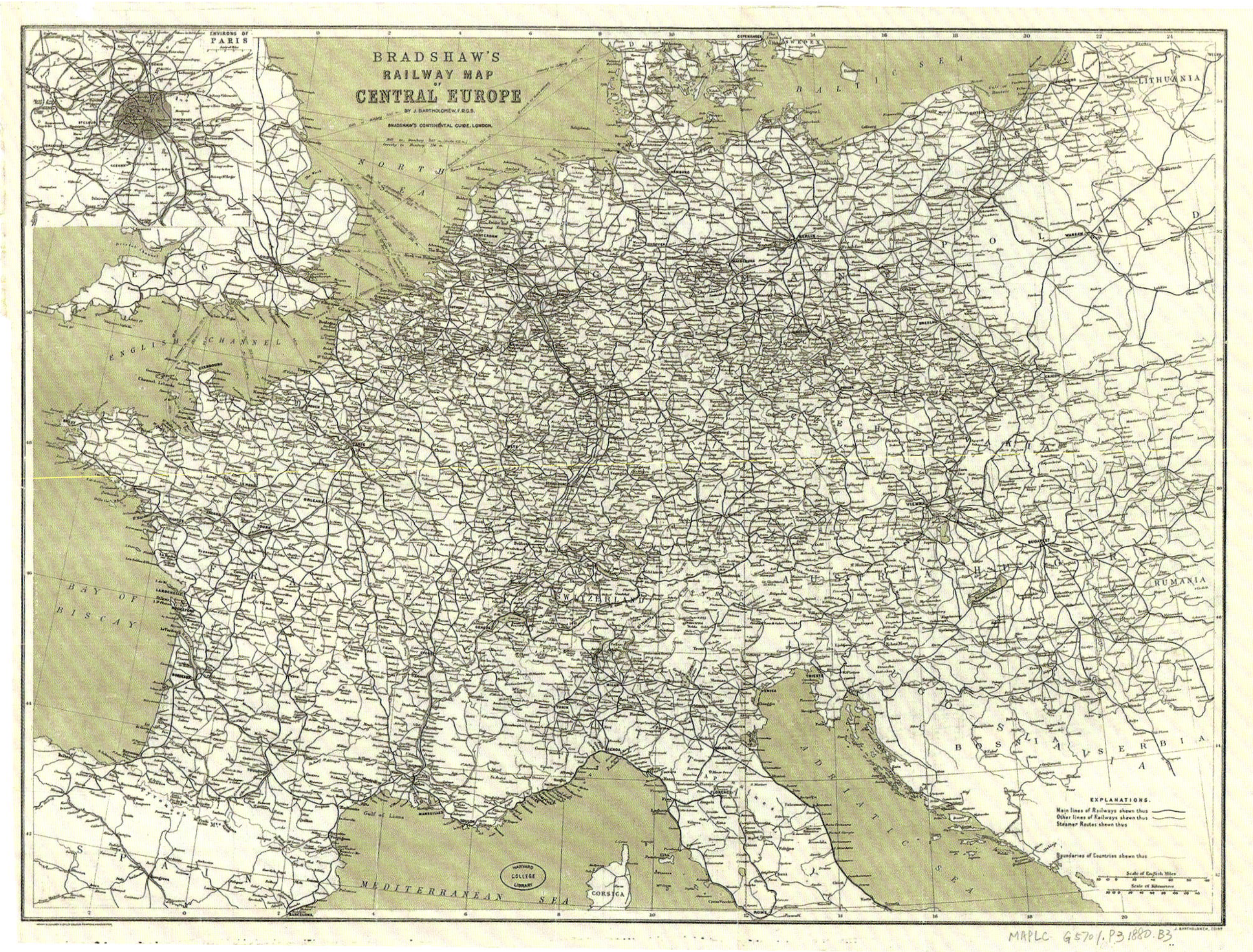

Fig. 24

Bradshaw's Railway Map of Central Europe, published by Harry Blacklock & Co., ca. 1880. Lithograph, 47 × 65 in. (119.4 × 165.1 cm). Harvard Map Collection, Harvard Library, Cambridge, Mass.

volume established important critical terms, in part likely supplied by Munch, that shaped the artist's subsequent reception in Berlin.[57] Przybyszewski would publish extensively on Munch's work, including important illustrated essays in *Moderní Revue* (Prague) in January 1897 and in *Życie* in Cracow in November 1898.

Przybyszewski and his wife, Dagny Juel Przybyszewska, served as agents on behalf of Munch in eastern Europe, where they cultivated collectors and facilitated exhibitions.[58] Przybyszewska, for example, attempted to make connections for Munch in Poland:

> Krywułt's Art Salon is the most prominent one in Warsaw and you can safely entrust him with your images. I also think that you can benefit financially from your exhibition there.... I will also speak with a friend, an art collector, who is well connected, so that one can make as much money as possible out of it.[59]

In another letter, she offered to sell lithographs on his behalf.[60]

One of the most consequential partners in the development of Munch's career was Meier-Graefe, a critic who became an art dealer, publisher, and one of the first systematic historians of modern art. In 1895 Meier-Graefe published a portfolio with eight of Munch's intaglio prints that included an essay (previously quoted here) staking a claim for Munch's status as an enlightened outsider.[61] According to Jay Clarke, Meier-Graefe "hoped that the print portfolio would add an air of legitimacy to his own critical reputation and budding business efforts, and was clearly disappointed that it had been unsuccessful."[62] She also notes that Meier-Graefe operated simultaneously as impresario, adviser, critic, and historian: he offered advice in the studio, curated and then criticized exhibitions, and finally enshrined them in his important art-historical writings. This complex and mutually referential interactive system of promotion would become standard practice within Munch's networks.

When Meier-Graefe published his important three-volume *Entwicklungsgeschichte der modernen Kunst* (*Development of the History of Modern Art*) in 1904, he traced a genealogical set of relations for artists such as Munch, who were considered radical or indigestible, legitimizing and naturalizing their work through ties with historical figures.[63] Robert Jensen has identified such a strategy of canonization as central to the burgeoning international art market.[64] After Meier-Graefe moved to Paris in 1895, he used his connections to Siegfried Bing at Maison de l'Art Nouveau to exhibit Munch's works there: "In eight days Bing's salon will open and perhaps I can arrange to put up one or more of your paintings. Send me something, for example *The Scream* or something like it. Strong things!"[65]

Meier-Graefe set into motion a network of patrons and supporters — some of them museum curators and directors — upon whom Munch relied in all aspects of his work. Among them was Eberhard von Bodenhausen, who copublished the periodical *Pan* with Meier-Graefe and who encouraged Munch to pursue graphic art: "It seems to me that printmaking is your true domain and I have no doubt that pecuniary results will come when you achieve even greater technical perfection."[66] Bodenhausen in turn introduced Munch to the collector Harry Graf Kessler, who gave the artist financial assistance in 1894 and then, a decade later, while director of the Museum für Kunst und Kunstgewerbe in Weimar, commissioned Munch to paint his portrait and introduced the artist to his own network in that city.[67]

Albert Kollmann, whom Munch also met in Berlin, began to function in a "public relations" capacity for Munch and helped to establish the artist's market in Germany. Like Meier-Graefe, Kollmann advised and collaborated with Munch on all aspects of his market. "I think the ideal option would be to exhibit my best works at Durand-Ruel despite the expense," Munch wrote to him in 1904. "Until I exhibit in Paris, it will be problematic in Berlin. The best would be a large exhibition in Vienna and also at Durand-Ruel next year."[68] Kollmann helped Munch to set prices, and the artist in turn kept him apprised of his commerce. For example, writing from Copenhagen in January 1909, Munch reported lively sales of graphic work in Helsinki, "much better than at Cassirer."[69] In 1911, while competing to win the competition to paint murals for the Festival Hall (Aula) at the University of Kristiania, he wrote to Kollmann from Norway, seeking a venue for his sketches for the murals in Berlin, "but where? Maybe the Berlin Secession, but is it available?"[70] Kollmann replied within the week, "The Secession has a great interest in your university decorations.... I also spoke with Cassirer."[71] Munch replied, "That would be ... great to be able to exhibit these works at the Berlin Secession.... Please give Cassirer a catalogue."[72] As Munch's prices rose, he informed Kollmann that he had to be mindful of his international market:

> One finds the works to be so enormously expensive — OK, but why not have bought them years ago, when they were so extremely cheap? Now they are costly, and I cannot set prices lower in Germany than in Scandinavia.[73]

Through Kollmann, in 1902 the artist met Max Linde, a prominent physician in Lübeck, who purchased graphic work, invited Munch into his home, which became a private promotional space, and commissioned various works depicting his residence and family. Linde introduced Munch, among others, to the art dealer Hugo Perls, who collected his work and commissioned portraits of himself and his wife.[74] Linde and the Belgian architect Henry van de Velde in turn introduced the artist to Herbert and Hanni Esche, whom they convinced to commission family portraits and collect graphics by Munch in 1905; through the Esches, Munch held six exhibitions in Chemnitz between 1905 and 1929.[75]

Munch's network continued to be remarkable for the number of its writers, who helped to forge his reputation. In 1902 Linde wrote a slim monograph entitled *Edvard Munch und die Kunst der Zukunft* (*Edvard Munch and the Art of the Future*). Illustrated with elegant photogravures, the work emphasized the artists's authenticity and enlisted a well-used metaphor that signaled vanguard status — the genius of the future whose anachronism is in the end redemptive: "Munch's soul is torn by the dilemma of modern times.... Artistic nature is bound by a thousand ties of our time to the rocks on which the artist, another Prometheus, bleeds to death."[76]

At Linde's home, Munch met the collector Gustav Schiefler, who in 1907 published a catalogue raisonné of Munch's prints.[77] Because at the time such catalogues were extremely rare for living artists, Schiefler's publication granted art-historical status to Munch's graphic production, elevating it from the exigencies of personal taste and critical judgment into a canon. As chronicled by Munch's voluminous correspondence with Schiefler in the years leading up to the publication of the book, the artist was actively engaged — albeit with some reluctance — in the process of systematizing his own work. Such a catalogue provided both a reference guide for connoisseurs, gallerists, and curators and an archival reference for those who might wish to build an authoritative collection. Munch, for example, urged the Bergen collector Rasmus Meyer to assemble a complete set of his works, which he was willing to offer at a reasonable price, so as to rival those of Linde and Thiel.[78]

Kollmann also introduced Munch to another of his future biographers, Curt Glaser, curator of prints and drawings at the Staatliche Museen zu Berlin.[79] When Glaser was commissioned by Bruno Cassirer to write a monograph on Munch, the artist collaborated in the process. Glaser wrote to Munch:

> I have spoken at length with [Bruno Cassirer] about the book he wants from me. I think it is better to do a less expensive work that will be easier to sell. What do you think about this? I believe it will be better than ... a publication that no one buys or reads.[80]

Munch's networks in Germany and throughout Europe spread through such writings and extended relationships. However, his own circle in Kristiania was especially tightly connected with the artist and with one another. Their correspondence with Munch and some of their memoirs following his death reflect a shared "all hands on deck" attitude.[81] Jappe Nilssen, seven years Munch's junior and a friend from the Kristiania Bohème, became one of the artist's most important interlocutors in Norway. Along with Jens Thiis, he was a significant collaborator in Munch's enterprise. When Munch was at Dr. Jacobson's clinic in 1908–9, Nilssen served as a factotum, arranging for him to exhibit his works at Blomqvist in two hangings, ordering frames built to Munch's specifications, and then helping to mount the show and to set the prices.

In fact, while convalescing in Copenhagen, Munch ran a remarkably active exhibition program. Nilssen wrote to Blomqvist to confirm the rights of Thiis, Ludvig Ravensberg, and himself to make the selections: "Thiis, Ravensberg, and I will furnish the locale, we can install the pictures, and WE ALONE have permission to determine what will be shown and what will not."[82] The exhibition was a success, prompting Munch to query Nilssen:

> I am wondering if it would be to my benefit to hold an entire Exhibition this Fall — in October. . . . Since my work continues to be sought after, why should I not exhibit? Of course, there are people in Kristiania who will be upset — and the exhibition is not likely to be a sellout. But I am also convinced that I could sell many of my works.

And he added, presumably in reference to their private negotiations, "We did cheat Blomqvist out of several percentage points."[83]

When, in 1910, Nilssen became the art critic for *Dagbladet,* he metamorphosed into Munch's propaganda arm, and a leitmotif of his writing was the conservatism and lack of sophistication of the Norwegian public. In April 1911, for example, reviewing the Dioramalokalet exhibition of Munch's full-scale sketches for the university murals, Nilssen served as the artist's cheerleader: "Edvard Munch is now at the peak of his power . . . among Norwegian artists he towers like an enormous tree over the underbrush."[84] A few weeks later, Nilssen equated the possibility that Munch's works would not be purchased as a blight on Norway's national prestige:

> We repeatedly permit our greatest works of art to disappear abroad. Other countries consider the sale of first-rate art to another country to be a great national loss. No wonder we consider ourselves a nation of peasants. Would it not be possible to find a wealthy man with the foresight to donate this unique work to the National Gallery?[85]

Parodying such rhetoric, and recognizing Nilssen as Munch's accomplice, the satirical Norwegian newspaper *Humoristen* published a caricature of Munch and Nilssen under the title *From the Munch Cloister* (fig. 25). It pictures Munch as headily absorbed in painting the sunny heavens in the manner of his Festival Hall murals while a miniaturized "Nielsen" pierces the darkness with a lantern: "Lucky Munch who has Jappe / Always racing in a flap / Shining his light low and higher / Looking for yet another buyer."

Similarly, another caricature published at the time, under the title *Summer Fiancés,* pictures Thiis as haplessly seduced by the artist (fig. 26). As the director of the National Gallery from 1908 to 1941, Thiis was one of the most powerful arbiters of both taste and history in Munch's home country. He was also one of the first to canonize Norwegian art with his book *Norske Malere og Billedhuggere* (*Norwegian Painters and Sculptors*), published as a series of pamphlets beginning in 1904 and then as a book in 1907. Thiis offered Munch a kind of wall-to-wall promotional coverage. As museum director, he regularly purchased Munch's works, sometimes to great public controversy when he was seen as acting unilaterally. He also published and lectured extensively about Munch and his work and, beginning in 1900, helped the artist to strategize his pricing, inserting himself as the middleman in some sales.[86]

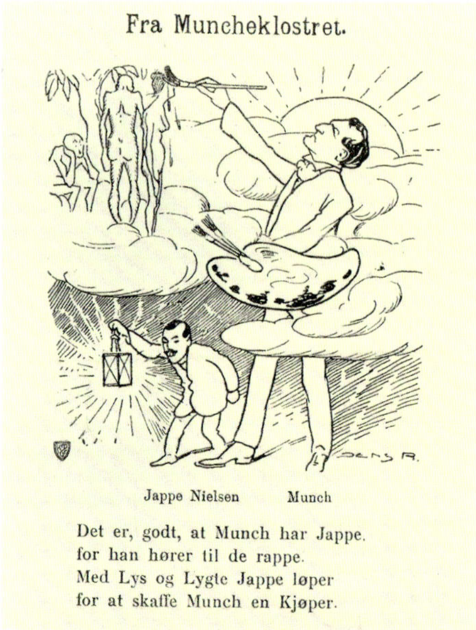

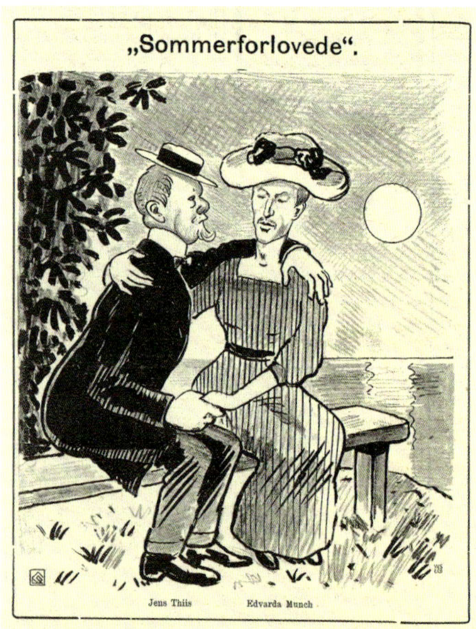

Fig. 25

Fra Munchklostret (*From the Munch Cloister*). From *Humoristen*, May 6, 1911

Fig. 26

Sommerforlovede (*Summer Fiancés*). From *Vikingen*, September 2, 1911

When Munch endeavored to exhibit his work in Trondheim and Bergen, Thiis characteristically offered a promotional infrastructure:

> Financial considerations aside, if you wish to exhibit at this time, please know that you will have my full support. No need to send anyone around to help; I will rent a space and supervise the show's hanging.... I also think I can promise you at least two newspaper critics.[87]

Serving on the adjudication committee for the University of Kristiania's competition for the murals to embellish its new Festival Hall, and therefore enmeshed in the mechanisms of the competition between 1908 and 1914, Thiis also advised Munch on how to position himself advantageously. In 1911 he suggested to Munch that he exhibit his mural proposals widely, including the one-man exhibition in Dioramalokalet of the works that coincided with the jury's selection meeting across town. He then helped the artist to arrange that exhibition, publishing articles extolling the merits of Munch's university paintings and later participating in the private purchase and donation of the works to the university.[88]

In 1933 Thiis published a comprehensive biography of Munch, for which he and the artist corresponded extensively in letters that testify to Munch's desire to manage his legacy. "We agree," he wrote, for example, "that the reference to an 'earlier circle of friends' will be deleted,"[89] presumably decoupling the artist from his old Bohemian associates and the networked path to fame. Munch drafted several letters chiding Thiis for not sharing his page proofs in enough time for Munch to make factual corrections: "[Pola] Gauguin, Glaser, and Schiefler all sent page proofs for my consideration and that of course is essential to do."[90] In the process, he did not want Thiis to disclose his own collaboration: "You must not cite me directly. It should not look like an autobiography."[91]

By the time he wrote those lines, Munch had collaborated in the authorship of his reputation.

In his biography of Munch, published in 1922, Curt Glaser had helped to shape this legacy:

> His art . . . finally received its due from the market. He, however, hardly paid it any attention. He noticed the wealth that came unbidden as little as he noticed the poverty that he gladly bore. To very few were the material exigencies of existence so foreign as to Munch. He strode through life without gazing to the right or left. He sees art. He sees life only through his art."[92]

Pointing to the embeddedness of such an identity, he wrote, "The name Edvard Munch signals a program."[93]

Part of the business of being Edvard Munch was not to be seen to be in business. In this, in the words of Ludvig Ravensberg, "While impractical, Munch is, paradoxically, quite practical."[94] Achieving exceptional success within the competitive art market, Munch supported the inventiveness of his painting and prints with his pioneering means of promotion:

> I have gradually built up a quite complicated and costly business around my artistic practice. . . . I have built up this apparatus during the past 20 years, and time has shown that it allows me to work a great deal and to sell a great deal.[95]

A painting as explosive and pathos-ridden as Munch's *Self-Portrait: Between the Clock and the Bed* (pl. 51) can also, as suggested by Reinhold Heller and by Allison Morehead in this volume, be understood as a depiction of himself as "curator" of his legacy. The painting reflects back on the business of being Edvard Munch.

Munch on the Periphery

Richard Shiff

Good advice: do not let emotion affect your judgment. Better advice: do not let prejudice and preconception repress your emotion. Thinking, directed by concepts and categories, interferes with feeling. It takes hold of our foreground of active sensations and our background of emotions and mood and molds all into normative form. But the various manifestations of feeling resist regularity and interfere with the cognitive process. We are split. Our immediate actions proceed with inadequate information and have unpredictable consequences. Our justification after the fact must account for inexplicable results. Heinrich von Kleist, addressing military officers who faced tactical decisions, acknowledged the dilemma of the human condition: "Thinking it over . . . seems only to confuse, inhibit, and suppress the necessary force of action, which has its source in wondrous feeling."[1] Rely on feeling as you press forward, and apply reasoning only to assess what comes to pass — this was Kleist's recommendation. With respect to creating a work of art, Paul Gauguin advocated the same order: "Emotion first! Understanding afterward."[2]

The conflict between feeling and thought is not absolute; it can be obviated. Consider the opposition of the two conceptual terms as an ingrained semantic quirk, more philosophical truism than human reality. Perhaps our language is split and we are not. Nothing compels us to maintain the division within the complex of our thinking and feeling, to indulge in an intrigue of dialectical contradiction. We can instead regard feeling as an active aspect of thought — the leading edge of thought — like a military advance or venturous aesthetic gesture. We feel a specific emotion because our immediate sensations are being cognitively informed at that very moment, channeled toward a set of connotations. Sensations may be processed by thought, but *through the same process* thought assumes an emotional form, a feeling. Many of Edvard Munch's verbally designated themes, such as "jealousy" and "melancholy," allude simultaneously to concept and mood, discursive narrative and sensory feeling. To judge by his art, he did not *feel* a division nor did he *think* one.

Munch resisted separating the human faculties into those generating concepts and those generating moods. The convergence of feeling and thinking is implicit in his art, which maintained its level of representational reference even as many of his twentieth-century admirers gradually reduced such qualities to feature immediate sensation in the form of abstract, material values. This characterization fits the later career of the German Expressionist Ernst Ludwig Kirchner (fig. 27). It also applies to a younger painter whom Munch supported, Ernst Wilhelm Nay (fig. 28); eventually, Nay eliminated representation entirely. Munch experienced less of an agonistic relationship between narrative conception and the projection of sensation than did many of his contemporaries. In both respects (conceptual order and sensory display), *Self-Portrait: Between the Clock and the Bed* (pl. 51), a work of old age, retains all the emotional intensity of the artist's earlier years. Clock and bed allude to an end to life — a poignant association — yet Munch painted this theme with insistent strokes of saturated hues, denying it the cliché of darkness. *The Artist and His Model* (pl. 37), a product of middle age, suggests multiple narratives, both biographical and allegorical; all the while, its vigorously brushed passages of heightened color are more than worthy of Munch's younger abstractionist contemporaries. His rendering of the bedding and the carpet exhibits the material freedom to be seen in Asger Jorn and members of the COBRA group as well as in the European Tachisme of the 1950s.

The two aspects of Munch, the literary or representational and the material or abstract, exhibit no dialectical tension. He was not struggling to preserve the one or liberate the other. For him, mood did not interfere with concept, nor concept with mood. Holding the two concerns in balance — they are as one — Munch never developed into a "pure" painter who would value the sensory impact of colors and forms above all else. Nor did he desire such purity, the indicator of an advanced modernity. Guillaume Apollinaire described the avant-garde attitude in 1912: "The subject no longer matters or

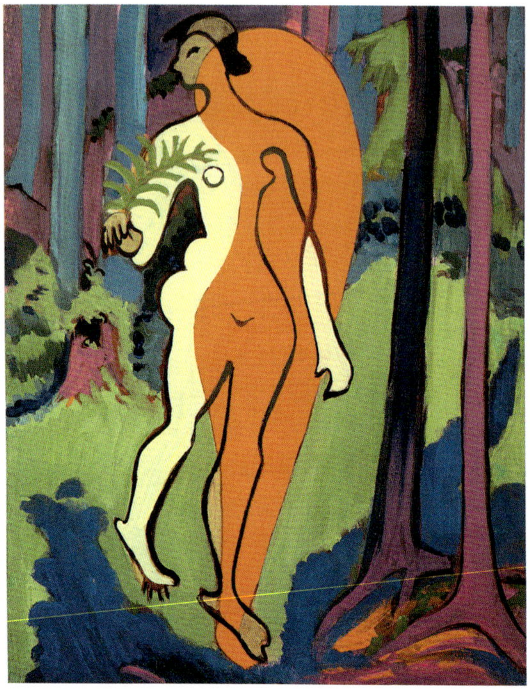

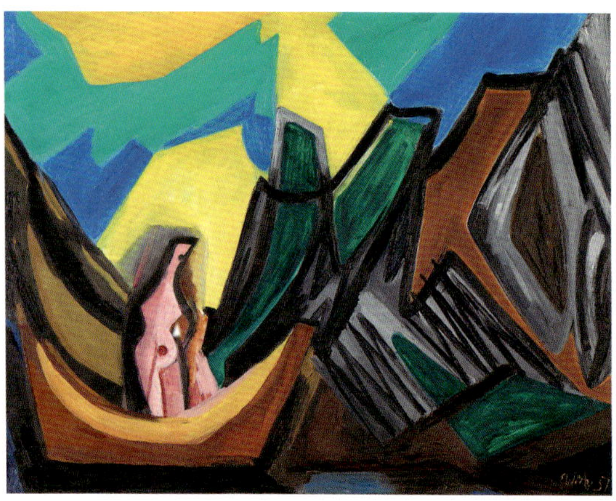

Fig. 27

Ernst Ludwig Kirchner, *Nude in Orange and Yellow*, 1929–30. Oil on canvas, 35 7/8 × 28 in. (91 × 71 cm). Kirchner Museum, Davos

Fig. 28

Ernst Wilhelm Nay, *Woman in a Boat*, 1937. Oil on canvas, 39 5/8 × 51 3/8 in. (100.5 × 130.5 cm). Nasjonalmuseet for Kunst, Arkitektur og Design, Oslo (NMK.2011.0260)

hardly matters. . . . We are moving toward a completely new art. . . . It will be pure painting [*la peinture pure*]."[3] For Munch, the subject continued to matter. Ironically, in the view of many prominent critics, his seamless expression of mood and concept excluded him from the avant-garde, because the narrative elements he featured seemed to suppress the material elements that, in their purity, ought to have dominated.

The painter favored by avant-garde critics of Apollinaire's time was Paul Cézanne (who, like Munch, would have declined the honor). An observer reported in 1904: "The more [Cézanne] works, the more his work removes itself from the external view [and] the more he abstracts the picture."[4] The nominal subject was dissolving into sensory paint-matter. As the early avant-garde position evolved into the more extreme position of the later avant-garde, Munch's exclusion became all the more obvious. "I know of nothing in art that affects me in anything like the way that his 'literature' does," Clement Greenberg wrote in 1967, referring to Munch's presentation of humanistic themes. "Yet the purely pictorial impact of his art remains something else, something less."[5] Munch retained the subject, contaminating his painting, which lacked avant-garde purity.

Because Munch did not recognize any disabling tension between representation and sensory expression, he had no motivation to "advance" from one mode of art to the other (representational to abstract). His position — ideologically free with respect to art world debates and for that reason potentially laudable — rendered him peripheral to art history as it was being constructed throughout the twentieth century. History favors the politics and strategies of military campaigns, and Munch did not wage one.

Outside to Inside

For a painter involved with the eye-work and hand-work of representation, a conceptual division between thinking and feeling need not matter, even in cases where the artist's own critical thought supports it. A scene depicted corresponds to the scene as it was felt — the only condition under which a scene can be observed or even imagined. It appears as it appears.[6] We (artists as well as everyone else) see what we feel. We gain a desirable degree of communicative clarity when we convert the idiosyncrasies of sensory experience into a normative form of representation or description, but we lose the intensity of our personal reality in the process. The divide between personal feeling and the social forms of its communication has long been recognized as a critical issue within debates over modern art. During the formative decades of Munch's career, idiosyncratic features of a style of representation were often defended, if not encouraged, as evidence of an artist's fidelity to his or her character, emotions, and vision. Aesthetic vision was inherently subjective, yet an artist could strive to maintain objectivity by keeping the subjective image as close as possible to its transitory appearance in a model. "We no longer make a true distinction between perception and the thing perceived," Henri Bergson concluded in 1896.[7]

Munch accounted for the character of his representational forms by invoking the emotional context, the mood:

> In an intense state of mind a landscape will make a certain impression on one — by depicting this landscape one will arrive at an image of one's own mood — it is this mood that is the main thing — Nature is merely the means.

Nature becomes the catalyst for conducting a transaction between self and self. Representation amounts to self-interpretation. Munch nevertheless faced an impasse, a certain paradox, when he mused over acting as his own interpretive critic: "To explain a picture is impossible — it is precisely because one cannot explain it in any other way than it has been painted."[8] An artist's vision — colored by the emotion of the moment — is already the interpretation and finds no adequate analogy in auxiliary critical discourse.

Every emotional delight, every emotional anxiety, is unique when experienced, whereas a critical discourse must generalize to become comprehensible. Munch strove to keep every feeling specific to its rendering. Some of his titles, because they convey generalities (*Anxiety*, *Melancholy*, *Separation*, *Attraction*), suggest that the pictorial expression reduces to the concept, as if the mood, too, were general rather than specific. To the contrary, a picture has a material presence that induces a particular feeling in the viewer even when its subject is a cliché. (This fact was stressed in the move toward "pure" painting.) Around 1907, Munch created two very similar versions of *Jealousy*. The figure of the jealous man virtually falls into the space of the viewer in both instances; the remainder of the scene becomes background screen, a narrative projection that excludes the jealous man. Munch rendered one of these studies (pl. 30) somewhat coarser than the other (fig. 29). The jealous man exhibits less refined features, and the wallpaper pattern is more reductive and insistent, which renders its greenness strident. I have to assume that the corresponding difference in mood belonged to Munch as he created the two paintings and not to an intended change in the character he twice depicted. More precisely, a mood adheres to the pictorial qualities of each image. It transfers to attentive viewers, who inflect it with their own receptive emotions.

Despite Munch's sense of the impossibility of explanation, he was skilled at a kind of exegesis that verged on poetry. He offered narratives evoking the sensory experiences that led him to create his various representations. Recalling his notorious images of *The Scream* (or *The Cry*) (fig. 8 and pl. 15), he spoke of his being affected by wave phenomena that activate the human senses:

> One evening I walk[ed] down a hillside path near Kristiania.... The fjord — cut in a cold blue — amongst yellow and red colors.... The lines and colors quivered with movement. These vibrations of light caused not only the oscillation of my eyes. My ears were also

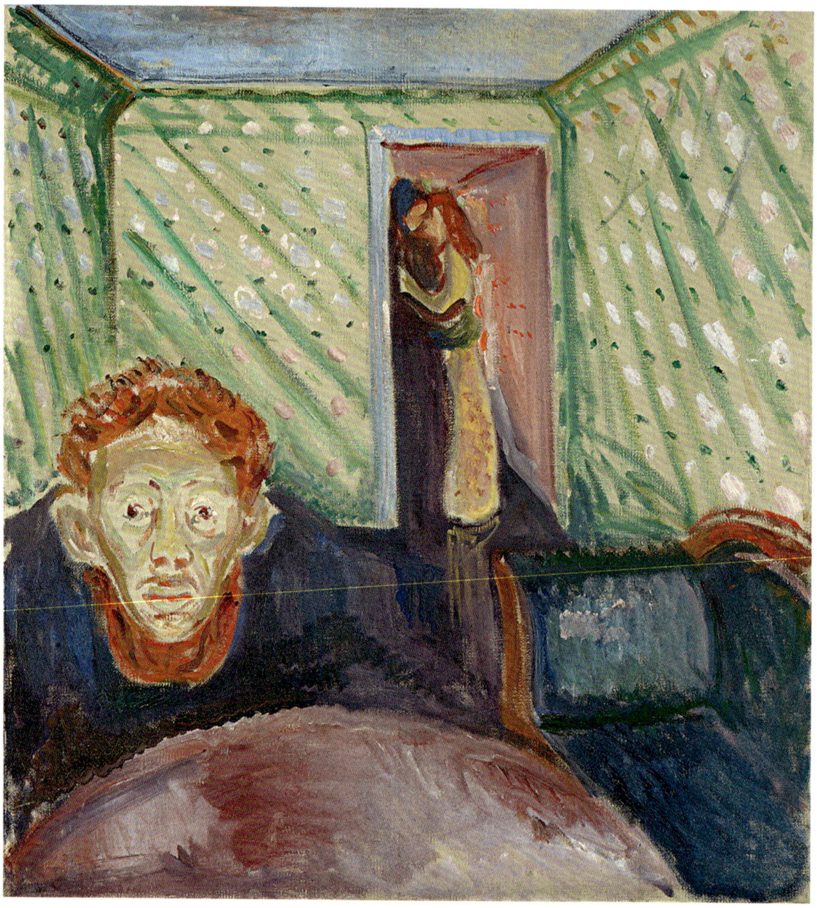

Fig. 29
Edvard Munch, *Jealousy*, 1907. Oil on canvas, 35 × 32 ½ in. (89 × 82.5 cm). Munch Museum, Oslo (MM M 573)

> affected and began to vibrate. So I actually heard a scream. Then I painted *The Scream*.[9]

In Munch's account, an impression of color instills an impression of sound. Both visual and auditory sensations derive from the vibrations or waves that generate all movement, the indication of life. The sound is universal, coursing through all matter; its source is not only nature but the human body that, like a medium of conductivity, vibrates with the wave.

"Light and movement," Munch stated, exist at the origin of life, which belongs not only to organic beings but to "the stone and the crystal."[10] Possibly, light-and-movement was a single quality for Munch, a unified wave phenomenon, undivided as organic and inorganic matter was undivided, or even as concept and mood might be undivided. Light, as the source of color, and movement, as the energy associated with the force of an artist's mark, constituted the fundamental elements of pictorial representation. In his paintings, Munch was recording vibrations that passed through the natural environment, traversing every substance as well as the body's sensory barrier. This theory of the wave, Munch's version of it, was as much current science as it was a modernist commonplace:

> Today I heard a lecture on the radio [explaining] that light consists of waves, and is therefore also matter. This is exactly what I wrote in my

> diary twenty — thirty years ago [circa 1900]. I wrote that everything is in motion, and that the fire of life may be found even in a stone.... The variety of movement determines the form and variety of the matter.[11]

Since movement reflects emotion (even etymologically), all matter has feeling.

Munch's alter ego in *The Scream* responds to a wave of sound. In the account quoted, the origin appears to be in nature but could also be in Munch, in his mood ("it is this mood that is the main thing," he said of landscape painting).[12] The human figure, or Munch himself, feels a "scream." We surmise that the wave has already penetrated the figure, which has been rendered with wavelike form. So a sense of touch must be involved as well as seeing and hearing. The body conducts the wave just as a rod might, and every cell is affected. It may be that the visual form, this human-as-wave, requires no explanatory gloss because it communicates its emotional state as directly as Munch perceived the colors of the sky to have uttered a cry. This was his feeling, not a rational deduction. The painting that resulted was his aesthetic venture — his intuitive, emotional advance.

A number of Munch's commentaries connect his understanding of the sciences to his impressionistic observations of daily life. He seems to have sought out theories to ground his intuitions, but all the while he inferred elements of theory on the basis of the very same intuitions.

> The Wavy line was ... linked to the discovery and premonition of new energy in the atmosphere — Radio waves and a premonition of a form of communication from one person to another. [With regard to] *Separation* [fig. 30]: I symbolized the connection between the separated couple with the help of the long wavy hair ... a kind of telephone wire.... Do you not find a similarity between *The Dance of Life* [fig. 18a and pl. 47] and the rhythm and movement in the dance of the past 20 years?[13]

Fig. 30

Edvard Munch, *Separation,* 1896. Oil on canvas, 37 ¾ × 50 in. (96 × 127 cm). Munch Museum, Oslo (MM M 24)

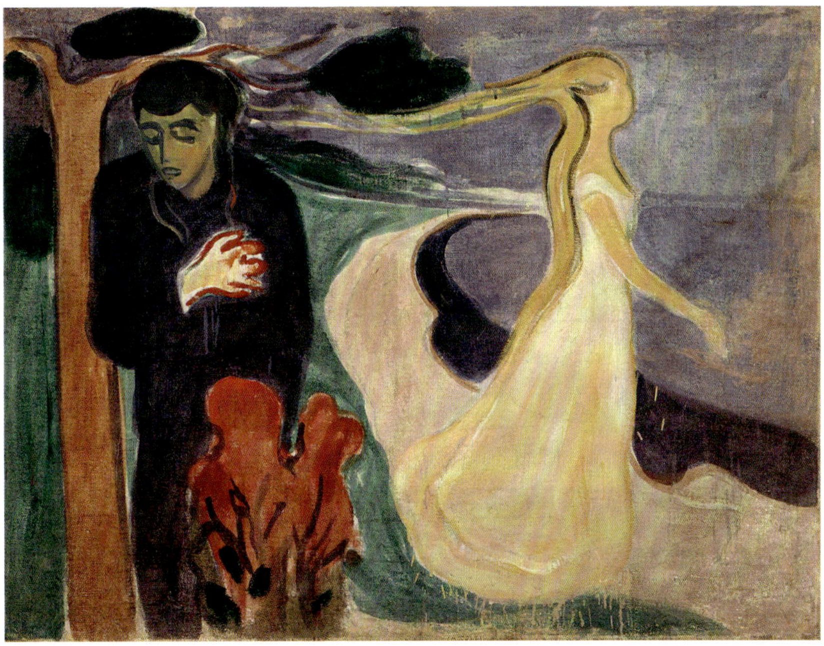

Munch's question implies that the connection between radio waves and popular dance ought to be apparent to feeling; it requires no reasoning. In *Separation*, the entirety of the woman's form constitutes a complex wave that extends to touch the man's head as well as to join the wave of the shoreline. Munch refers to symbolization and offers the metaphor of the telephone wire, a mechanism for contact over distance. As I view this configuration of forms, however, the links between body and body, body and matter, and matter and matter are so evident that literary devices such as metaphor reduce to what critics at work during Munch's final years called "literature." I have already quoted Greenberg to this effect; the term "literature" was derogatory, referring to superfluous thematic elements where form should have been sufficient as the communicative device.

Using analogous wave forms, Munch immersed the foreground figure of *The Scream* within the environment of the Kristiania fjord; neither the figure nor its pictorial background acquires a naturalistic appearance. He held the figure to the landscape by rendering its hands as elongated curves that reiterate the arc of the landmass at the figure's side (land presumably below the level of the bridge yet appearing to rise upward, contributing to an oceanic perspective of feeling that knows neither up nor down). The primary figure has been cast unusually far forward into the plane of viewing, as if a camera lens were too close to the object of focus.[14] Munch often took this compositional feature to an extreme, with a figure seemingly pressed into the viewer's space, as in *Red Virginia Creeper* (pl. 23) and the two versions of *Jealousy*, already mentioned. Frontal staging of this type raises the possibility that a background is dreamlike and itself a projection, a fantasy image drawn forth from an agitated mind in which feeling is determining thinking. Munch's wavy body in *The Scream* — physically distorted, evocative of both physical and emotional distress — might be conjuring the fantastic forms and colors behind it. Yet, the inverse is unavoidable. We recognize that the figure has itself been assimilated to the pictorial context it conjures, becoming the subject, but not the master, of its fate. Waves know no boundaries: the photographic record of Munch's studio practice indicates that he enjoyed placing his paintings side by side and creating friezelike compositions. Just as waves are continuous, feelings — whatever their origin — are infectious. This is why we respond to representations rendered with feeling. From the outside, we move inside. A wave of sensory emotion transports us.

Inside to Outside

Consider the nature of aesthetic debate during the late nineteenth century, when Munch entered history as a professional artist. The old aristocracy and the social groups that identified with its interests favored an art of rational principle and order, promoting the moral messages associated with traditional religious and historical themes. Such rational art, "classical" in both style and meaning, could be perpetuated by standardized methods maintained within a controlled educational process. Because of its association with institutions of long standing, this normative art was "official" and "academic." Its counterpart among the newly empowered bourgeoisie featured motifs of quotidian observation and acquired the labels "realist," "naturalist," and (somewhat later) "impressionist." Munch associated Impressionism with "interpreting strong emotions whilst working directly from nature — or nature seen in terms of strong emotions."[15] This art of the bourgeois, entrepreneurial class featured signs of personal experience as opposed to presentations of received wisdom. To the extent that artists of the bourgeoisie regarded themselves as agents of social change and intellectual advancement, their art self-identified as "avant-garde."

The various naturalist modes were not the only alternatives to the various classical ones. Underlying the practices of both the old aristocratic order and the new bourgeoisie was a type of art that represented a ground zero of human experience and expression — art relegated to the periphery, but at the developmental periphery, recalling remote sources. Such art was loosely associated with "primitive" mentality. It was not the work of a primitive being, but a product of a state of mind utterly direct and reactive with respect to human feeling. This art was naive and natural, as opposed to naturalistic. If we were to rank the various modes of visual representation in terms of the strength of emotional affect, the naturalist styles would win out over the classical ones, but any "primitive" manner would rank still higher. Its directness would cause the nuances of observation inherent in naturalistic practices to appear artificially refined — an affectation diminishing the intensity of feeling. Nineteenth-century critics often expressed admiration for evidence of genuine naïveté, whatever the shortcomings, as in this comment on a group of amateurish landscapists in 1847: "Less able in execution than most others, barely initiated into the subtleties of their craft, they copy like grownup children, [yet] their painstaking incapacity is not without a strange seductiveness."[16] The description approaches the condition of Munch: "I used to look for landscapes to paint.... [But] in my state of depression or elation I was unable to paint what I could see."[17] Nineteenth-century criticism had an explanation: "You see nature agitated or at ease, according to what is happening within yourself."[18] In the incapacity that his emotion brought about, Munch resorted to painting his feeling; and feeling is both self-seductive and seductive of others. But he was neither intellectually nor technically naive.

Sensitive to the critique of naturalism among French painters and writers around 1890, the time of a Parisian sojourn, Munch definitively shifted the connotative emphasis of his art from observation to feeling. From the beginning, his painting had been exceptionally physical in character — already marked by emotional intensity (*Self-Portrait*, 1886; pl. 2). His Parisian reorientation may have been a deliberate strategy, or he may simply have yielded to the compelling force of his mood. His representational details became boldly abstracted, yet with no pretense to capture anything other than common emotional states and the human condition. Despite its excesses, Munch's art remained this-worldly; it did not become other-worldly. His *Death in the Sick Room* (1893; pl. 5) yokes a compelling narrative to an insistent rhythm of interlocking formal elements. The tilt of the head of the figure at the extreme left mirrors the reverse tilt of the head of the figure to the right of the woman who faces forward. The shadow cast against the wall and floor at the left margin — introduced selectively (it does not appear in a variant of the composition) — joins the baseboard so that the angles echo those of the chair in the immediate foreground and the bedding dropping to the floor in the furthest background. This contrapuntal conjunction of lateral movements and abrupt shifts forward and back thoroughly undermines the logic of perspective inherent in presenting bodies and other objects at different scales. To the same effect, Munch allowed the prominent brown-orange of the floor in *Death in the Sick Room* to remain unarticulated and unmodulated; it rises as an assertive abstract shape rather than receding with diminishing chromatic saturation.[19] Like good staging for a theatrical production, the rhythm of the forms animates this scene of life and death without interfering with the essential human drama.

Munch invented radically expressive ways of presenting familiar themes of human joy and despair. He had no need to venture beyond the scope of his personal experience: "I came into the world as a sick being — in sick surroundings. My youth was spent in a sickbed, and life was a brightly lit window."[20] He painted aspects of life outside the window, but ceased doing so naturalistically. Taking him at his word, one imagines that his emotional identification with his imagery was too intense for him to do otherwise. "To copy nature," he stated bluntly, as if with a sigh of futility: "We couldn't touch nature anyway, so perhaps it was better to express one's feelings. How could one copy in a naturalistic manner sobs and tears as they really were, when one was completely dissolved by them."[21] In 1891 Munch's compatriot Christian Krohg associated the vitalism of his line with the new French Symbolism: "A long shoreline that moves inwards over the picture and becomes a delicious line ... [rendered] according to a mood.... This relates to Symbolism, the latest tendency of French art."[22] In 1904 Julius Meier-Graefe, an influential German critic with Parisian sympathies, identified Munch as "the youngest child attending the school of Gauguin."[23] The Sonderbund exhibition held in Cologne in 1912 celebrated Munch alongside Cézanne and Vincent van Gogh. Its official handbook described Munch's technique as "unthinkable without his Parisian schooling."[24] Gauguin and Parisian culture in general had advanced the modern aesthetic. Munch absorbed it all, yet did not become a "pure" painter, nor join the nominal "avant-garde."

The critic Thadée Natanson made a series of comments on paintings Munch exhibited in Paris during the 1890s. His assessments indicate that Munch struck a fine Symbolist balance between the emotional states associated with a range of human feeling (grief, lust, envy) and the various "pictorial emotions" (the likes of rhythm and lyricism — features of depiction appreciated for independent sensory qualities, whether linked to an identifiable emotional state or not). Natanson's observations recognize the division between one expressive pole and the other: "[Munch] neglects to some degree the pictorial emotions for the sake of expressing above all the human emotions."[25] This statement of 1895 could not have been applied to Cézanne (fig. 31), whom Natanson would discuss appreciatively less than a month later. He noted Cézanne's "coarse" and "uncultivated" material qualities that made no mitigating allusion to human character.[26] Yet this was not a detriment. In contrast to Munch, an artist of the human subject, Cézanne became notorious for the "loss of subject"— the indifferent subject, rendered opaque or meaningless by an overbearing material technique. "The subject disappears," claimed one of Gauguin's associates in praise of Cézanne. "There is only a motif"— an abstracted movement or form (like Munch's wave, perhaps).[27] Natanson reviewed Munch again in 1896: "His hastily drawn forms, violently colored, are expressive and emphatically meaningful. One imagines a [Constantin] Guys at wit's end [*quelque Guys exaspéré*]"— that is, the rendering of an edgy social observation, in which the form has nevertheless become more compelling than the subject.[28] In 1897 the same critic reviewed Munch once more: "His violence and rawness pursue pictorial expression of an exalted lyricism."[29] This last observation might have suited Cézanne as well, but Munch, unlike Cézanne, set his material intensity in service to his thematic development.

Natanson's allusion to Guys, an artist of Parisian nightlife, was responding to Munch's *Rose and Amelie* (1893; fig. 32), a painting that depicts two prostitutes with a caricatural flair worthy of Georges Seurat, Henri de Toulouse-Lautrec, or Guys himself. The two women form a single wave of rounded faces, shoulders, arms, and breasts. The prominent shadows (or chairbacks?) punctuate the rhythm and extend it fully into the pictorial environment. A sine curve passes through this pacific image of doubling, just as a shrill, oscillating cry passed through the Kristiania fjord. Two different themes, two different emotions (lust and anxiety): each, in its specificity, appears to have inspired a wavelike whole. Because Munch's sense of an integrating rhythm or motif seemed to generate excessive distortion within his human figures, his various exhibitions provoked caricatures of themselves, with the waves becoming exaggerated signs of graphic disorder.[30] We ought to expect such caricature of caricature, because whatever a unique temperament finds expressive is likely to appear as caricature to others. Yet not all viewers would be derisive. Some would be of similar mind and sympathetically inclined or, more likely, caught in a wave of *involuntary* sympathy, having been affected by the expressive forms. *Rose and Amelie* has a curiously crude, untutored quality that might generate a version of the "strange seductiveness" that nineteenth-century critics perceived in the works of naive artists.[31] For all its sophistication, Symbolist art (Munch's included) often verged on what critics of the time considered "primitive."

Fig. 31

Paul Cézanne, *Still Life with Fruit Dish,* 1879–80. Oil on canvas, 18 ¼ × 21 ½ in. (46.4 × 54.6 cm). The Museum of Modern Art, New York, Fractional Gift of Mr. and Mrs. David Rockefeller

Fig. 32

Edvard Munch, *Rose and Amelie,* 1893. Oil on unprimed canvas, 30 ¾ × 42 ⅞ in. (78 × 109 cm). Munch Museum, Oslo, Rolf E. Stenersen Collection (RES.A.216)

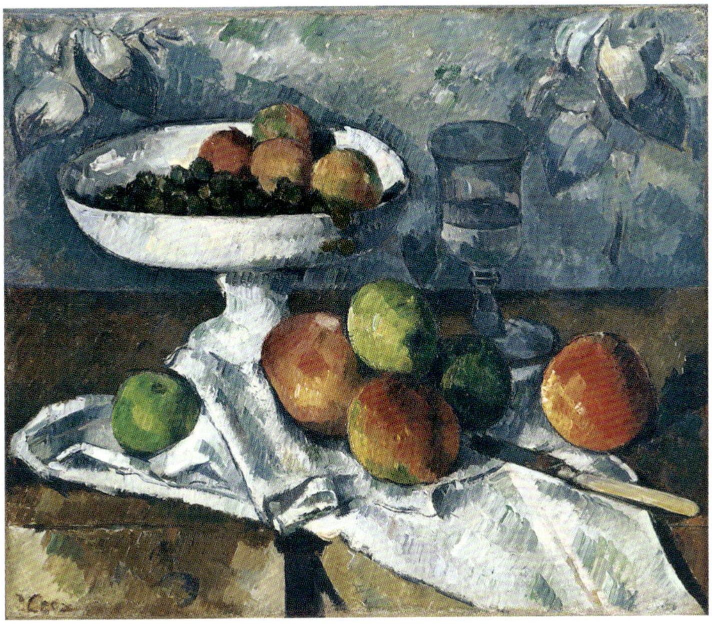

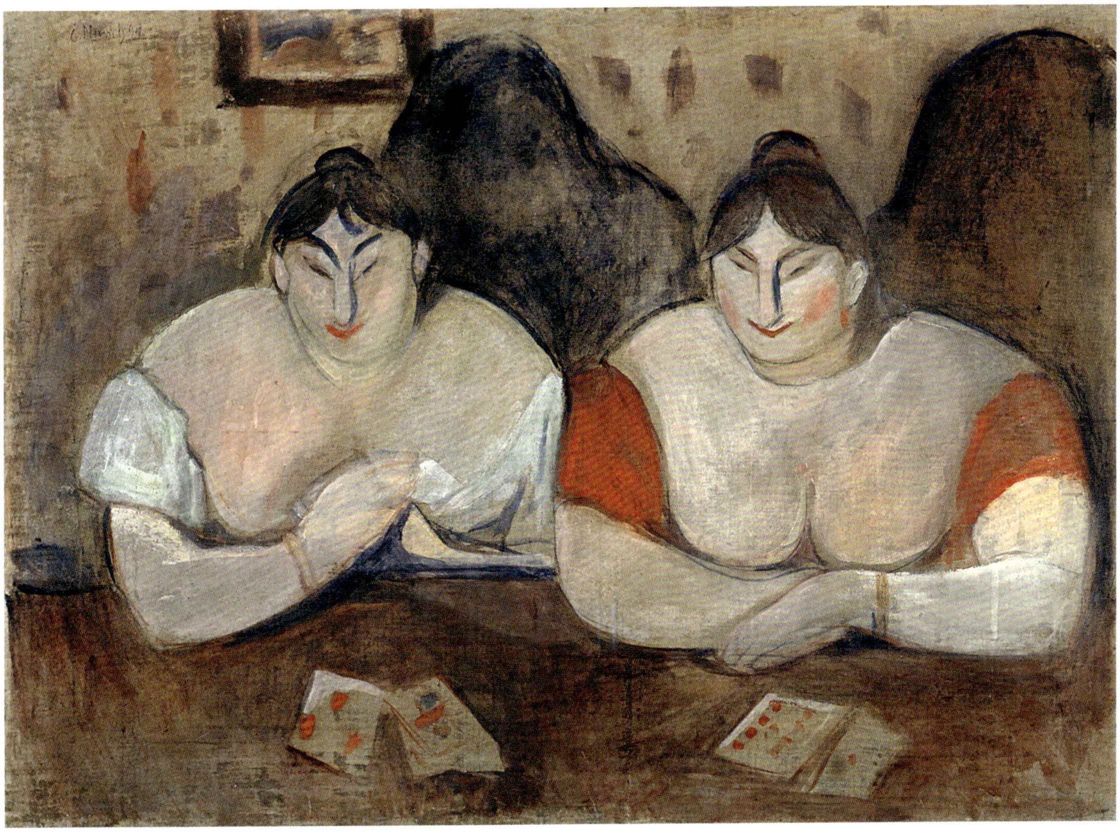

From the rudimentary character of a primitive technique to the emergence of avant-garde abstraction the distance was remarkably short. Bold linear motifs (Munch's waves), intensified chromatic effects, and aggressive marking were potentially "primitive" features of the representational painting identified as Symbolist, features that manifested a substantial degree of abstractive reduction. Abstraction of the details enhanced the overall emotionality, whether or not a specific emotion bearing a name was evoked. In Parisian Symbolism, every aspect of sensation became emphatic; the meaning of an artwork would depend first on relations of form and color, and only secondarily on considerations of genre, narrative intent, and other thematic factors. Gauguin's "symbolist" lesson amounted to this: "Does the shadow look rather blue? Don't be afraid to paint it as blue as you can."[32] The notion became prevalent in avant-garde circles: visual art becomes more powerful — in fact, revolutionary — when it releases its formal expression from the restraint of literary, thematic content. Despite his own involvement with complex allegories and details of representation, Gauguin encouraged painters to allow their material means to develop formal effects freely: "Art is an abstraction; draw it out from nature in an imaginative dream, and think more of [this act of] creation than of what will result."[33] The extreme end of practices of representational abstraction — as in Wassily Kandinsky and Piet Mondrian — evolved into early forms of abstract art.

Initially located on the periphery of acceptable practice, modes of abstraction were eventually written into the history of modernism as its high points. For liberal critics, the abstract art of the avant-garde signified advanced thought, social reform, and political freedom. An early example of the argument appears in the appreciation of Cézanne published by Charles Morice, Gauguin's literary collaborator. He stated that Cézanne's neglect of social themes, his "painting with the aim of painting," amounted to "a tacit protest" against the political position implicit in conventional representational art.[34] "Painting with the aim of painting" was another way of saying "pure painting." A late form of the argument comes from art historian Meyer Schapiro, who, in his title for an article, encapsulated the message: "The Liberating Quality of Avant-Garde Art." With references to spontaneity and release from representational constraints, he alluded to American Abstract Expressionism as the new paradigm.[35]

Like Gauguin, but in a more physical way, Munch developed a radical sense of materiality within representational painting. He scraped and scratched his surfaces, allowed visible drips and spatters, subjected his canvases to weathering, and incorporated thin and thick areas within a single composition. All the while, he focused on the human condition — the course of life, death, and rebirth (in his terminology, "metabolism"). As years passed, the material pole of expression increasingly dominated the critical evaluation of modernist art, promoted by the likes of Meier-Graefe in Germany, Roger Fry in England, and Greenberg and Alfred H. Barr, Jr., in the United States. Because he continued to emphasize the human subject as more than merely a model, Munch became an anomaly, a peripheral figure within the avant-garde periphery. In contrast, the lineage of Cézanne (Gauguin's primary inspiration) included the likes of Henri Matisse and Joan Miró, and eventually Jackson Pollock and Barnett Newman — artists who reduced the narrative potential or eliminated it entirely. In Greenberg's view, Cézanne's art succeeded historically because it demonstrated that "every sensation produced by the motif was equally important once its 'human interest' was excluded."[36] In this regard, Cézanne anticipated Pollock's "all-over" compositions of the 1940s, with their evenly distributed marking. Through the trajectory of his career, early and late, Munch continued to depict the human subject as a focal point of interest, even though he embedded it within an accentuated sensory environment of what could readily be viewed as "pure painting." He welded the portrait subject of *Christian Gierløff* (1909; fig. 33) to its harbor background by tracing a wave of dotted marks and linear strokes around it, an aura of materiality. As with Cézanne, Munch's physical effort is evident in all parts of the canvas, yet the composition does not become "all-over" in Greenberg's sense because the conceptual motif of the human subject can be drawn forth from it.

By the late 1940s, the materiality that had characterized the avant-garde of 1900 was no longer located at the periphery of what was acceptable; it had become firmly established as the center of modern aesthetic practice. Not long after Munch's death in 1944, Greenberg stressed the identification of modern art with abstract, material values by using Cézanne, Van Gogh, and Henri "Le Douanier" Rousseau as his examples. These were three representational painters, each of whom, Greenberg argued, attained his avant-garde status unknowingly. Each happened to develop the material features of painting with such innovative force that the significance of the representational theme became inconsequential; the nominal subject no longer constituted the social meaning of the art. Rousseau's case in particular revealed a new cultural analogy between art and society:

> His flat, direct, almost crass colors, contours, and modelling gave to many painters the first real impression they ever got of what life, reduced to solely empirical considerations and without the deception (but also protection) of faith in anything, looks like in art.

An aesthetic of material values reflecting a materialist culture, an elemental art signifying "elemental existence" devoid of faith in anything higher — this constituted modernism in 1946.[37] For Greenberg, the situation was the fault of the society, certainly not the artists, who, in their homeopathic way, were merely treating the societal sickness by mirroring the general state of mind, with the effect of shocking people into the realization of their condition. In the context of the immediate postwar years, any other type of art would be willful fantasy.

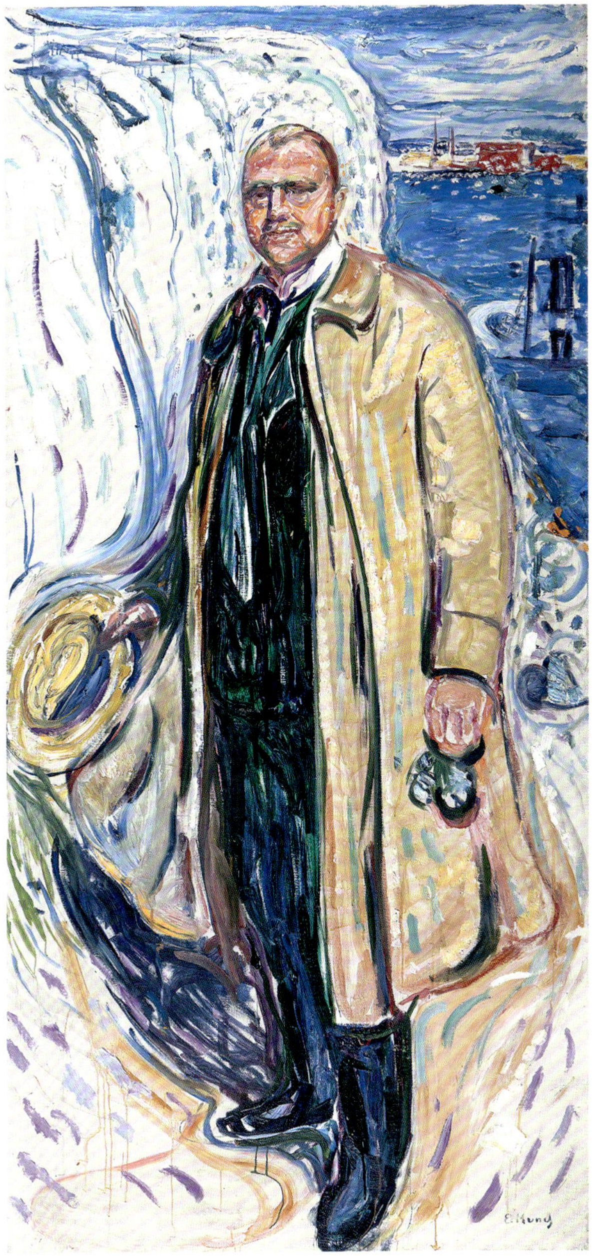

Fig. 33

Edvard Munch, *Christian Gierløff*, 1909. Oil on canvas, 81 ½ × 39 ⅝ in. (207 × 100.5 cm). Göteborgs Konstmuseum

The situation of the 1940s moved the art historian Hans Sedlmayr in the opposite direction. In 1948 he issued a screed against modern art, aptly titled *Verlust der Mitte (Loss of the Center)*. Sedlmayr indicated that the core of art had been ceded to modernist practice, which had no spiritual center. "Modern art transcends man, not because it strives to move towards a higher [spiritual] plane, but, on the contrary, because it moves towards a lower [material] one."[38] Material values — inverse transcendence — no faith. God should have been occupying the center but was absent. By concentrating on "pure seeing," Cézanne, one of Sedlmayr's many targets of opprobrium, had eliminated moral content, converting the reverential, contemplative "stillness of still life" into "stillness without life."[39] *Verlust der Mitte* mentioned Munch only twice despite being written for a European readership; he was neither spiritual enough to be praised, nor "pure" enough of a painter to feature among the modernist villains. Munch had "genuine artistic power," yet was among the first whose art "cast a doubt on the true [spiritual] nature of man," revealing "the nightmare that was riding Europe in its great cities."[40] Sedlmayr advocated restoring religiosity to art, an option that Greenberg rejected with irony: "In the name of 'profundity,' we still long to dissolve our art and ourselves in some ultimate vagueness or confusion. And what promises this better than religion?"[41] He preferred the matter-of-fact honesty of "crass colors" with no false profundity to muddy them. Neither critic worried over Munch's anxiety. He was absent.

Life Goes On

Our canonical history of modern art is not a history of human sensation and emotion. If it were, Munch would be more of a presence, and even central. The structuring of society has oriented our traditional story of art to reflect its self-image, placing emphasis on religious, national, political, ethnic, racial, gender, class, and family identities, all enlisted to explain the character and significance of particular areas of achievement. The mid-twentieth-century commentaries of Greenberg and Sedlmayr, which represent opposite ends of the critical judgment of modernism, are founded in the usual social structures. Sedlmayr stresses spiritualism and religiosity — here, referring sardonically to the Impressionists: "In the nineteenth century [artists saw] the gleam of Heaven in the 'natural light' which shone down upon all things."[42] Greenberg stresses materialism and class identity, as when locating the call for religious values in "bourgeois society's refusal to confront the difference between its ideals and its actuality."[43] Munch found no place in either of these influential versions of history, antimodernist or modernist. He remains apart, a perennial outsider on the periphery of normative history and its multiple categories of identity, none of which does his art justice.

Munch's distinctiveness may lie in his ability to present emotion apart from the controls of conventional pictorial structure — thematic and conceptual, formal and material. His practice of exposing his canvases to weather introduced unpredictable changes, as if the emotion were still in the process of its expression, having been offered a chance to ferment and mature.[44] We are used to viewing a type of representational art (and abstract art as well) that commits its quality of emotion, oddly enough, to abstraction — to *intellectual* abstraction. The image no longer generates an emotional aura; it becomes a surrogate, externalizing the feeling so that its problematic qualities might be mastered and transcended. Viewers apply the dialectical finesse that comes second nature to Western thinkers. As an intellectual abstraction, the image passes immediately from sensation to interpretation. To the contrary, Munch's art incorporates no such escape route to transcendence. His evocative titles, often amounting to poems of a single word, either provide unneeded glosses on his imagery or were intended to remain just as they are: instances of a thought lacking an interpretation — an emotional leading edge. Our thoughts of a scream will not contain the emotionality of *The Scream*. Its surface communicates something far more complex than our imagination of the depicted event, its locale, its sound, its color, its illumination. The surface constitutes a whole that resists being fragmented, whether by general analytical methods or by analyzing Munch's various accounts of the incident.[45] Paradoxically, the way to deny the generalized abstraction of feeling — its conversion to a set of named emotions and their causes — is to present the markers of emotion in their minimal form. The material marker or sign will seem to arise from a primitive ground, reduced already at its origin.[46] The Munch effect is so direct that its material abstraction, like its thematic material, is immune to any (further) reduction. Obvious examples are the convergence of two faces as a single form in *The Kiss* (1897; pl. 21) and the frontal stare of pinpoint eyes in many of Munch's figures. These features require no historical context, no biography, no interpretation.

An exceptional artist relegated to the historical periphery nevertheless attracts others, especially those who may be peripheral in some other regard. In the beginning, one is central only to oneself, not to history. Bridget Riley recalls that during her student years in London in the early 1950s, she turned to Munch as a guide to converting her mastery of tonal values to a more evasive chromatic order: "How he managed to connect with Matisse's fauvism reflected my own aspirations."[47] For Riley, who studied representational practices as the foundation for her development of abstract art, Munch was not secondary to Matisse (as in Greenberg's view) but parallel — a judgment she reached by sensation rather than the concept of a "modern" art.

The Dane Per Kirkeby recalls that Munch was the first artist who affected him, as one marginal figure to another: "Munch was always there. When you are young and in the periphery of things, you go for Munch and Van Gogh." An emotional attachment to his Scandinavian predecessor has remained: "I have always dreamed of equaling Munch in his late years."[48] Munch's combination of representational theme and material abstraction appealed to Kirkeby and, similarly, to his German contemporary Georg Baselitz; over the years, the two artists distinguished themselves by developing numerous novel formats for the abstract presentation of representational imagery.[49] "Munch was my first experience with art," Baselitz states:

> I have often thought about the concept of the avant-garde after 1900. Picasso as representational painter, Kandinsky as abstract painter — yet in both cases, their sources were objects — the same true of Mondrian and [Marcel] Duchamp. So was Munch an avant-gardist? No, at least not in the same sense. His greatness comes from being no avant-gardist at all.

Baselitz continues by referring to other members of the canonical avant-garde — from Cézanne to Pollock — all of whom received modernist credit for suppressing their representational content to whatever extent necessary, developing abstraction in its stead. Yet they maintained a degree of residual representation ("Pollock sustained the object"). Musing over Munch, Baselitz concludes:

> I am emotional in my love for paintings [their materiality] and then possibly also touched by humanity — yes, this [combination] can be and [accordingly] I have always loved Munch's paintings. With Munch, there is no need to think about the loss of the object [the narrative theme] or the center [humanity].[50]

The allusion may be to Sedlmayr's complaint: loss of the spiritual, human center. Baselitz perceives that Munch kept concept, mood, and materiality in harmony rather than exploiting aspects of their conflict. For this reason, he could never be admitted into the canonical avant-garde, which evolved to lead Symbolist-like representation into practices that were either abstract (Pollock) or conceptual (Duchamp). Munch, "no avant-gardist at all," remained peripheral to both branches of the historical lineage.

Katharina Grosse, from a younger generation of German artists, has also been touched by Munch.

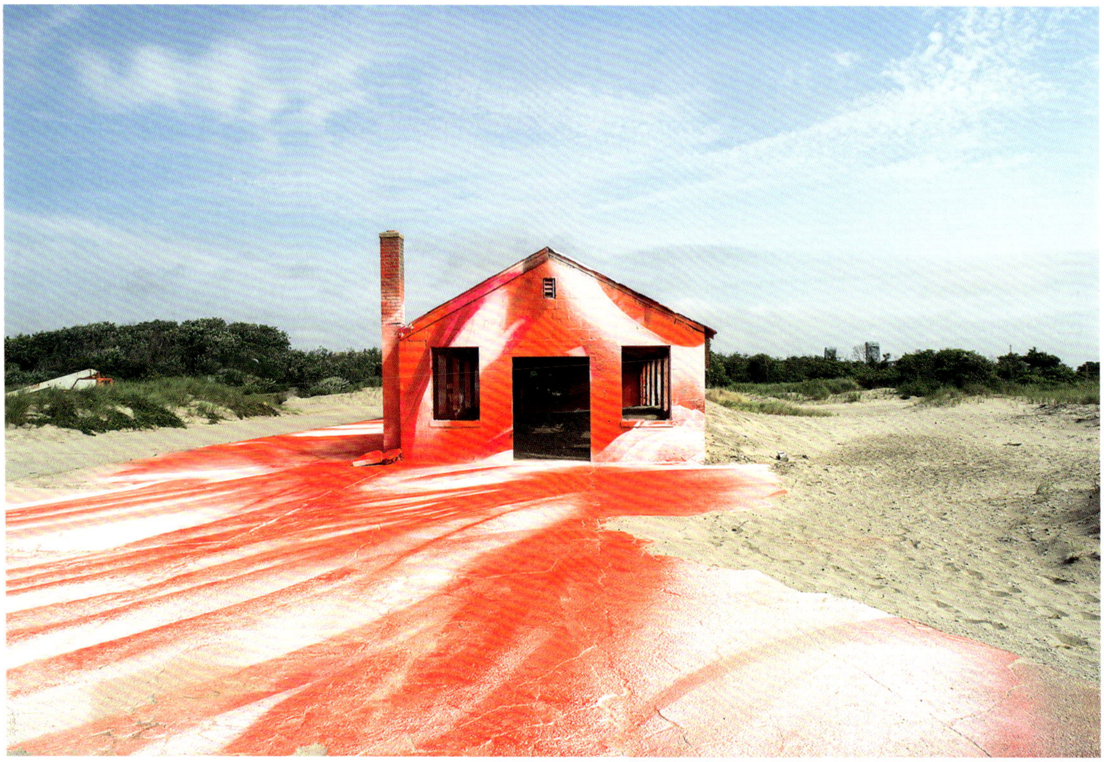

Fig. 34
Katharina Grosse, Rockaway project, 2016

Like Riley, she has valued his art not so much for its thematics, but for its raw sensory impact:

> A painting can appear anywhere.... This thought is central to my work and it got inspired early on in my life by... Munch. He left his paintings outside... given to the ever-changing weather and light.[51]

Many of Grosse's projects have involved spray-painting over large objects, interior environments, or outdoor land formations (fig. 34). Her expansively colored surfaces change over a lengthy period of time as the layers of pigment weather; they also change in the shorter periods in which a viewer traverses the area of color, observing it from different perspectives and under transient conditions of ambient illumination. Because the work is changing at two different temporal rates, it remains impervious to an analysis that would reduce and fix it to abstract components — if, indeed, it has any. Grosse remarks:

> We [customarily] use an artificial structure to filter the feeling, emotion, sexual longing, that is, to transcend it. In my case, I invent formal layers in order to return to some very direct means. Otherwise I would be abstracting these things [the feelings].[52]

Grosse is an improbable heir to the estate of Edvard Munch. The imperviousness of her art to a structural analysis nevertheless strikes a chord with her predecessor's painting. The details of Munch's biographical, social, and political context provide a background narrative for his career, his reception, his successes and failures; we understand *him* through such information, which fits a general historical template. But his images — their figuration, their interlocking contours, their color, their texture, their ever-present wave — exist only on the periphery of the historical construction we use to channel the varieties of our experience. A Munch image appears at the center of our attention at the moment that we feel it, unfiltered. Each of his paintings stirs the emotions like a psychic probe, too direct to be deflected. Historical exegesis may be an aid to some future era, but not to this one, not *now*. We have experienced the feeling of this art already, before ever attempting to identify what it is.

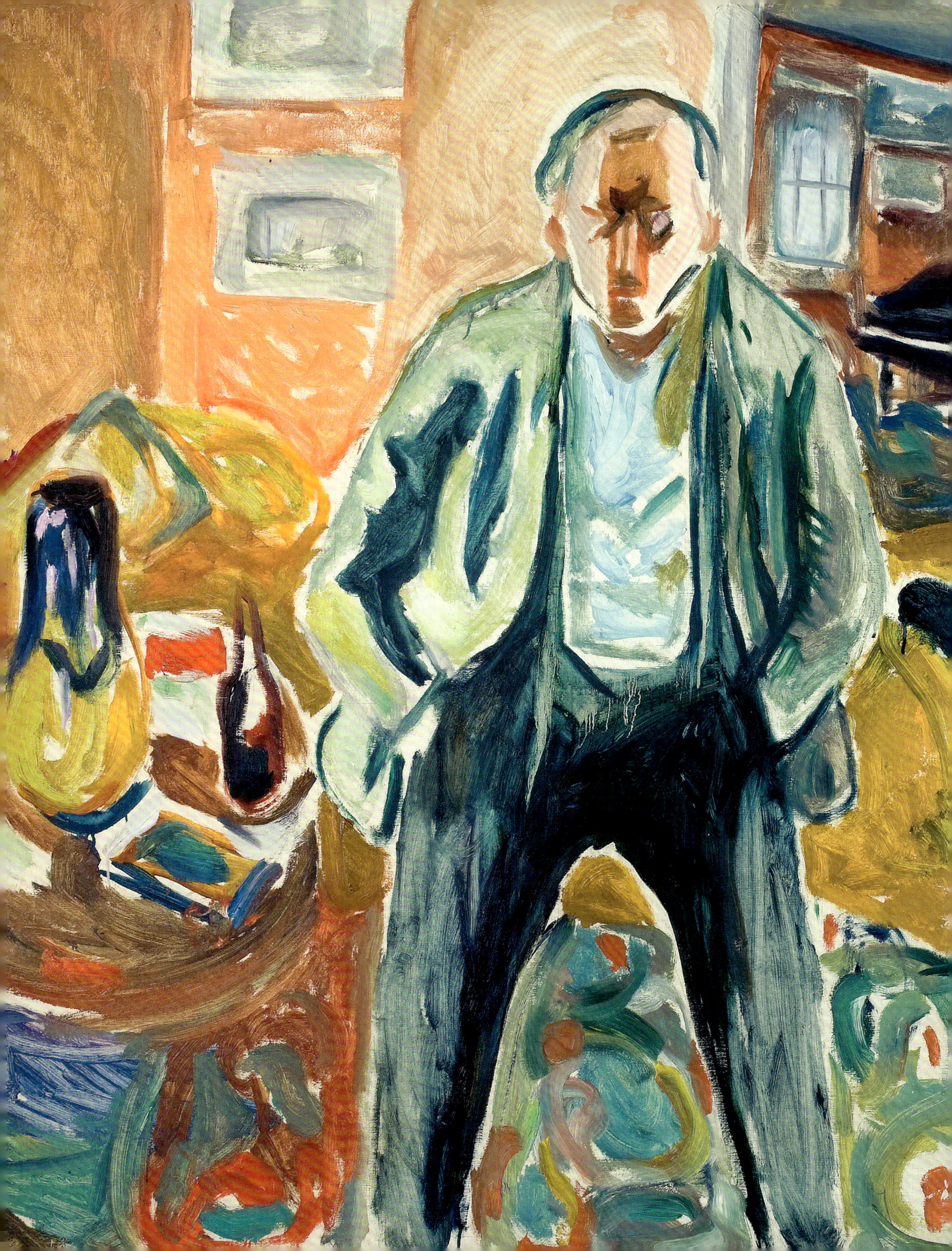

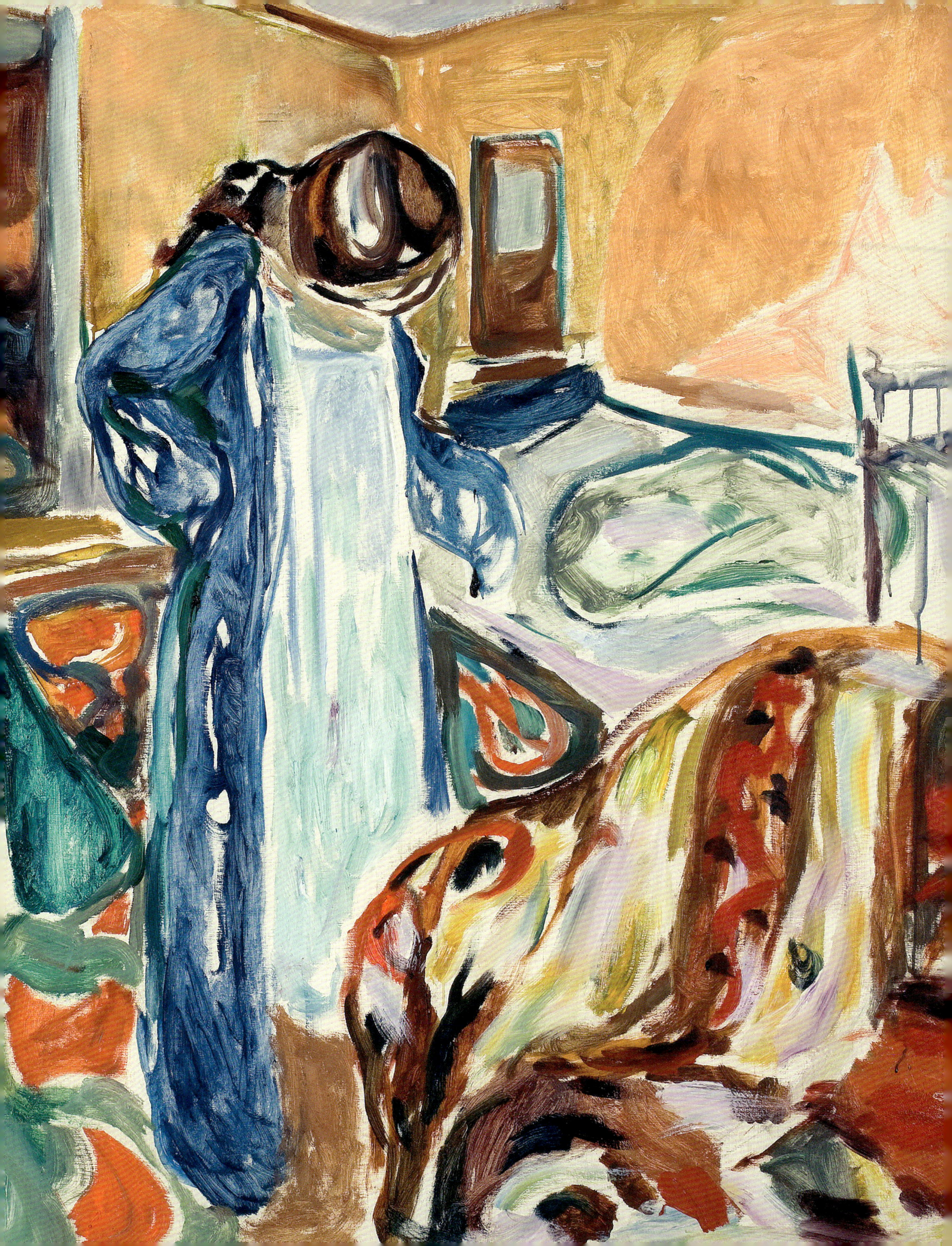

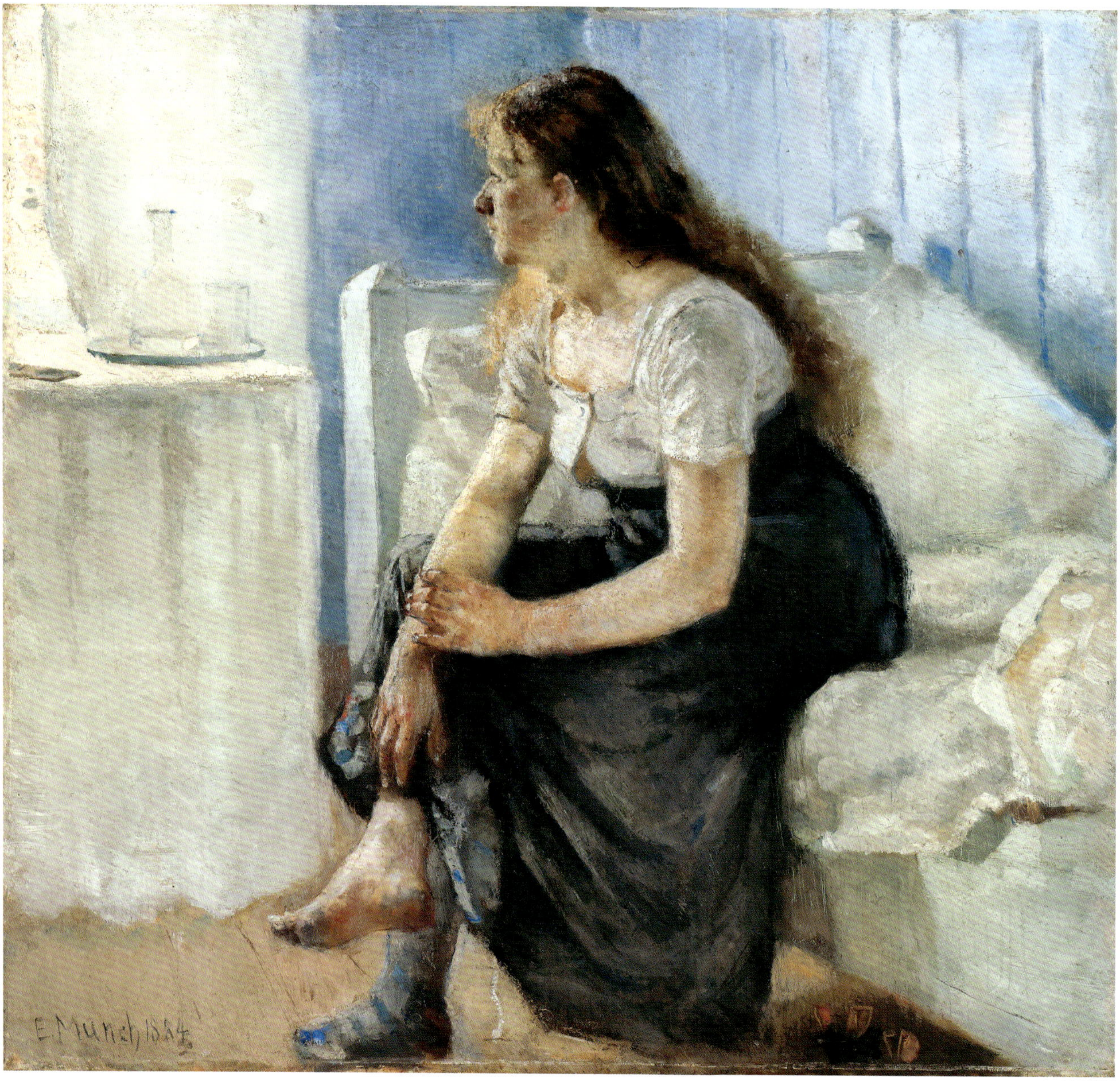

1

Morning, 1884. KODE Kunstmuseene i Bergen, Rasmus Meyers Samlinger

2

Self-Portrait, 1886. Nasjonalmuseet for Kunst, Arkitektur og Design, Oslo

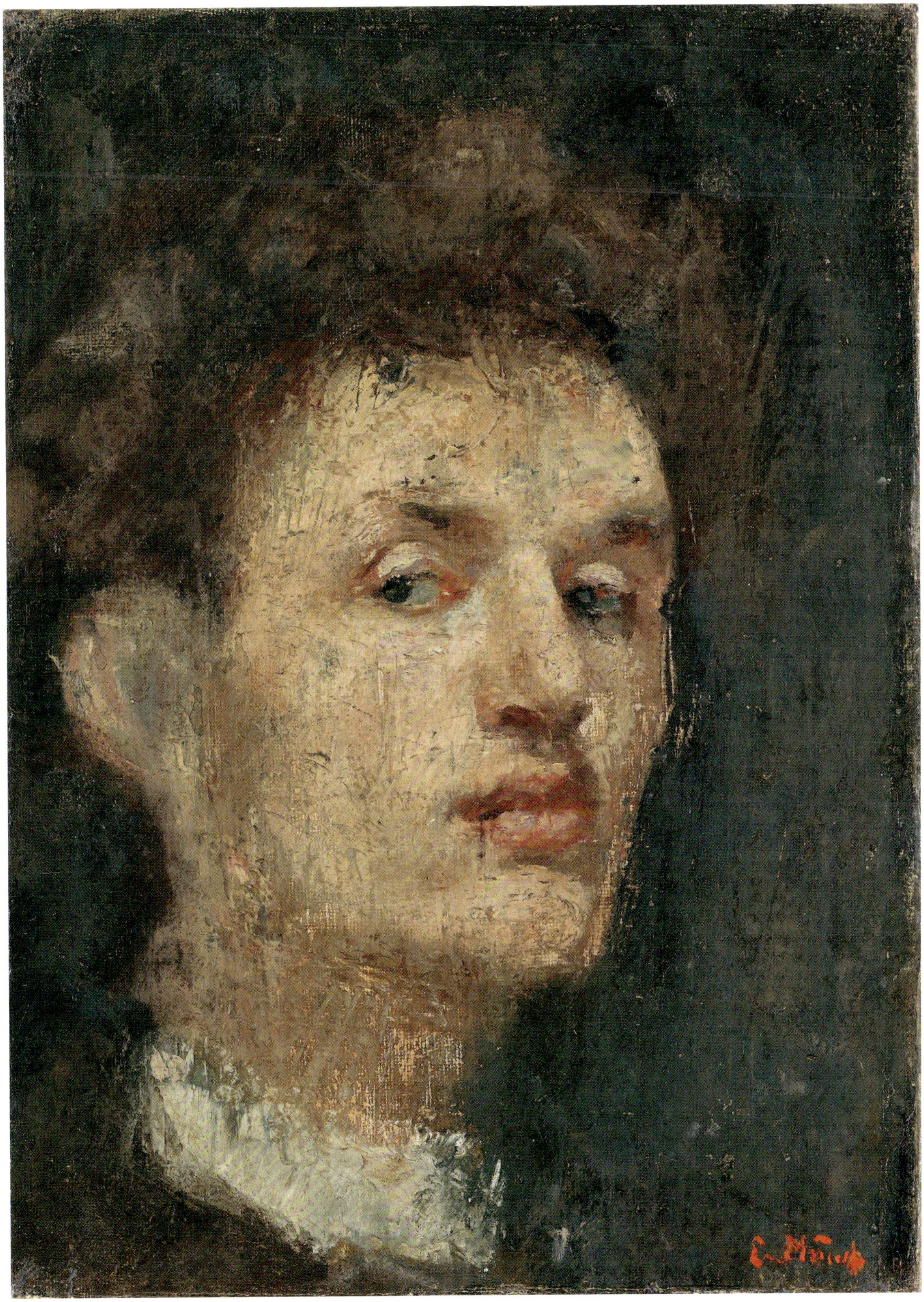

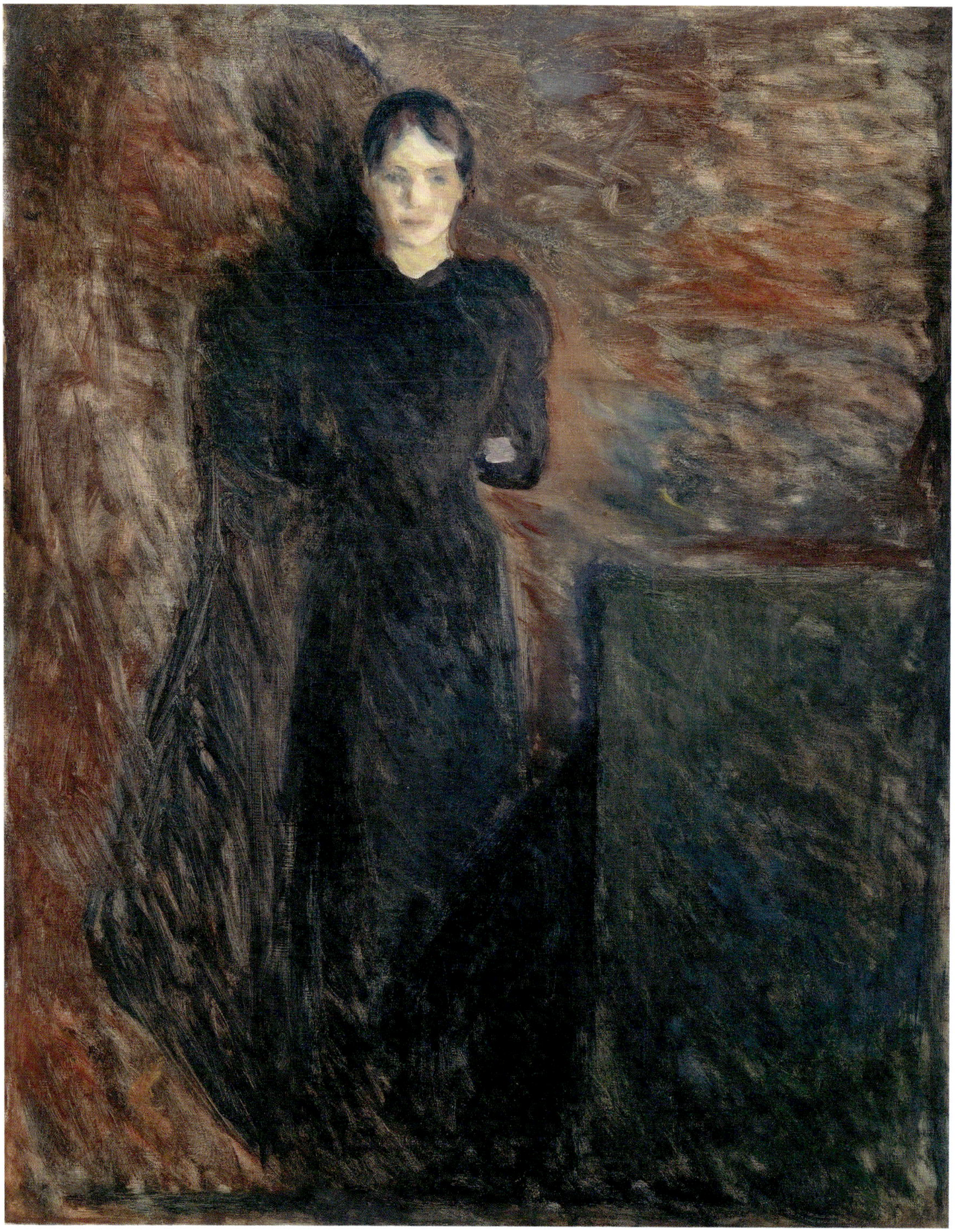

3

Lady in Black (Olga Buhre), 1891. Statens Museum for Kunst, Copenhagen

4

Sick Mood at Sunset: Despair, 1892. Thielska Galleriet, Stockholm

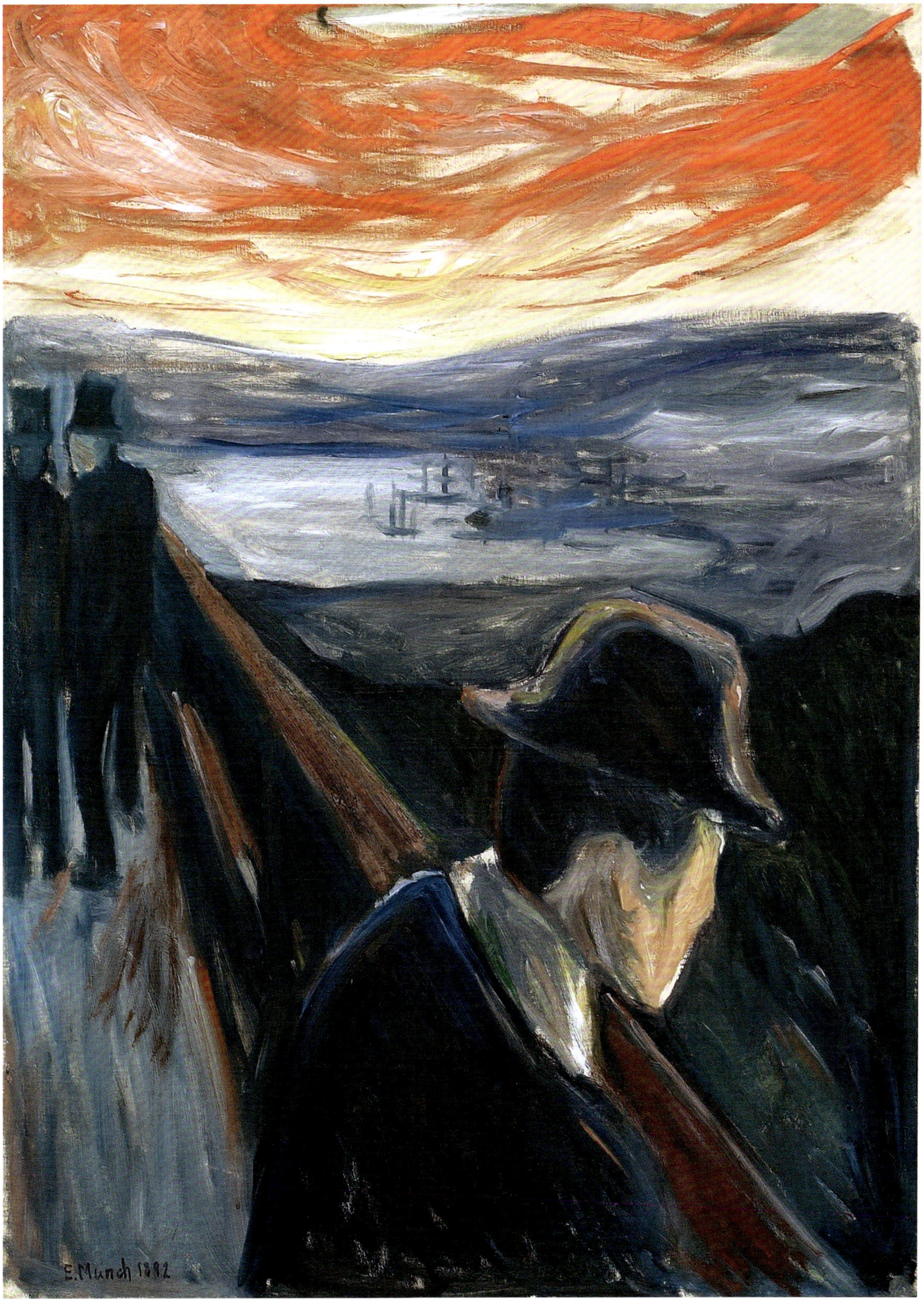
E.Munch 1892

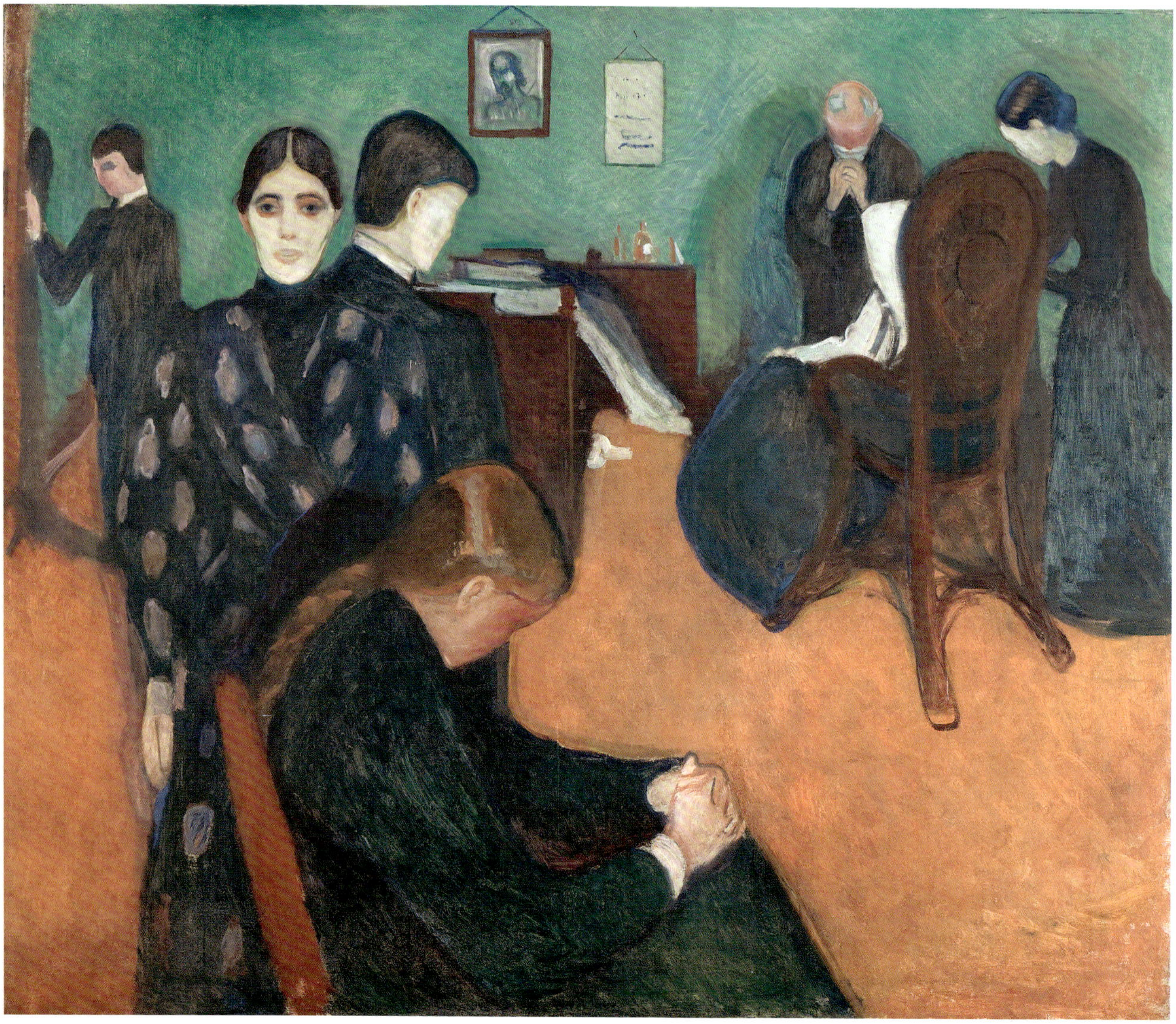

5

Death in the Sick Room, 1893.
Munch Museum, Oslo

6

Moonlight, 1893. Nasjonalmuseet for Kunst, Arkitektur og Design, Oslo

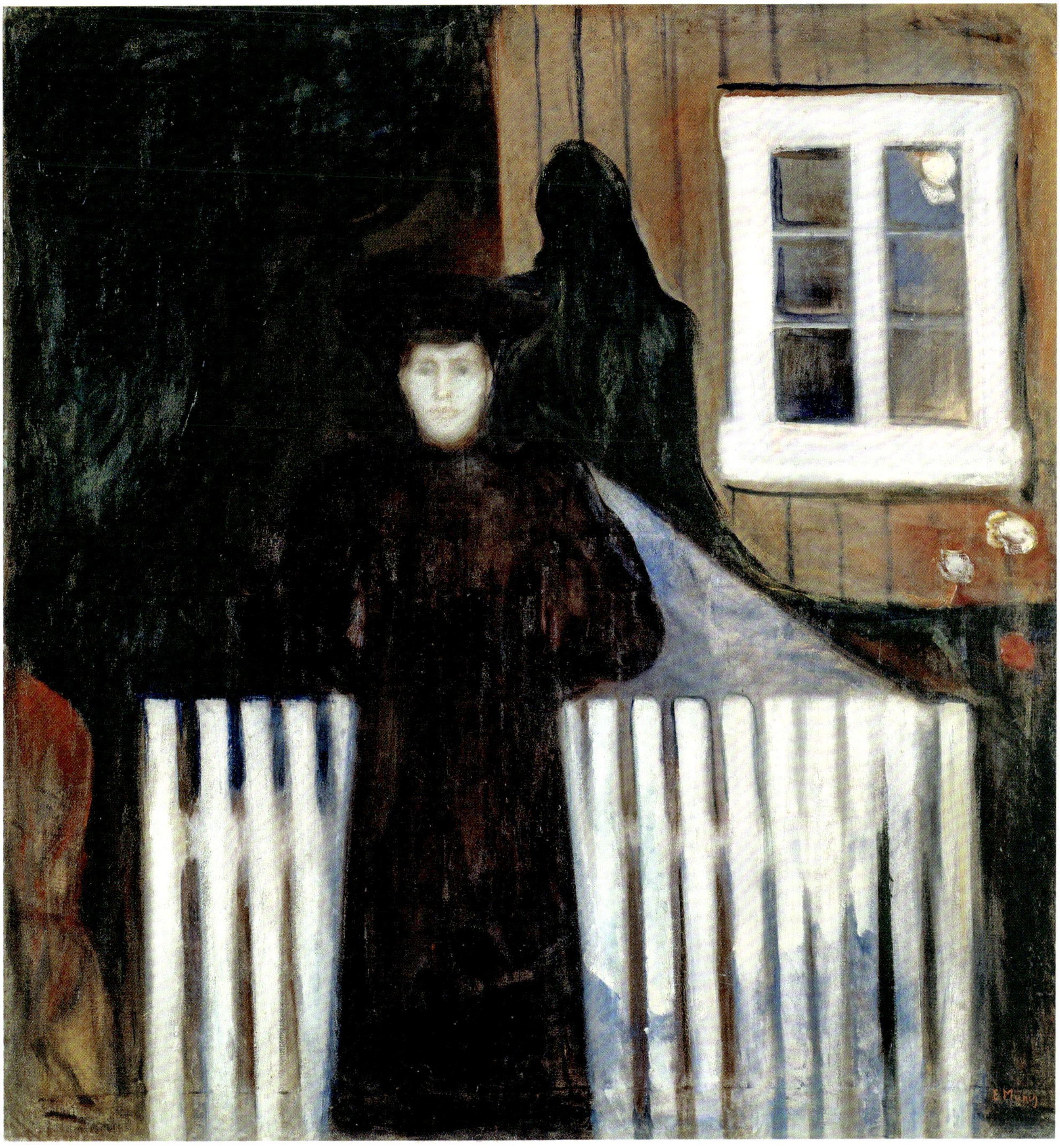

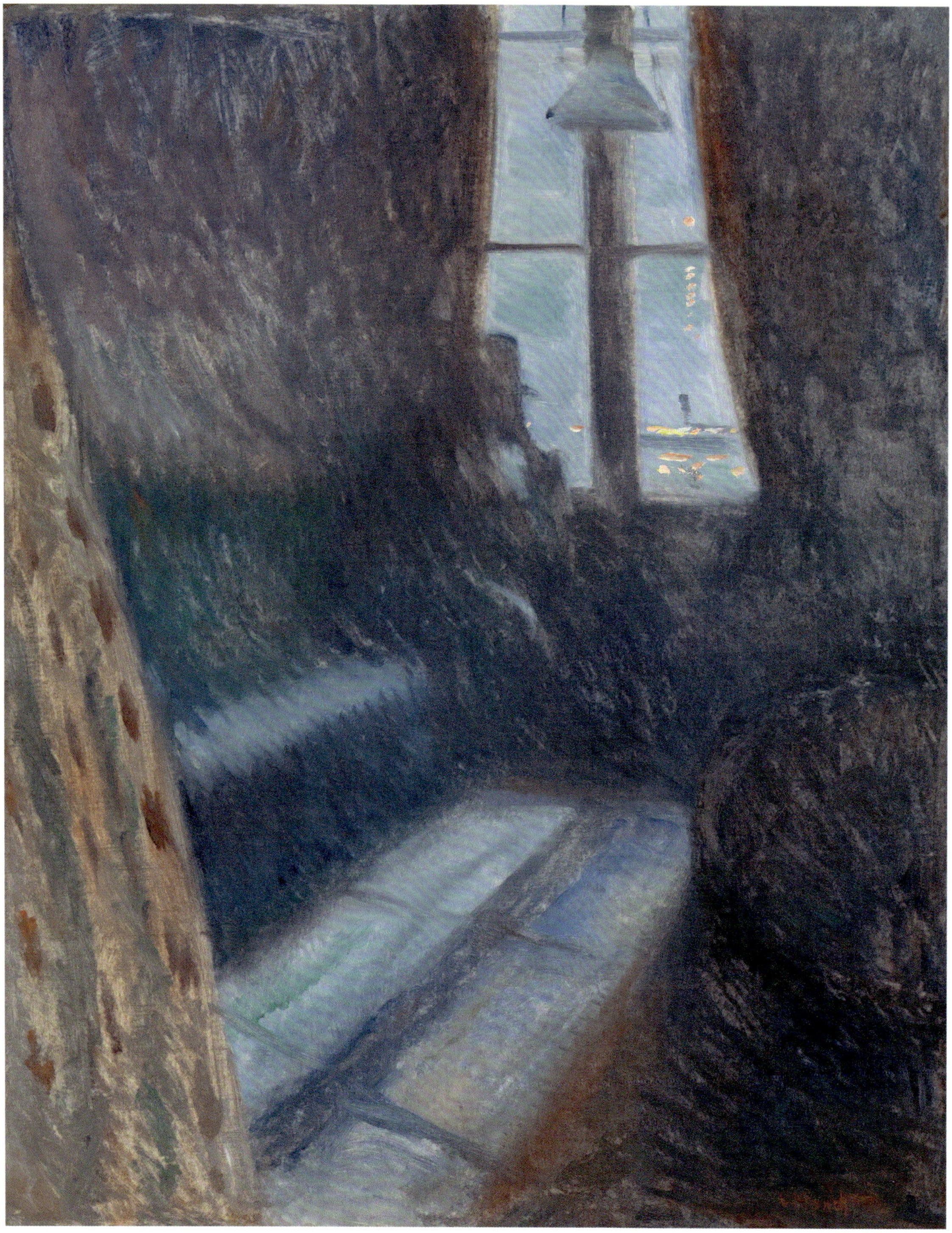

7

Night in Saint-Cloud, 1893. Private collection

8

Self-Portrait under the Mask of a Woman, 1893. Munch Museum, Oslo

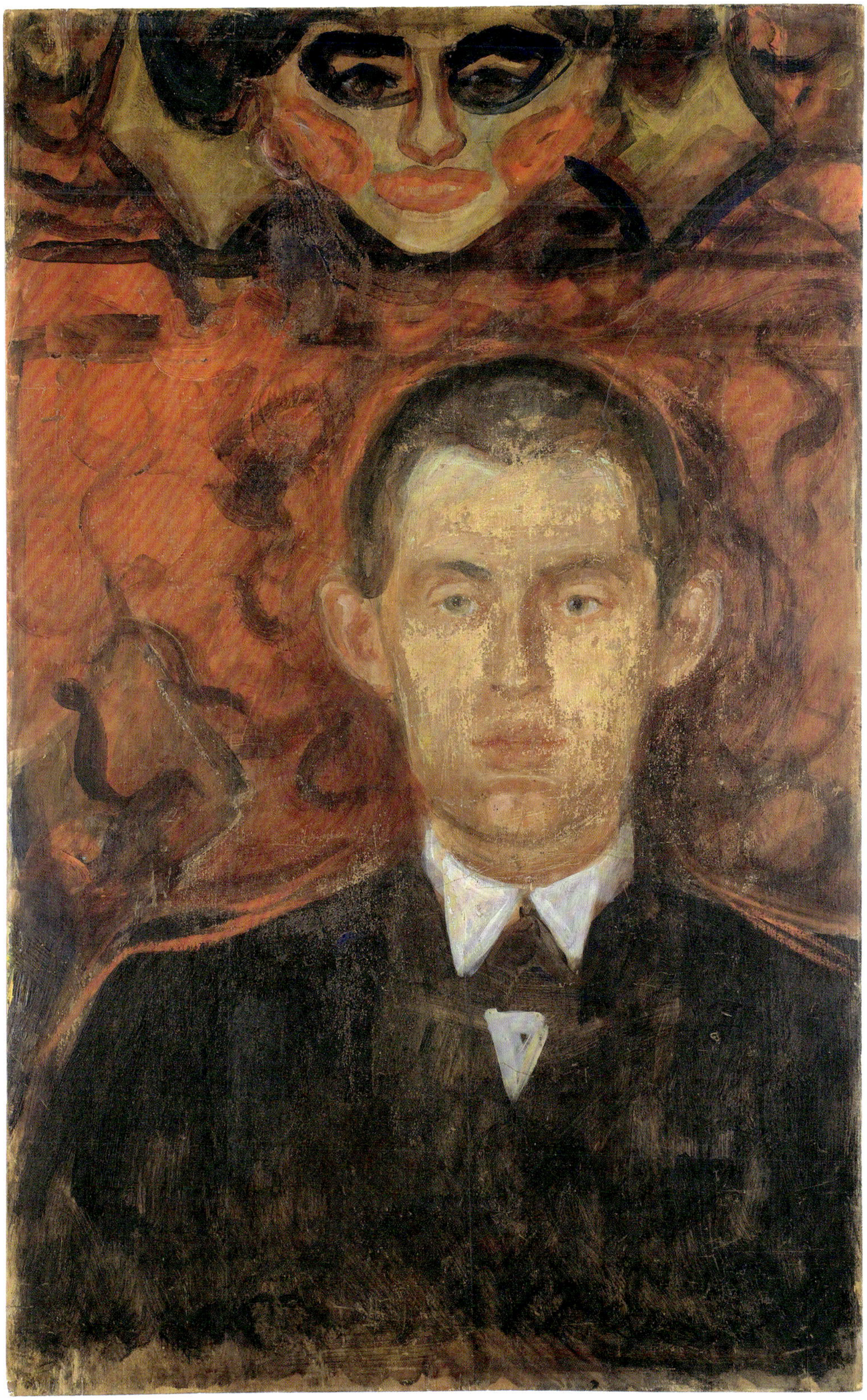

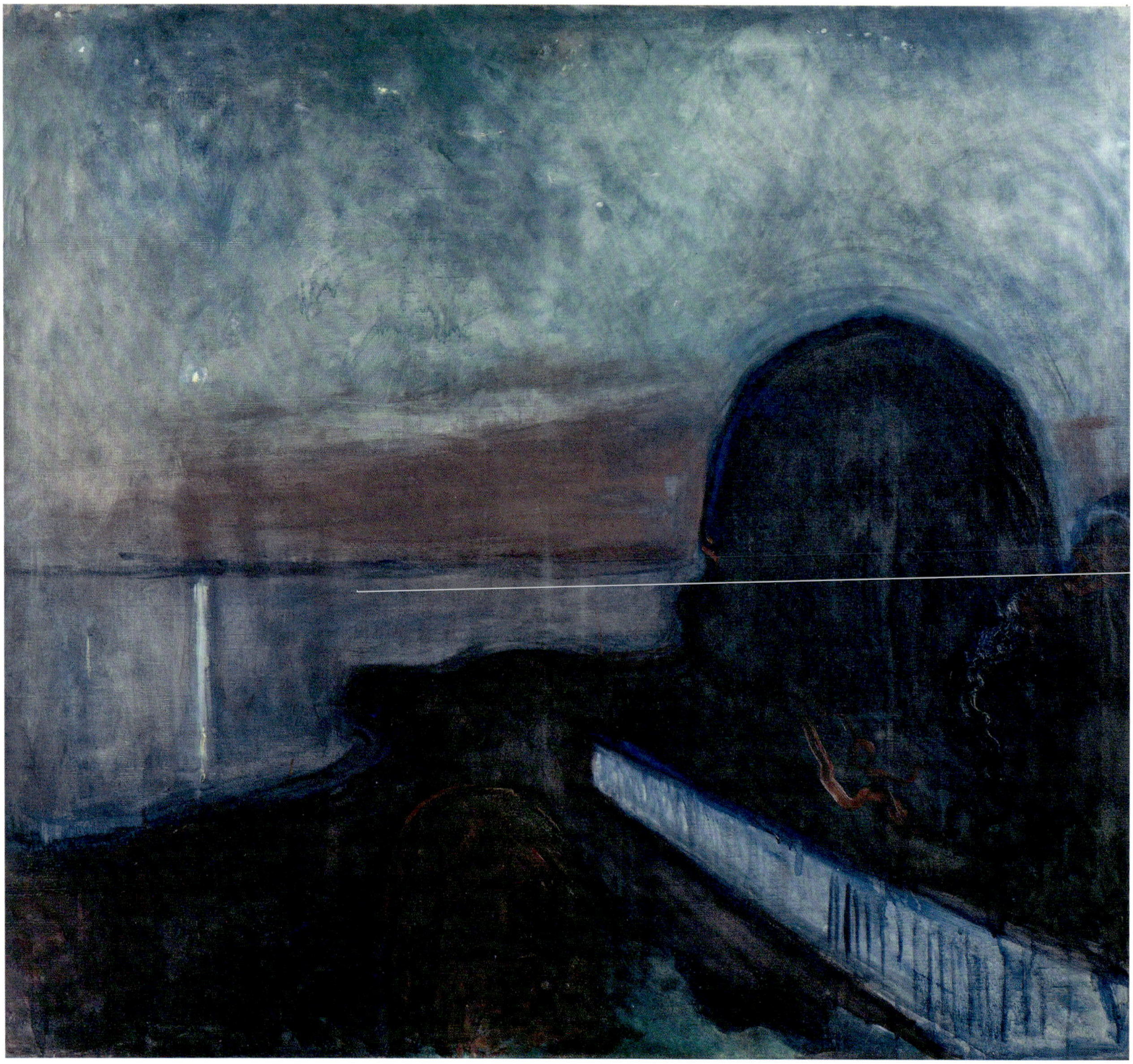

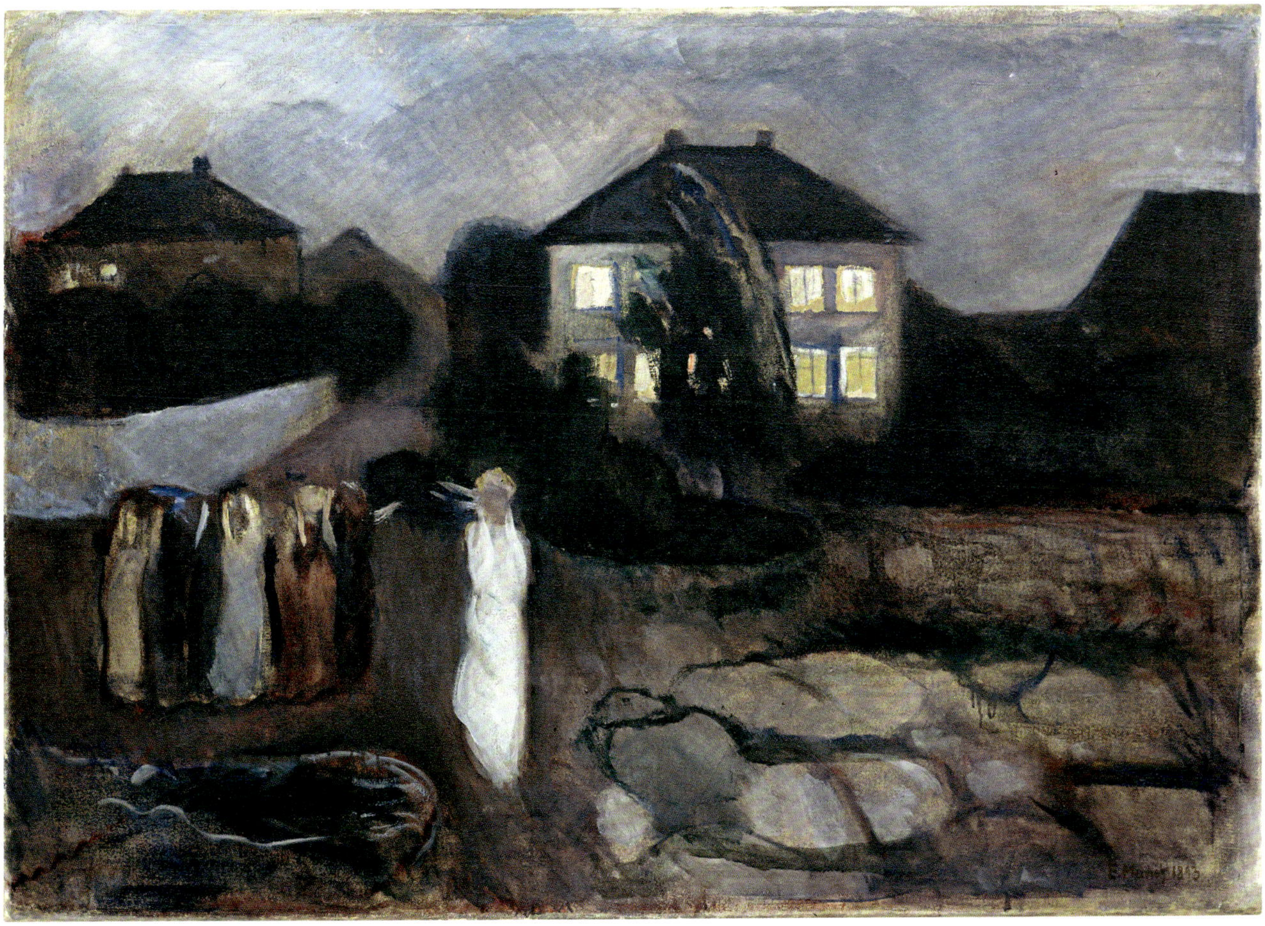

9

Starry Night, 1893. Von der Heydt-Museum, Wuppertal, Germany

10

The Storm, 1893. The Museum of Modern Art, New York. Gift of Mr. and Mrs. H. Irgens Larsen and acquired through the Lillie P. Bliss and Abby Aldrich Rockefeller Funds, 1974

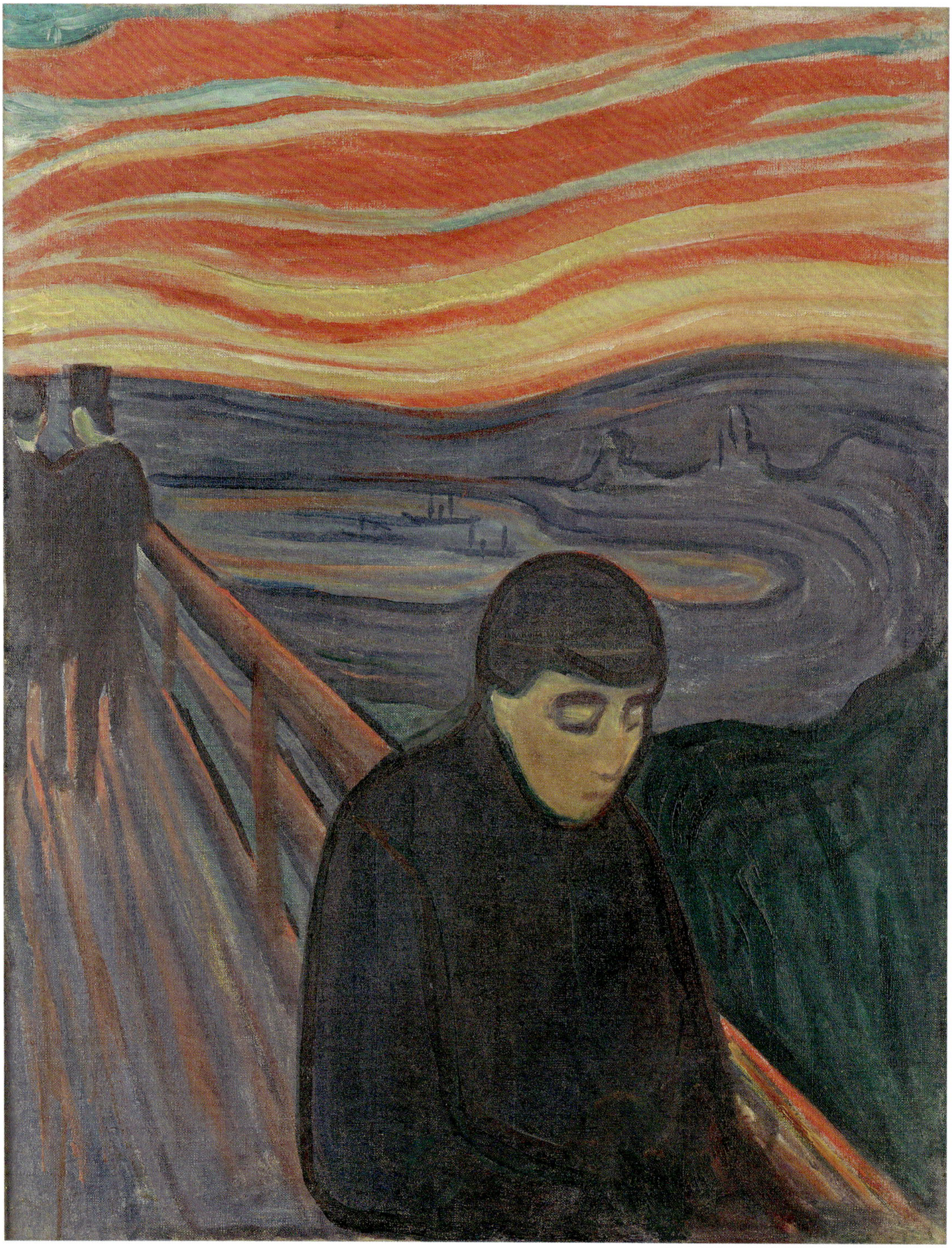

11
Despair, 1894. Munch Museum, Oslo

12
Madonna, 1894. Munch Museum, Oslo

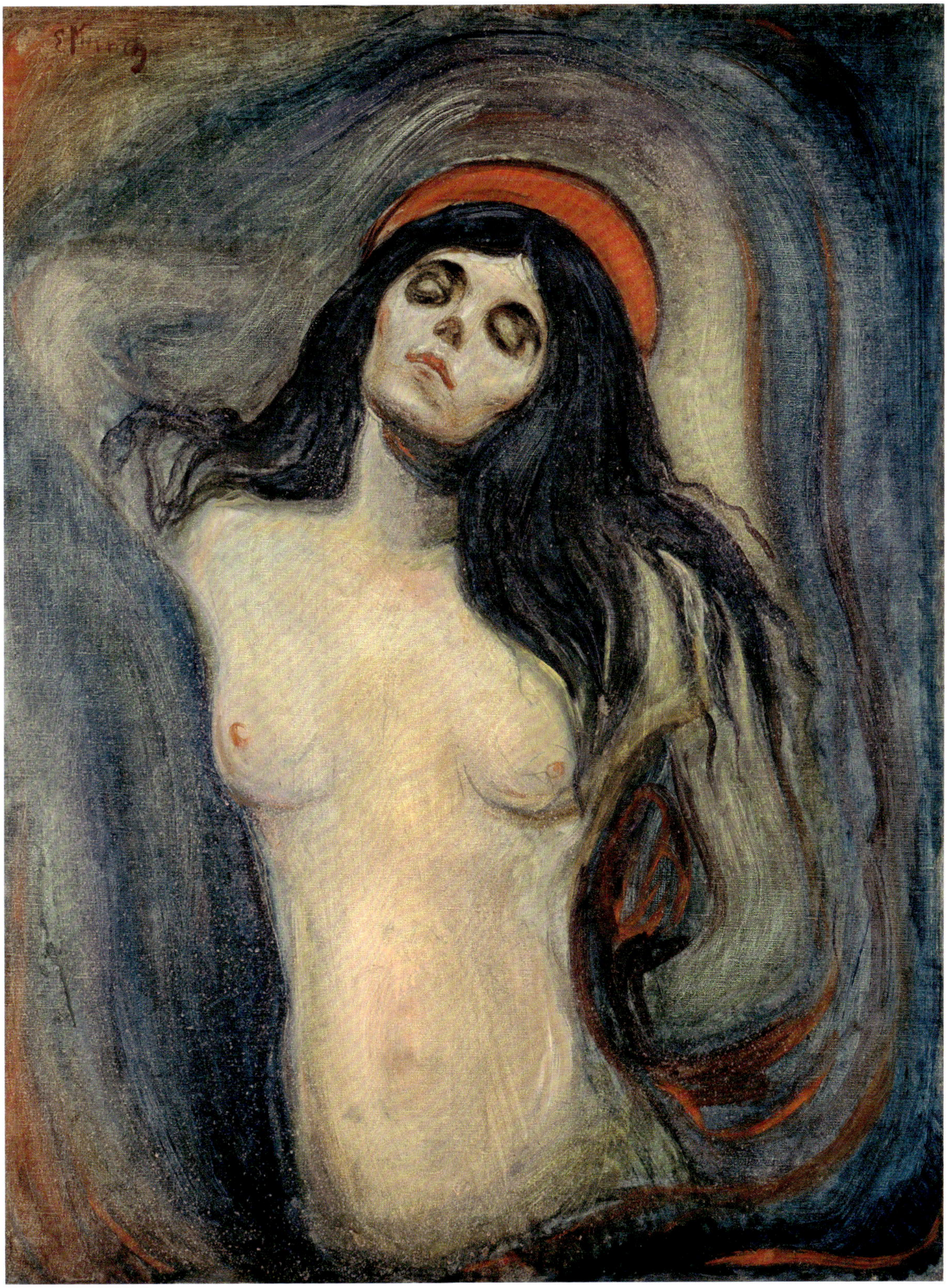

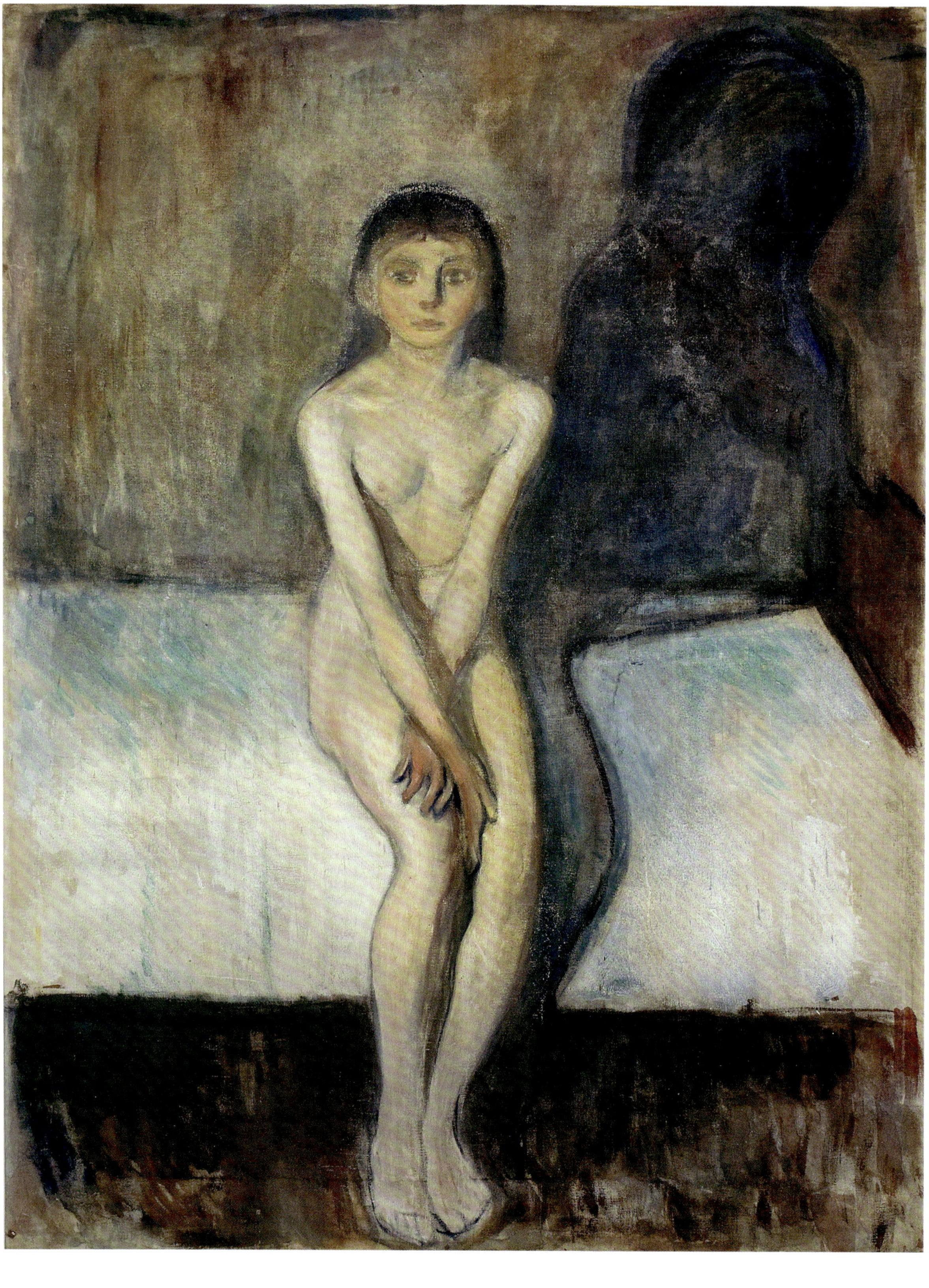

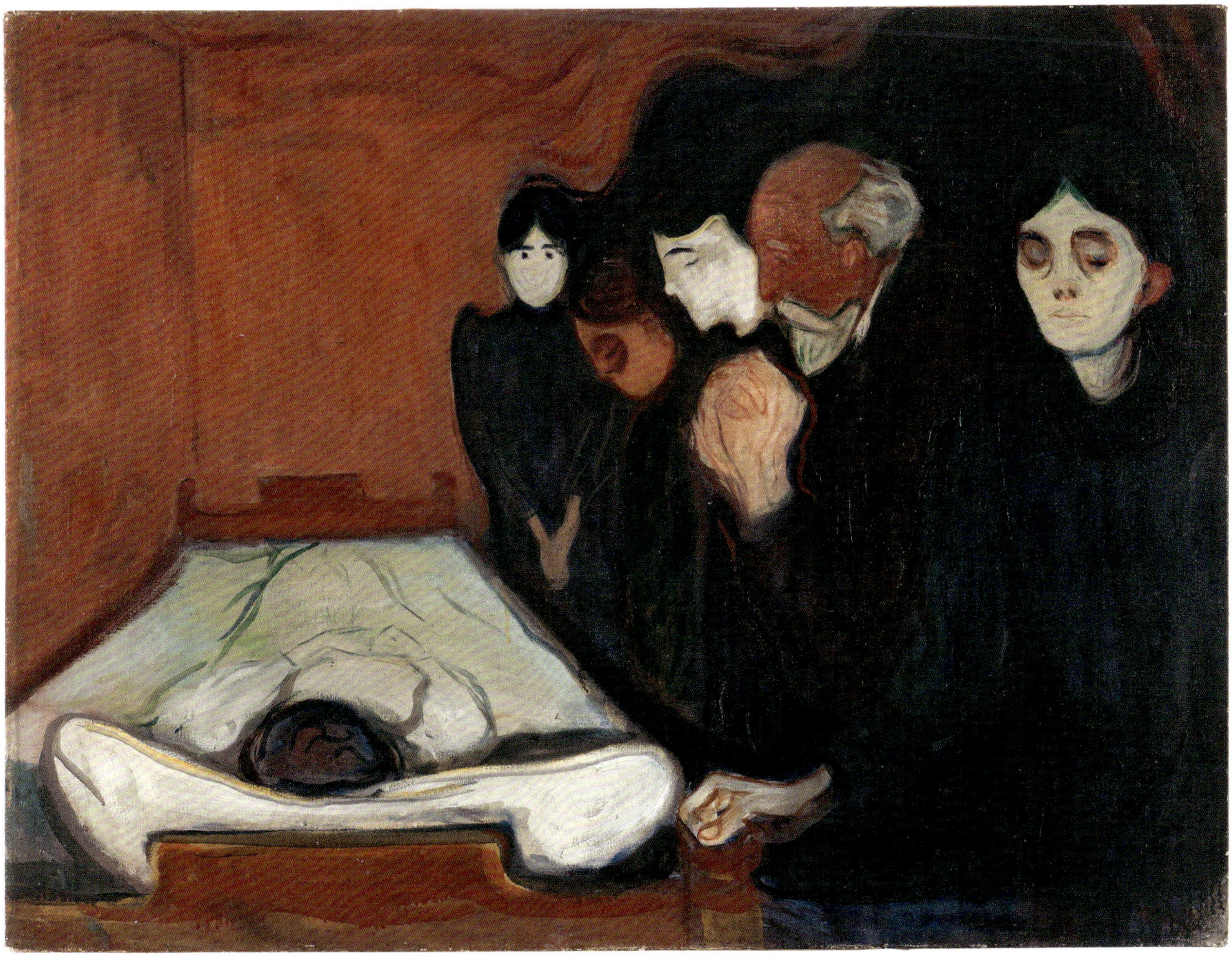

13

Puberty, 1894. Munch Museum, Oslo

14

At the Deathbed, 1895. KODE Kunstmuseene i Bergen, Rasmus Meyers Samlinger

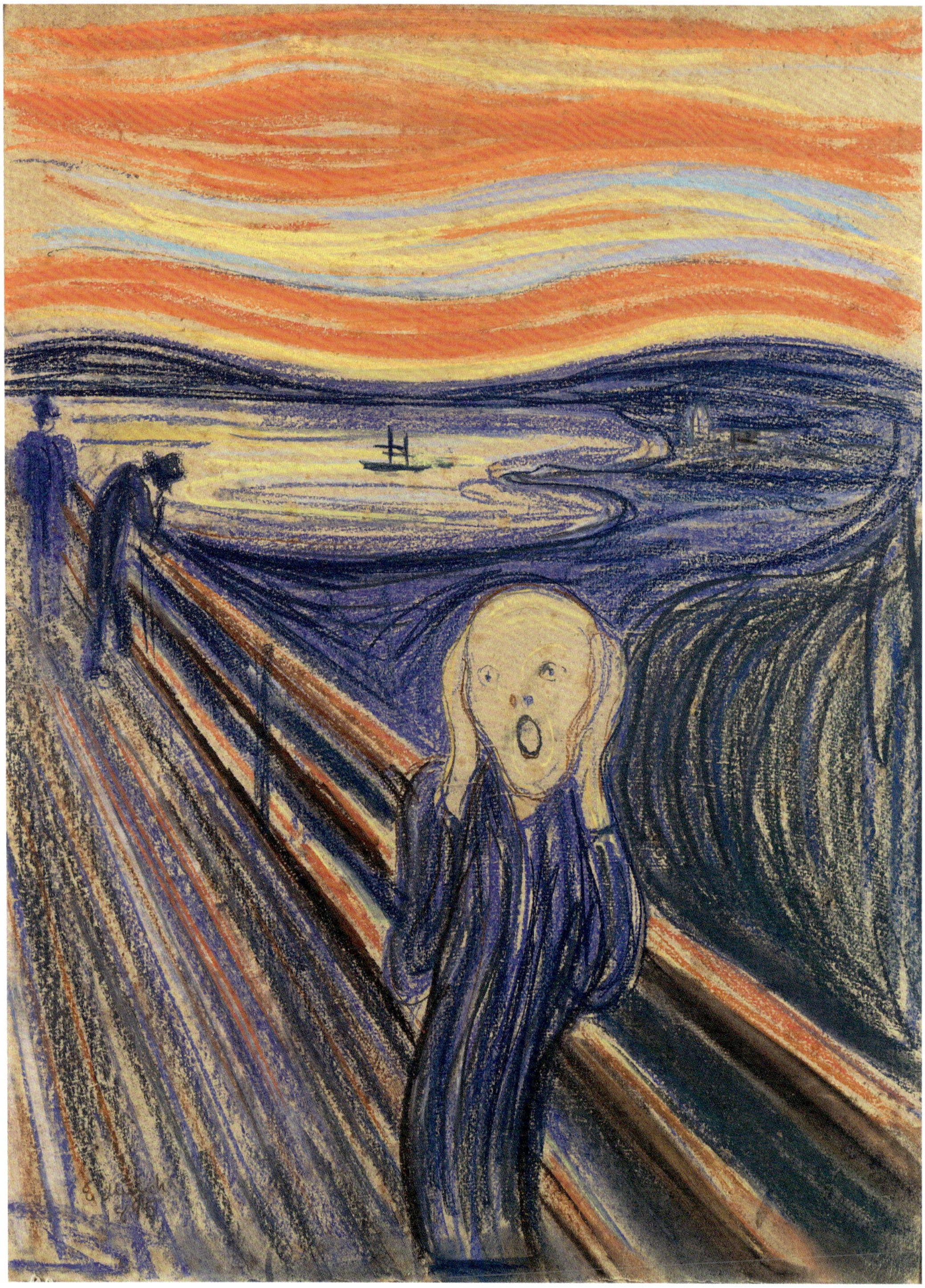

15

The Scream, 1895. Private collection

16

Self-Portrait with Cigarette, 1895. Nasjonalmuseet for Kunst, Arkitektur og Design, Oslo

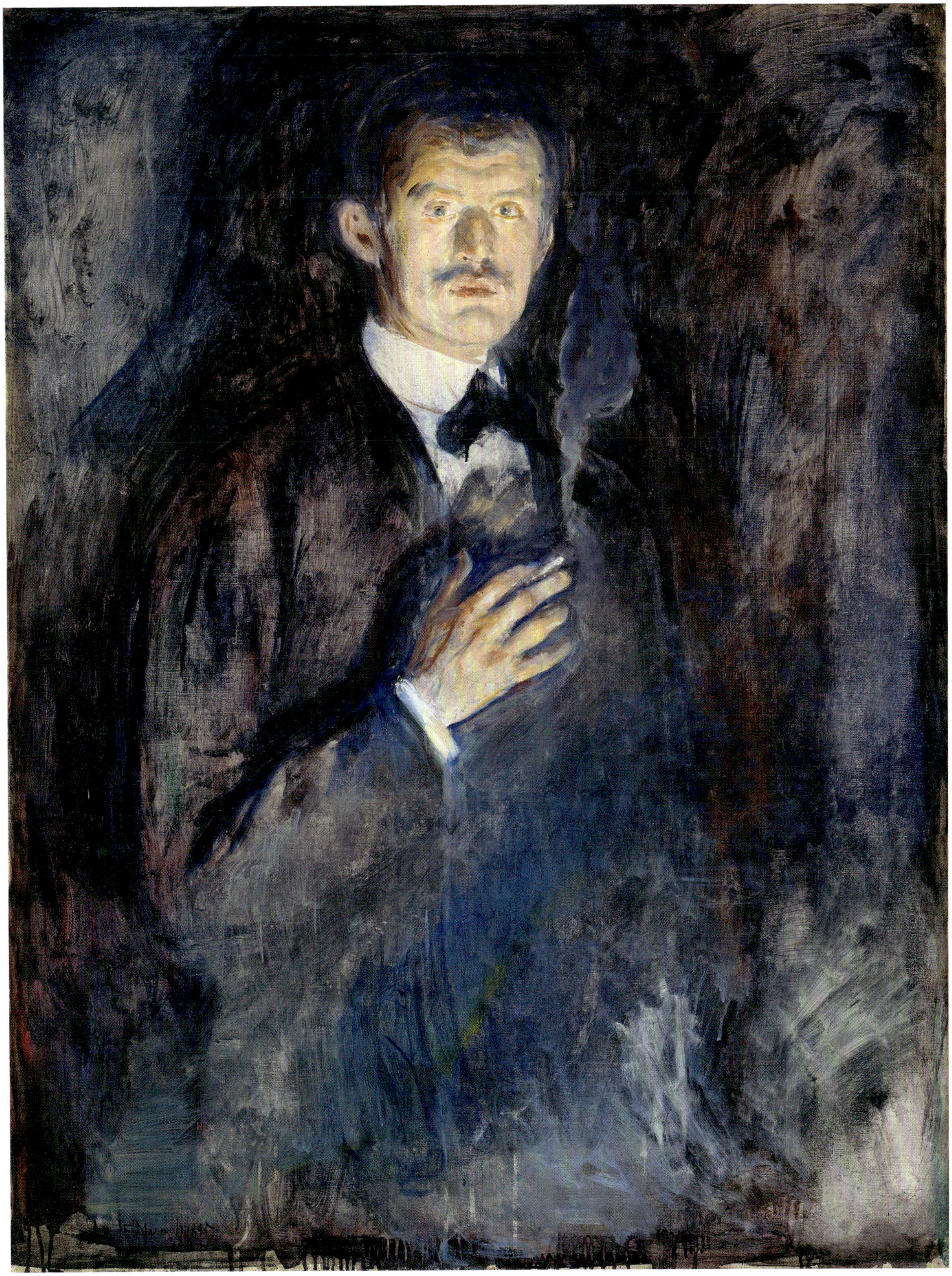

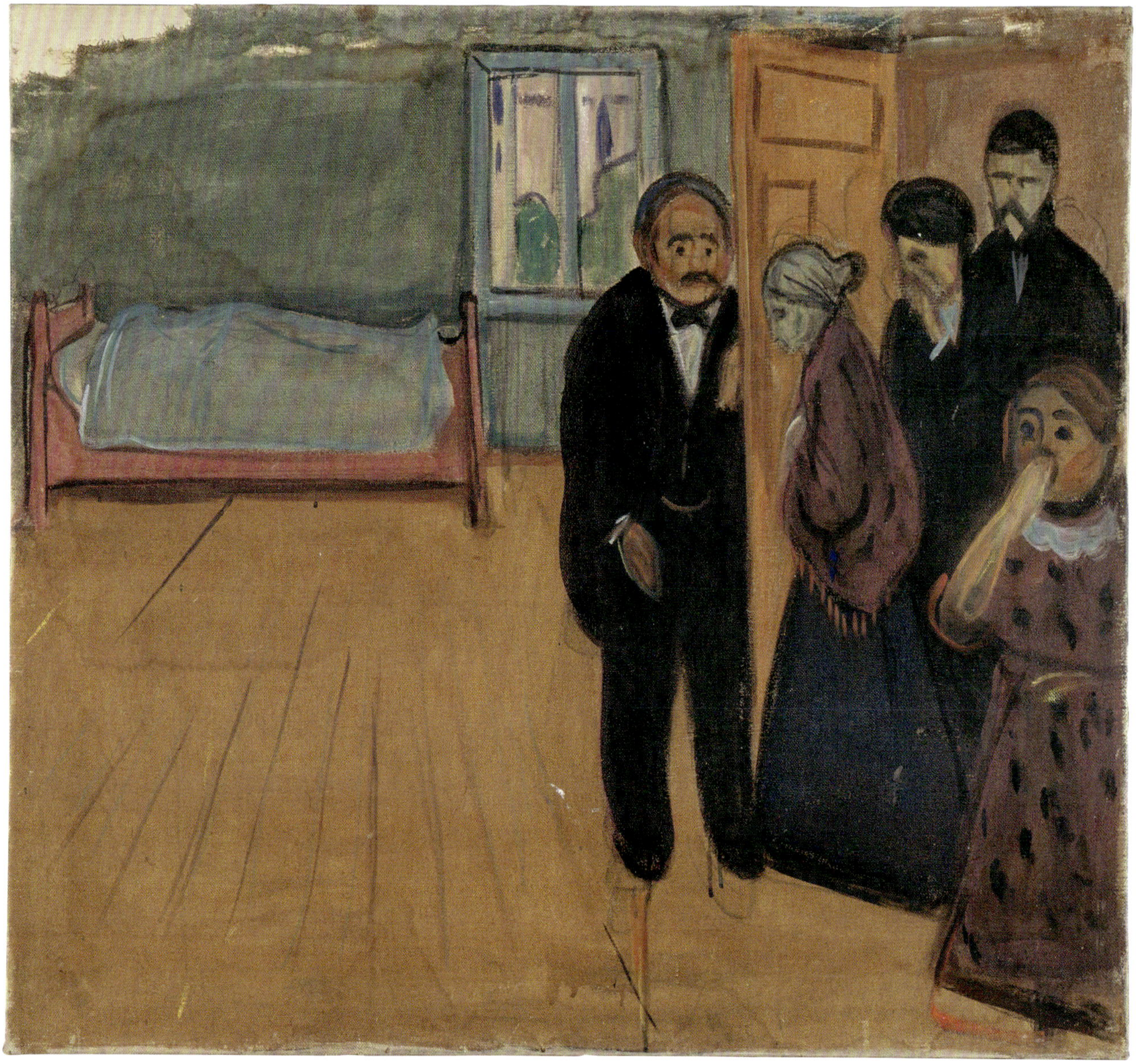

17

The Smell of Death, 1895.
Munch Museum, Oslo

18

Madonna, 1895–97.
Private collection

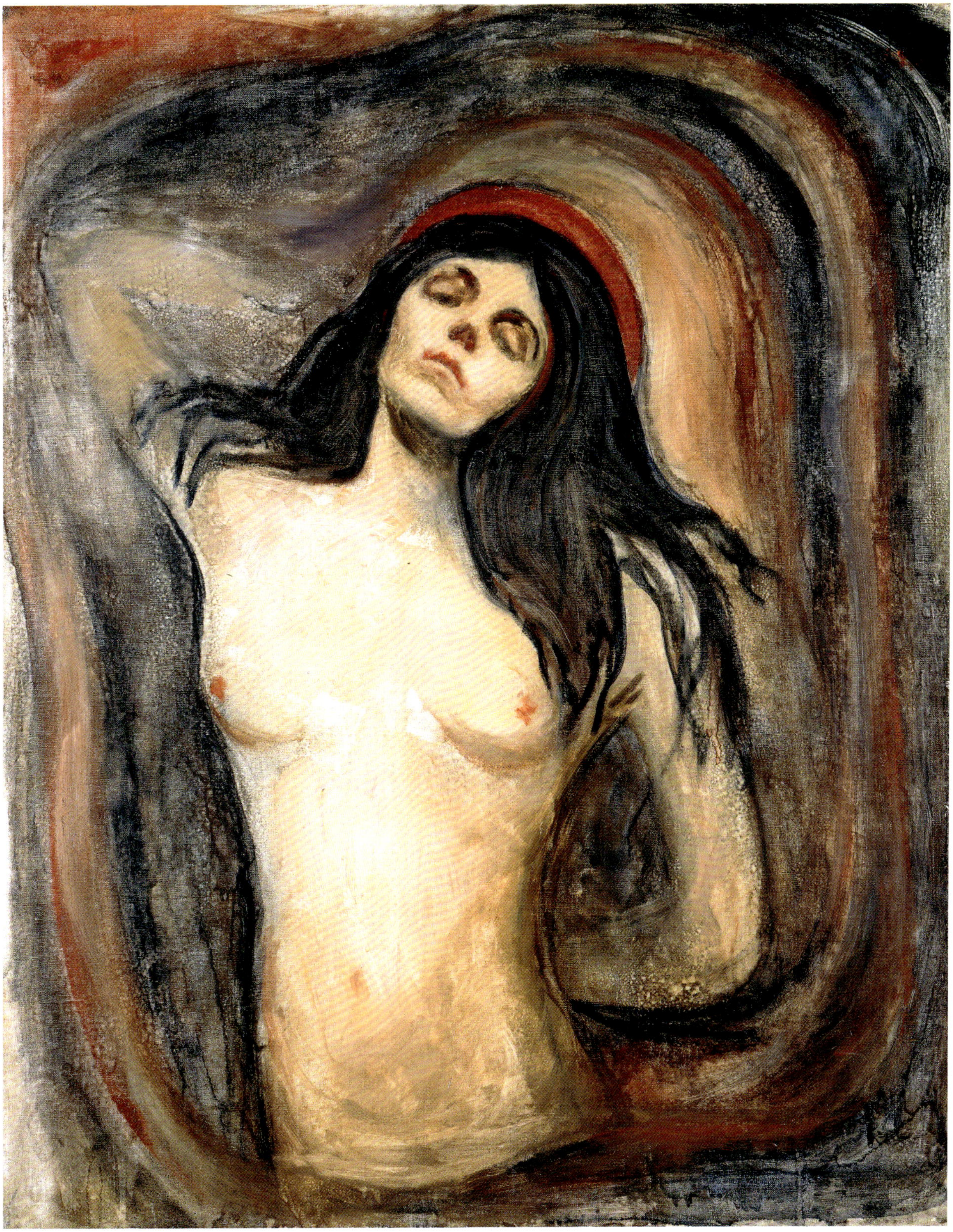

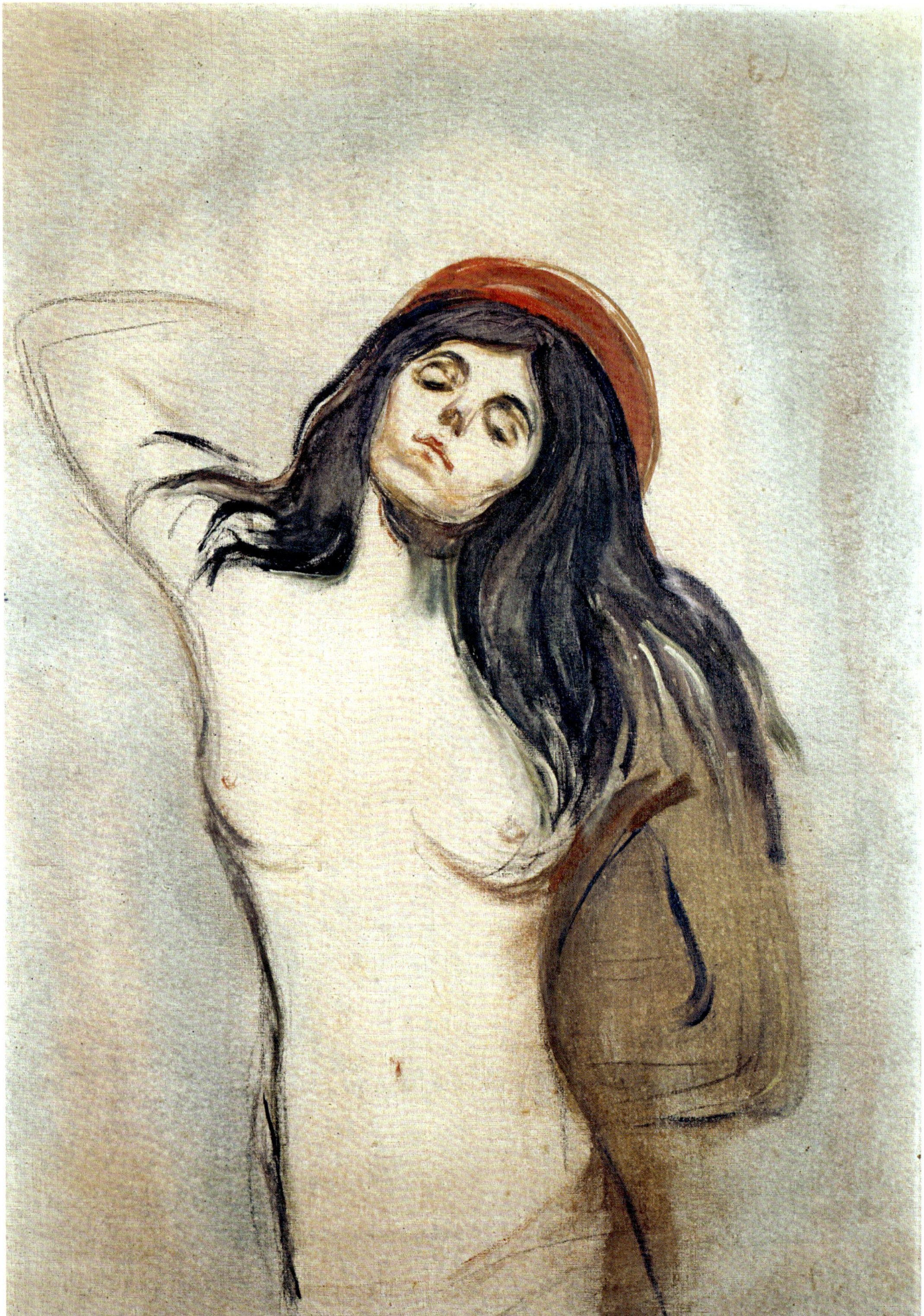

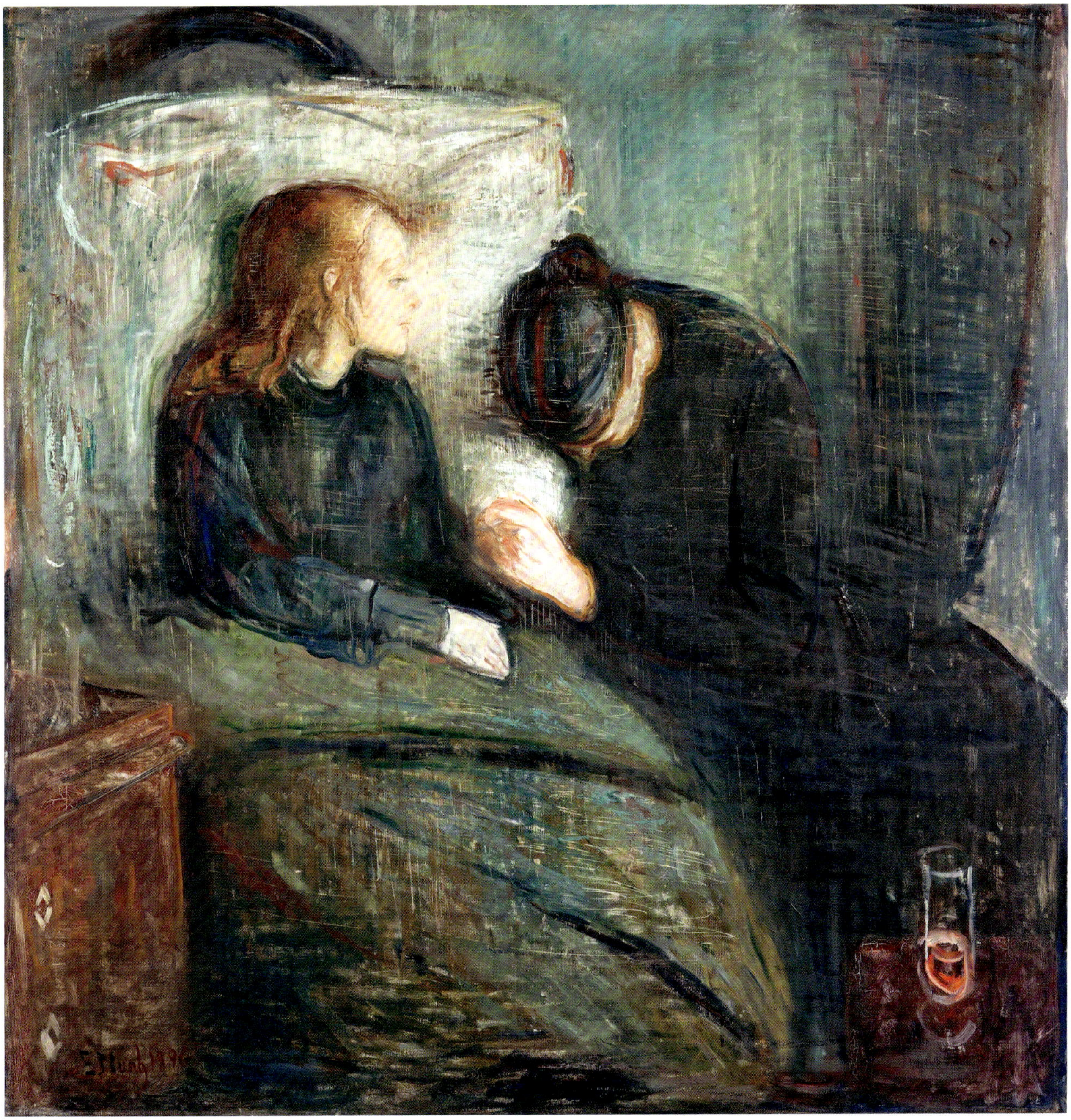

19

Madonna, 1895–97(?). Collection of Catherine Woodard and Nelson Blitz, Jr.

20

The Sick Child, 1896. Göteborgs Konstmuseum

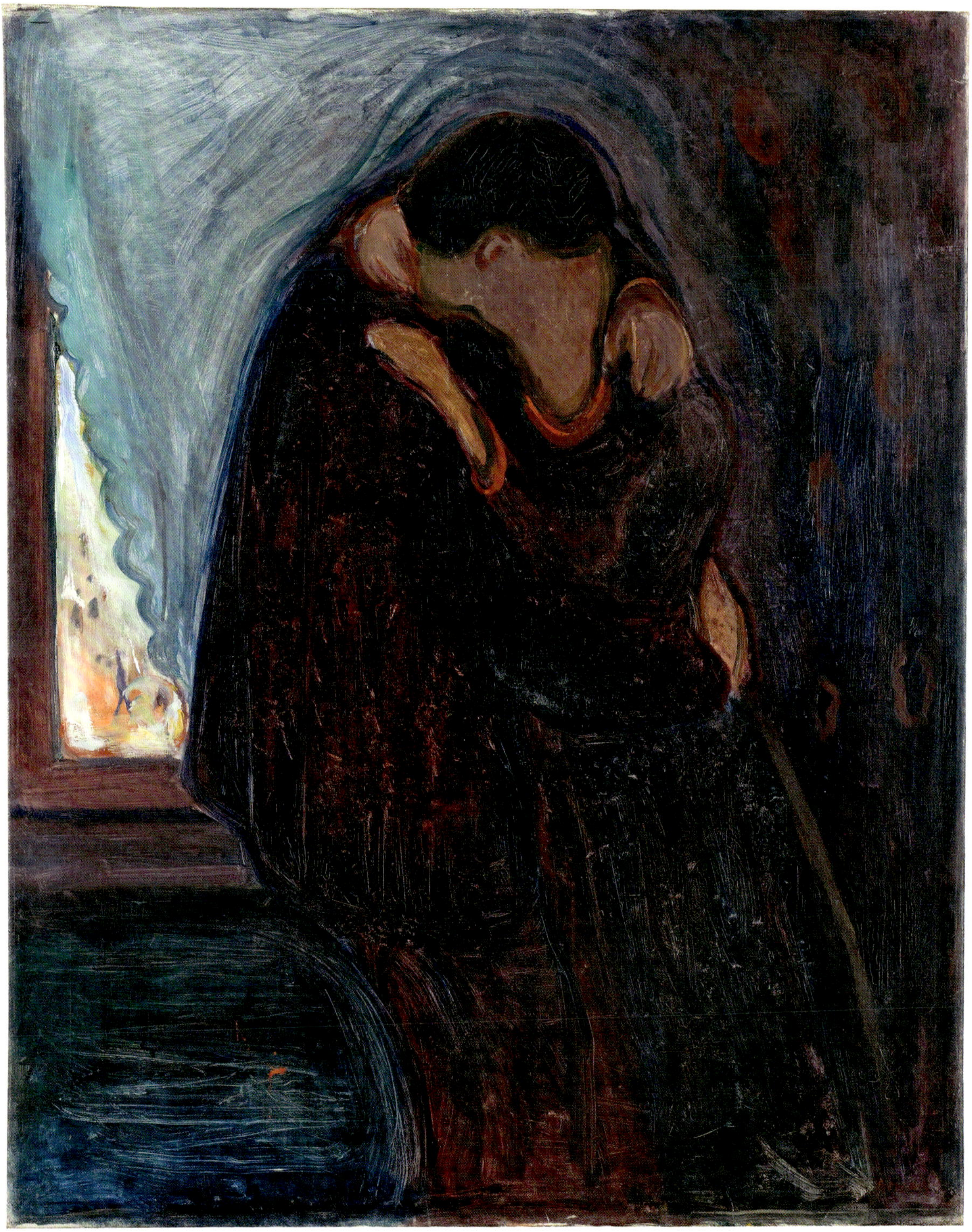

21
The Kiss, 1897. Munch Museum, Oslo

22
Inheritance, 1897–99. Munch Museum, Oslo

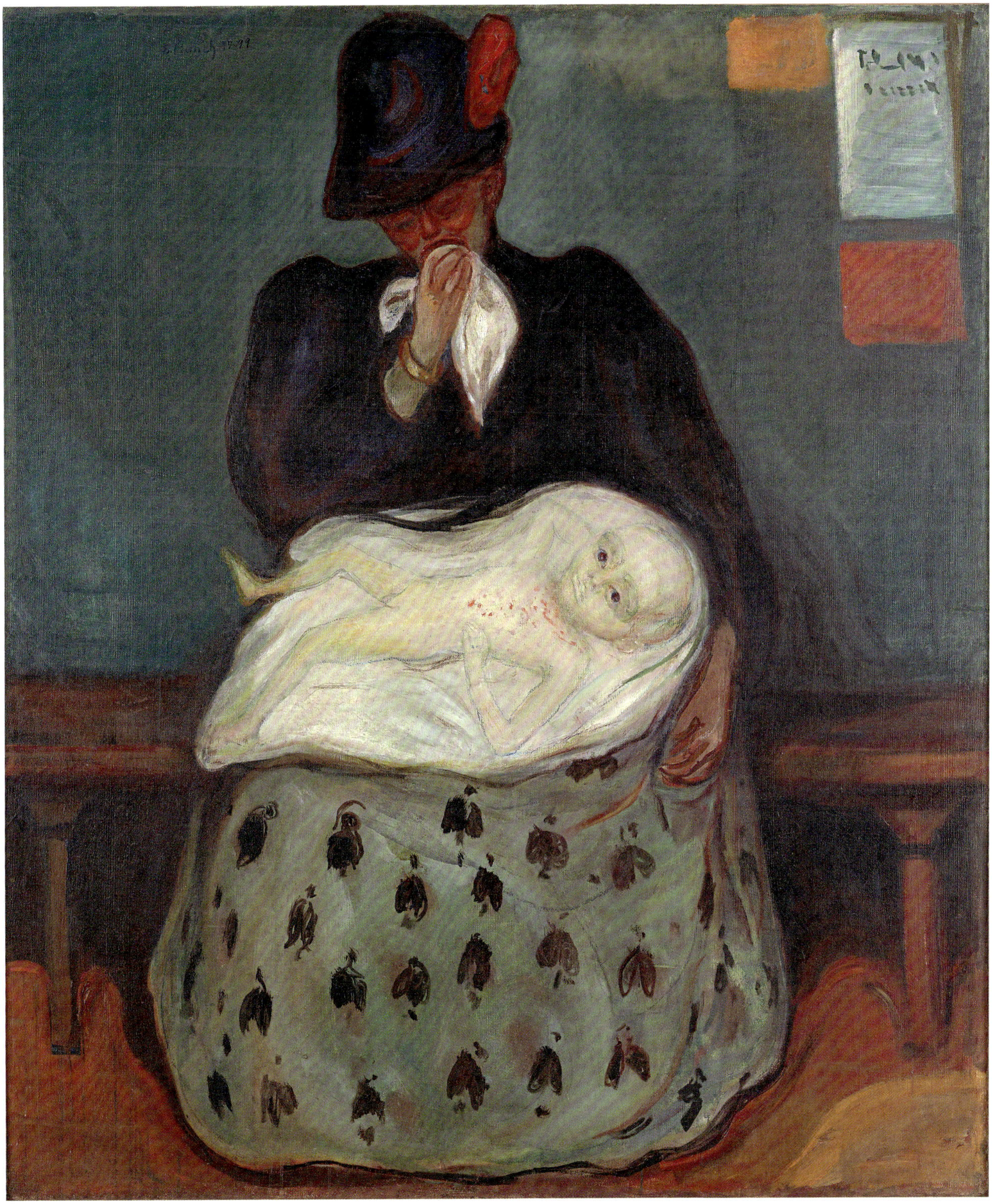

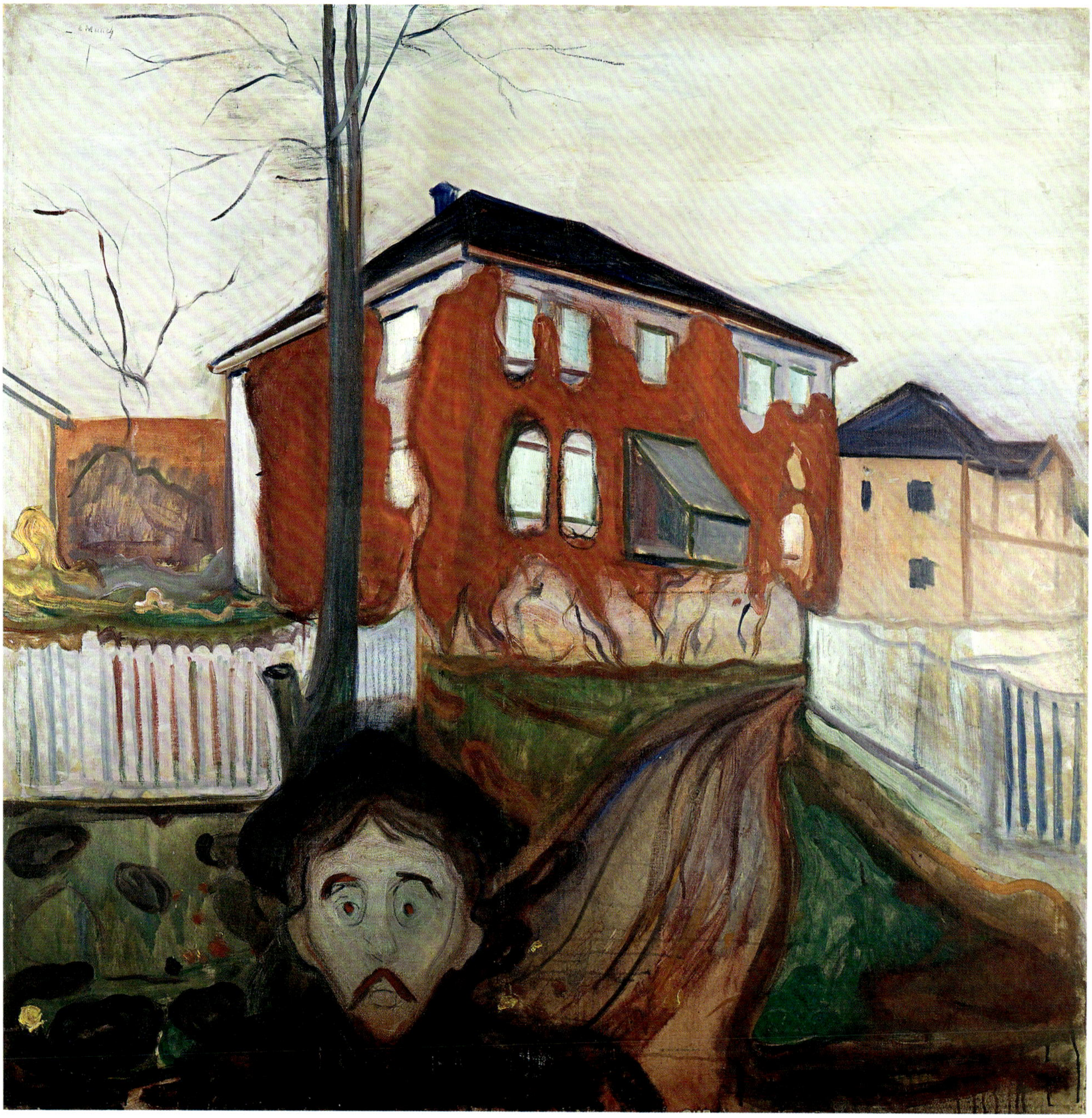

23

Red Virginia Creeper, 1898–1900.
Munch Museum, Oslo

24

Eye in Eye, 1899–1900.
Munch Museum, Oslo

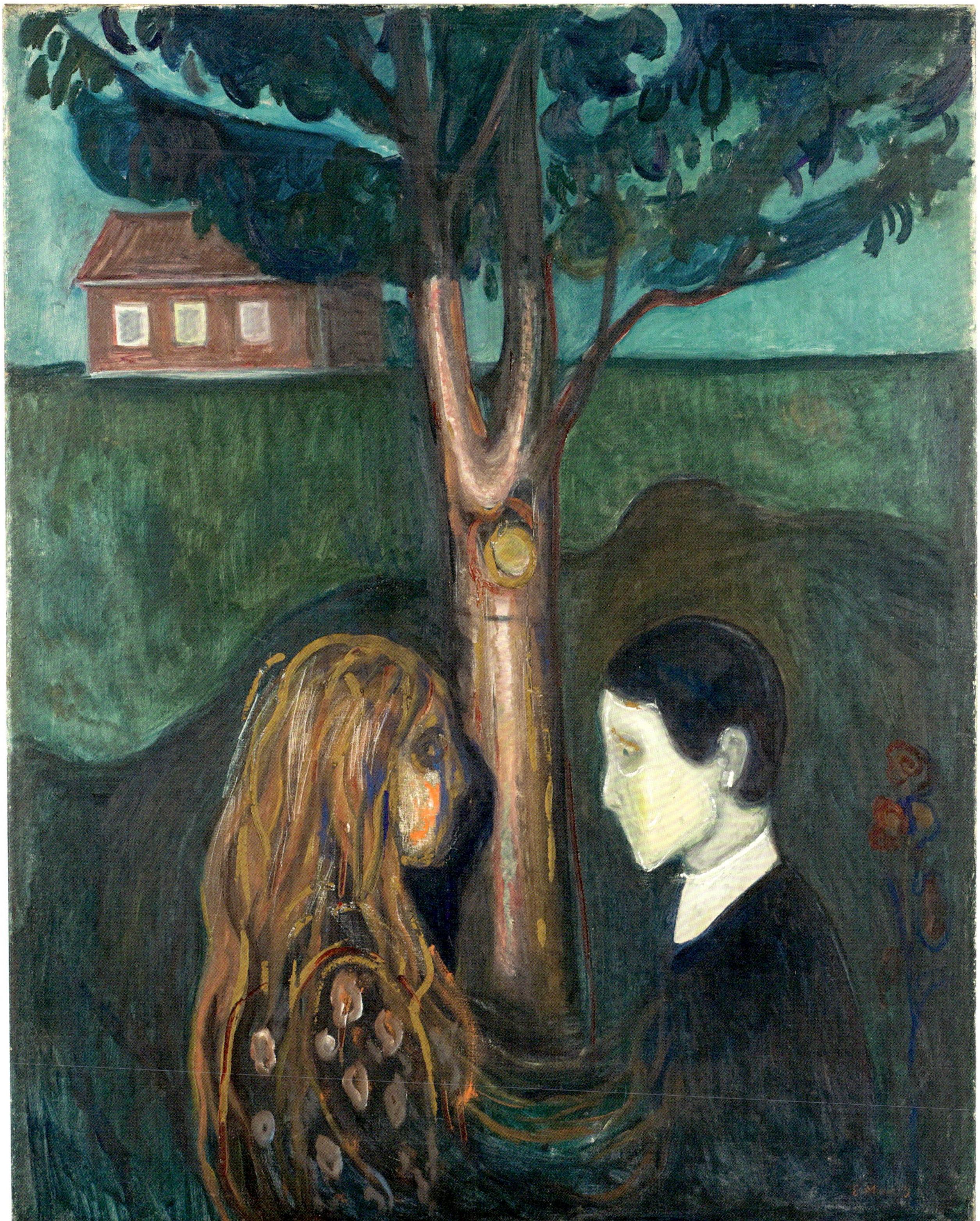

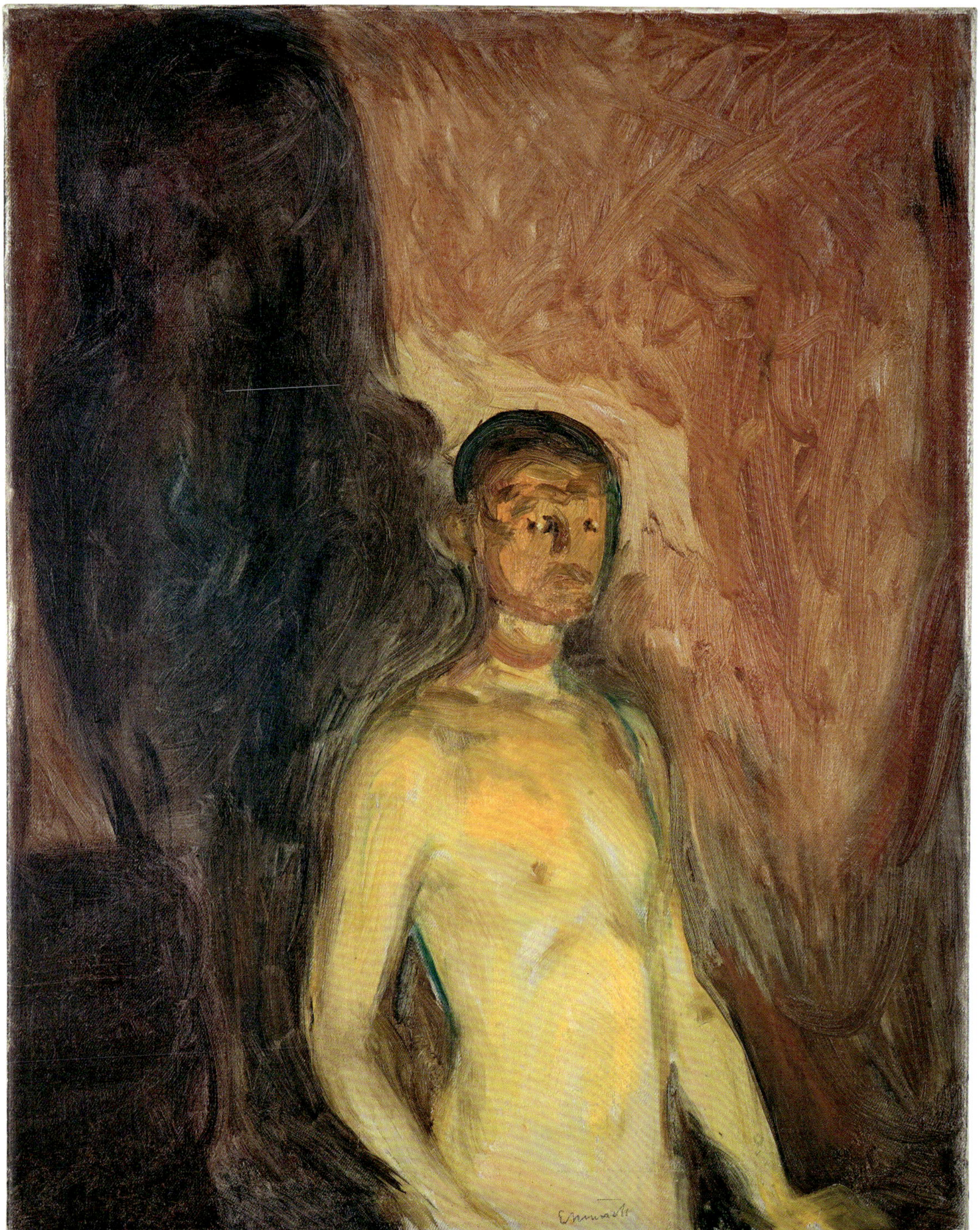

25
Self-Portrait in Hell, 1903.
Munch Museum, Oslo

26
Self-Portrait with Brushes, 1904.
Munch Museum, Oslo

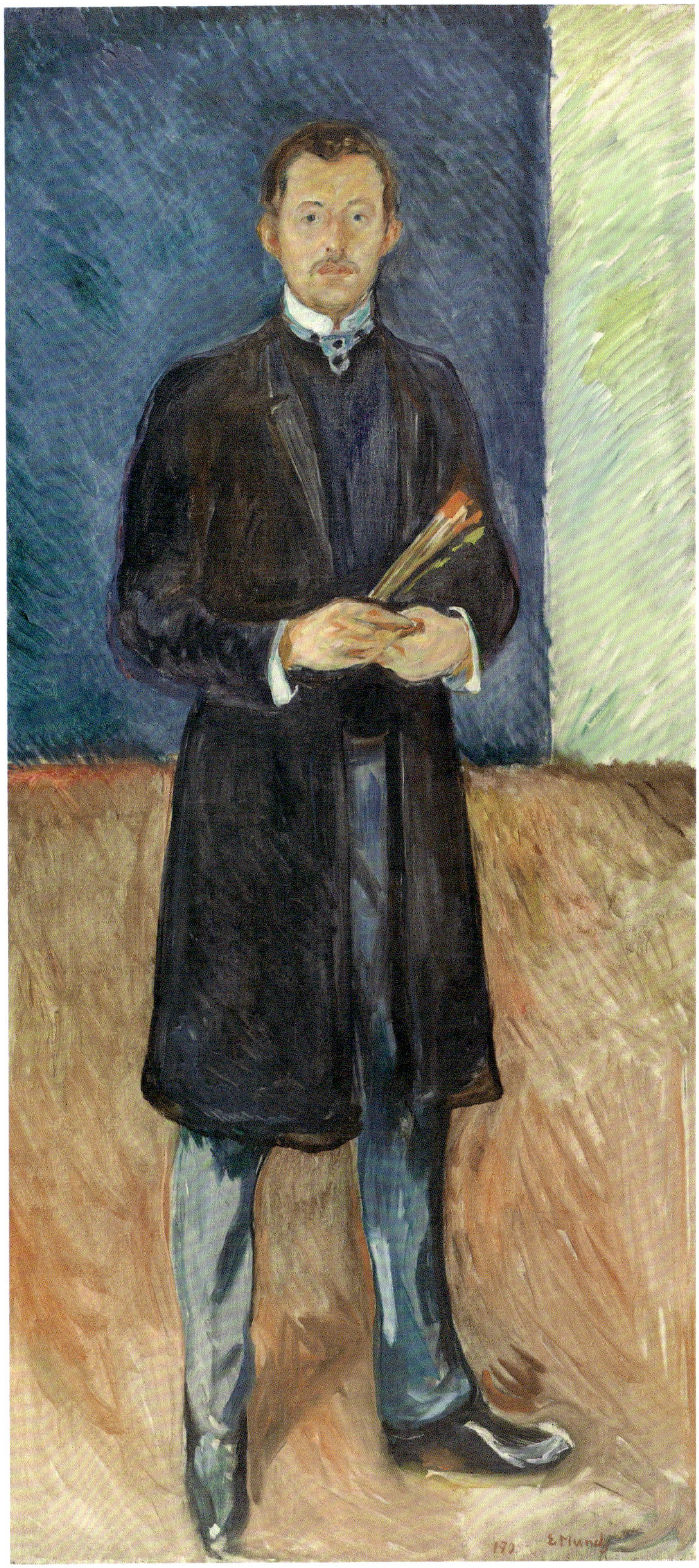

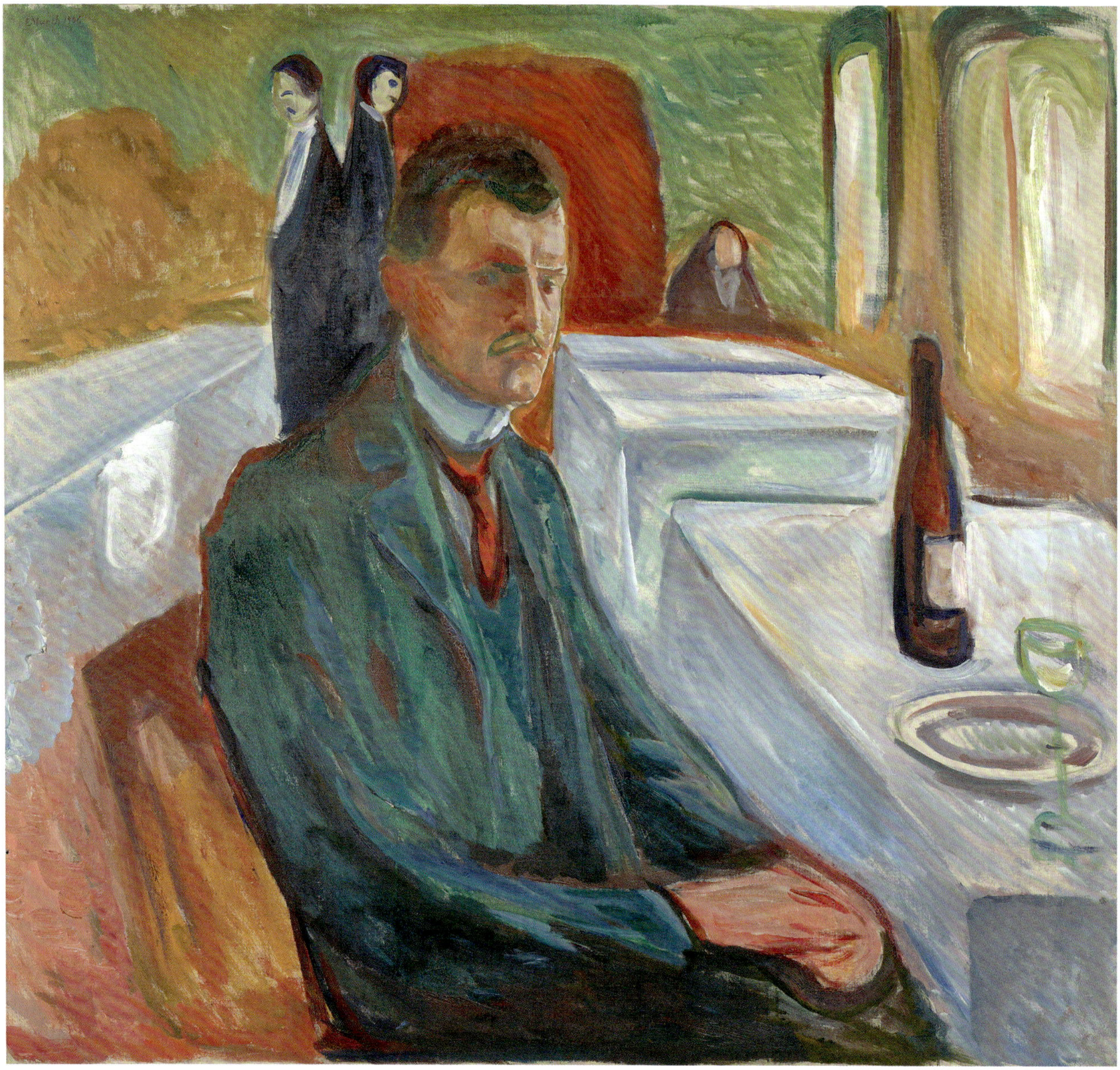

27

Self-Portrait with a Bottle of Wine, 1906.
Munch Museum, Oslo

28

The Death of Marat, 1907.
Munch Museum, Oslo

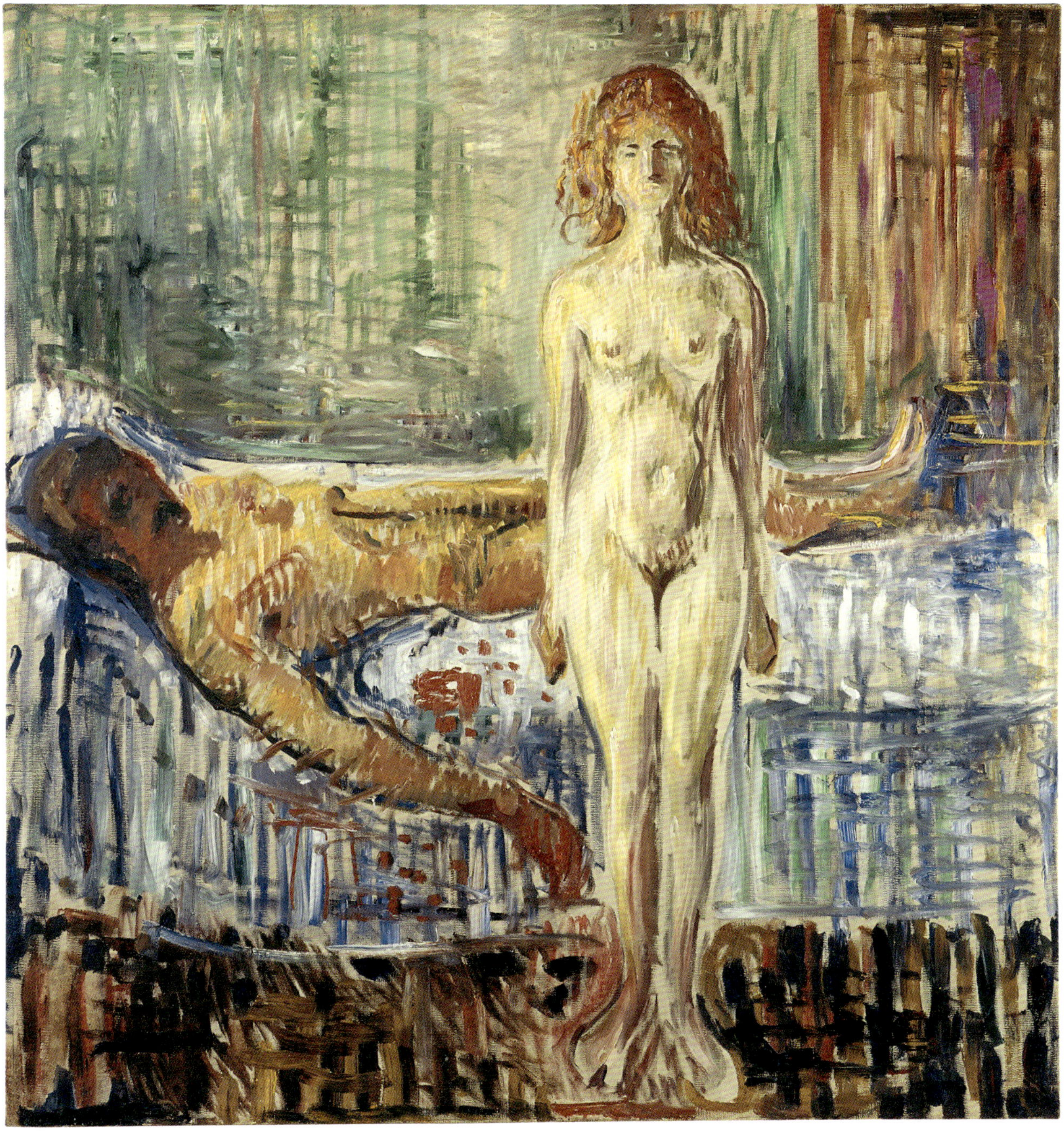

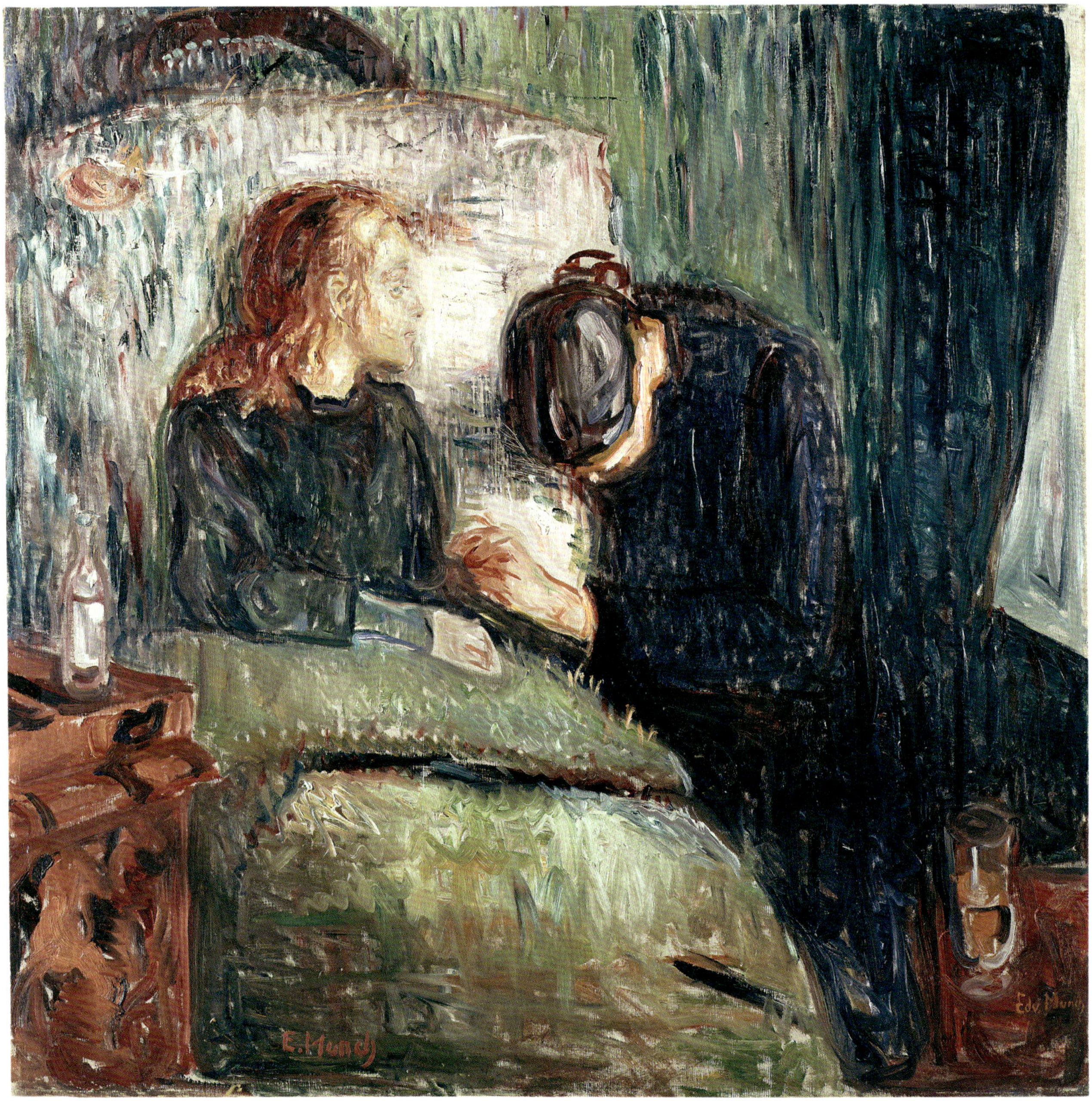
E.Munch

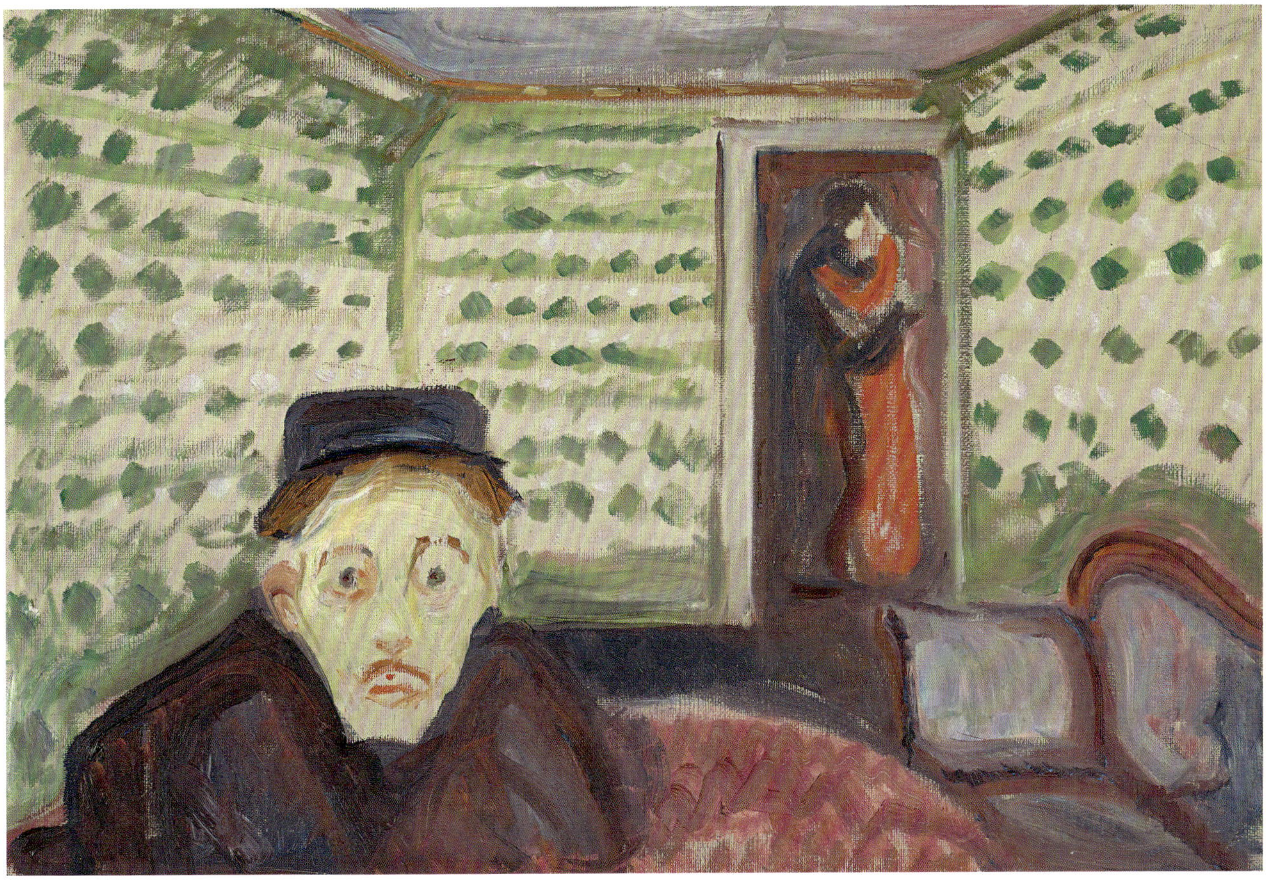

29
The Sick Child, 1907. Tate Modern, London

30
Jealousy, ca. 1907. Munch Museum, Oslo

31

The Scream, ca. 1910.
Munch Museum, Oslo

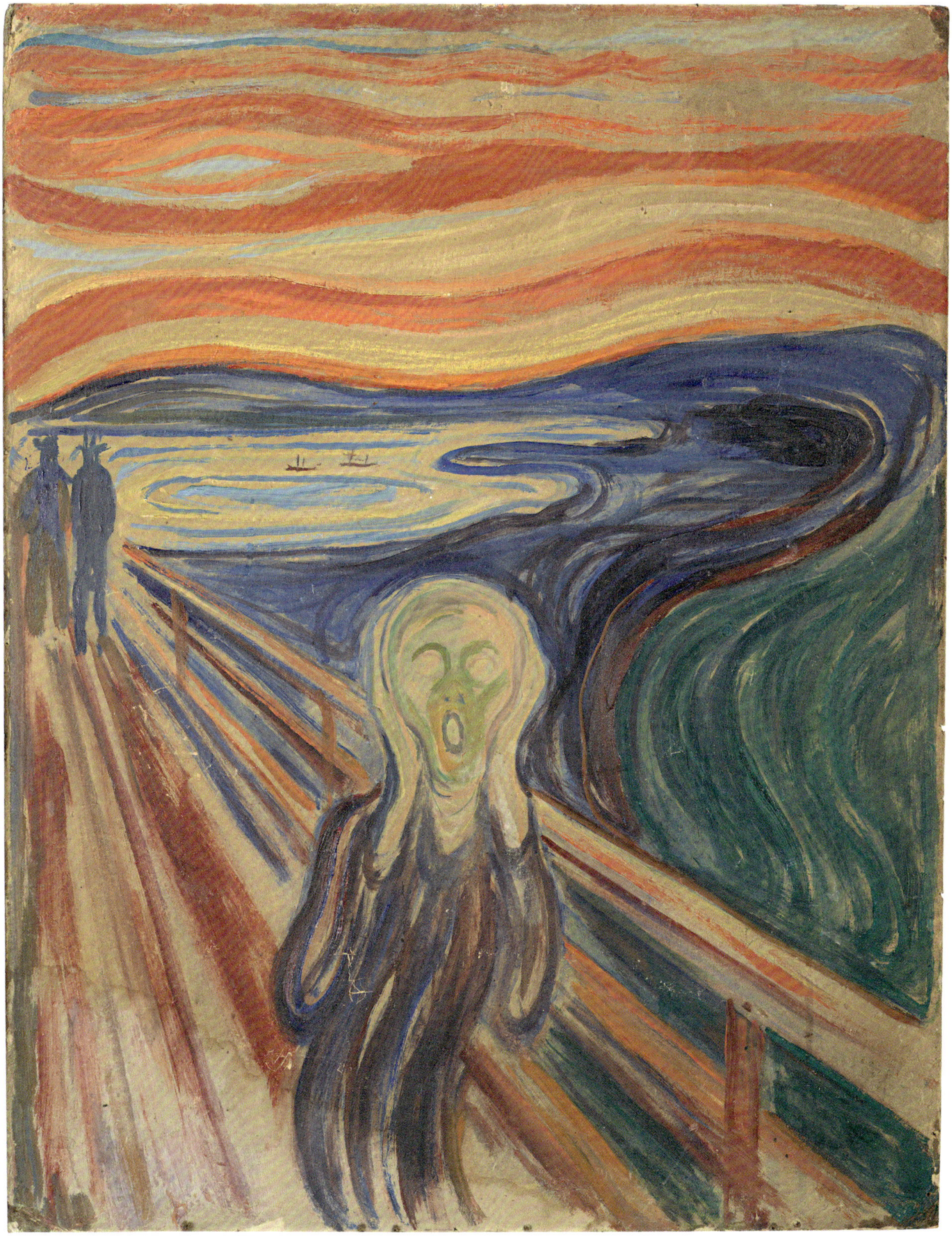

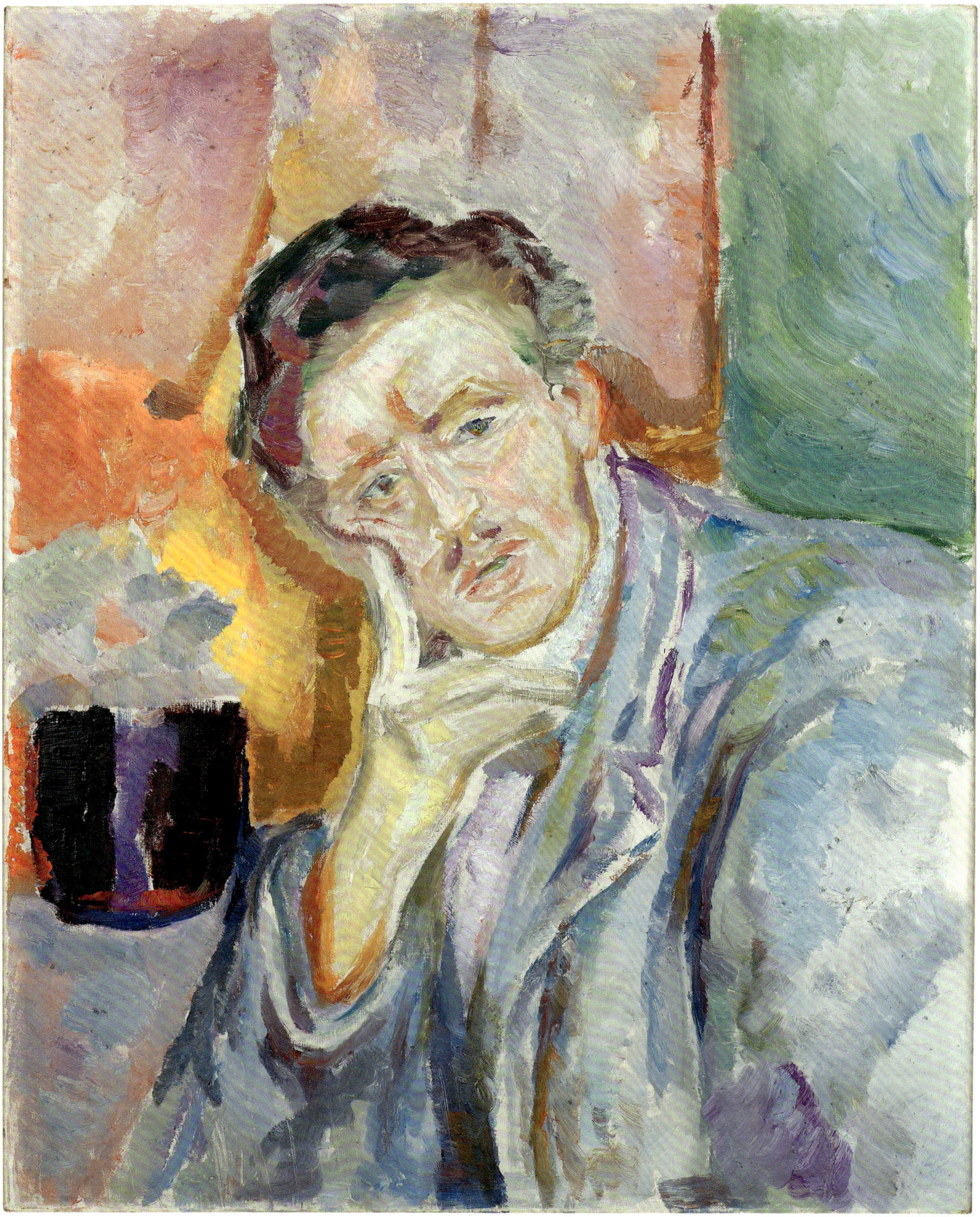

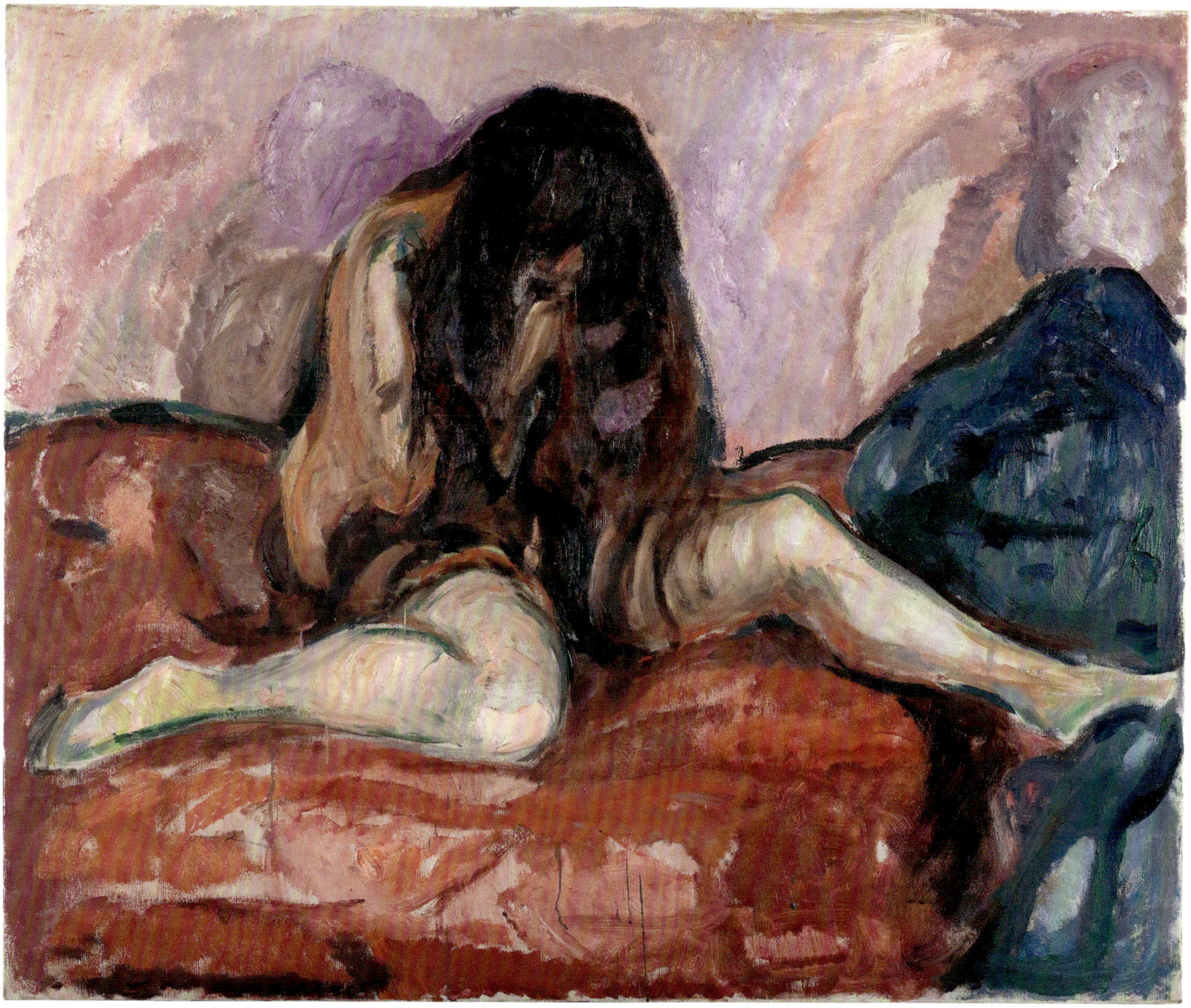

32
Self-Portrait with Hand under Cheek, 1911.
Munch Museum, Oslo

33
Weeping Nude, 1913–14.
Munch Museum, Oslo

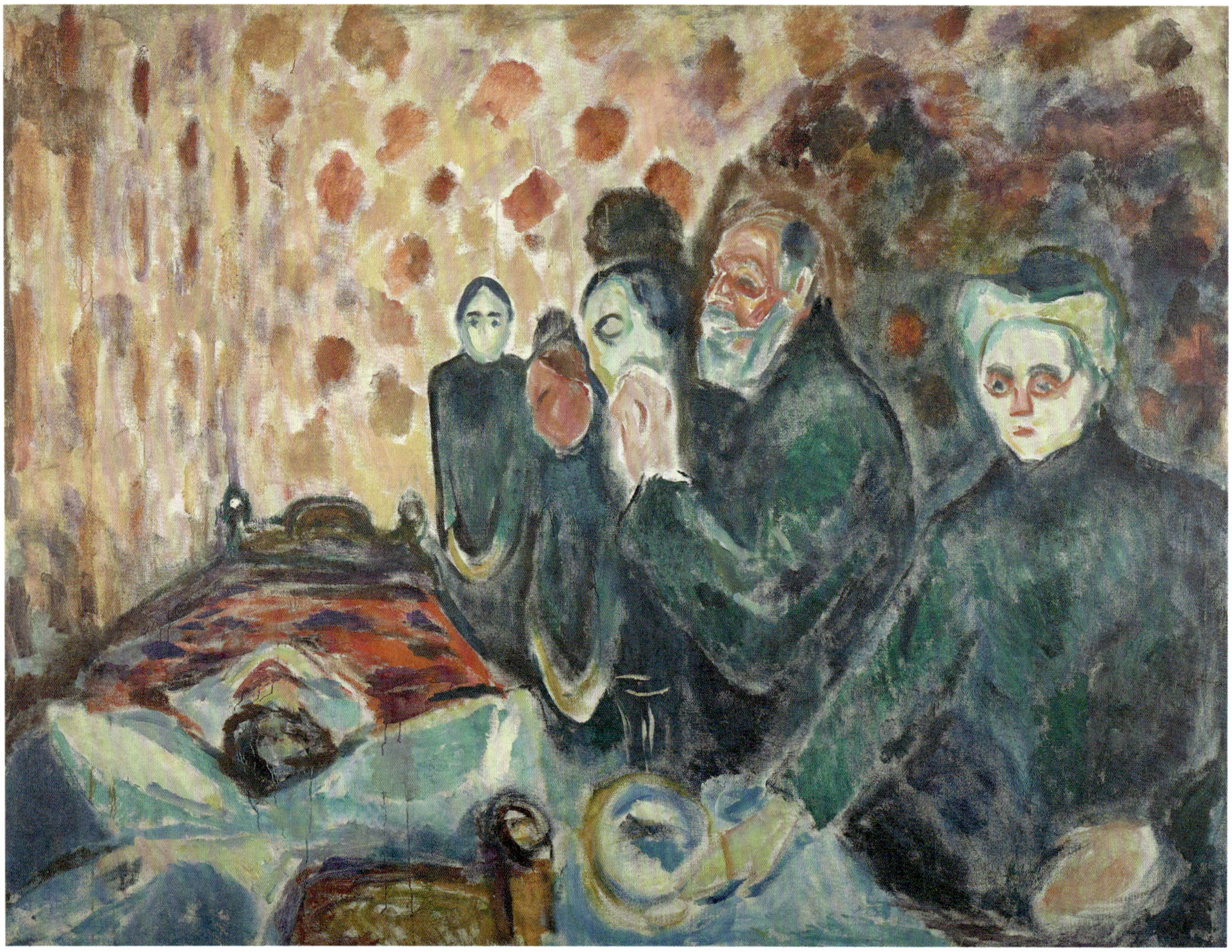

34

Death Struggle, 1915.
Munch Museum, Oslo

35

Self-Portrait with the Spanish Flu, 1919.
Nasjonalmuseet for Kunst, Arkitektur og Design, Oslo

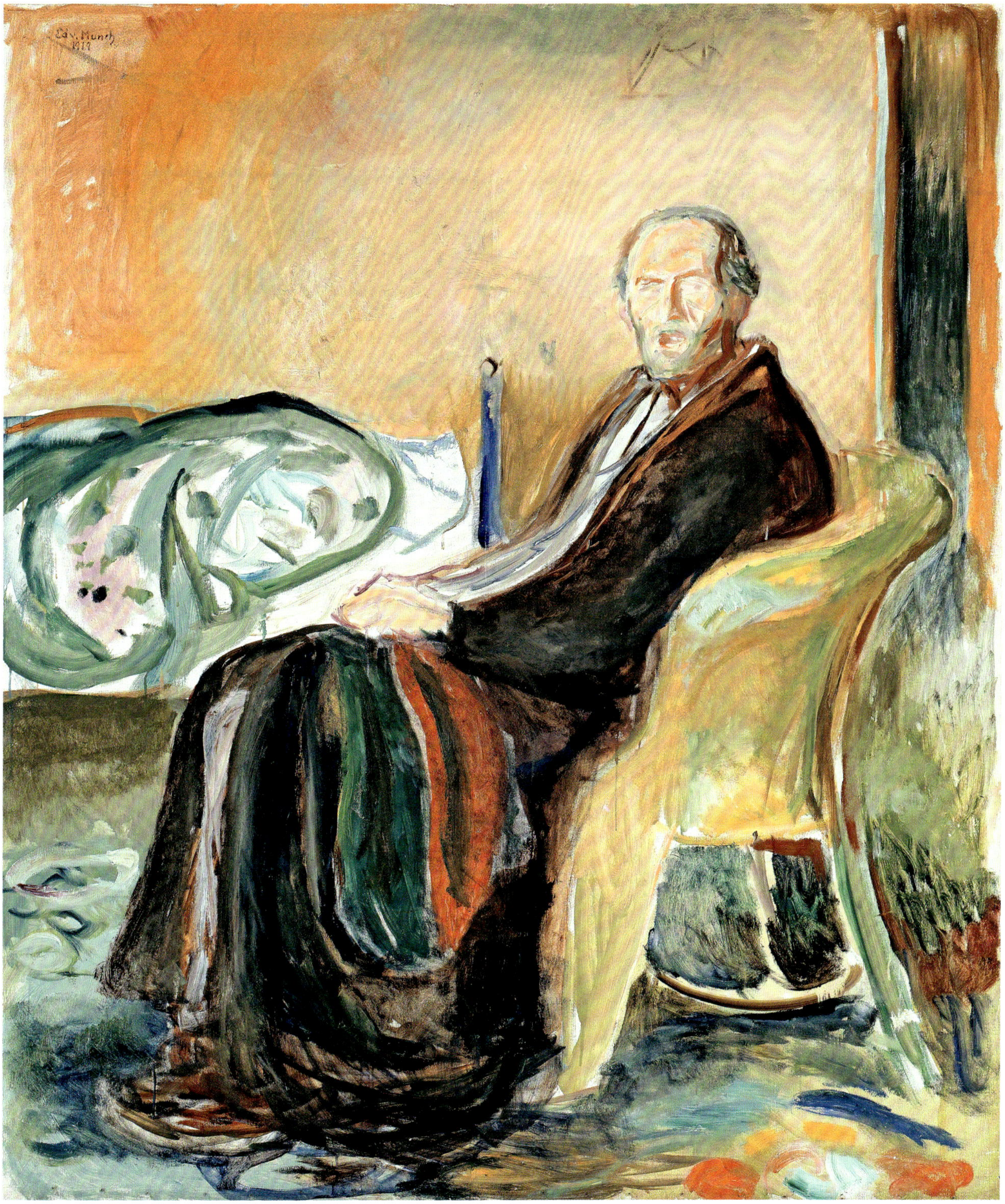
Edv. Munch

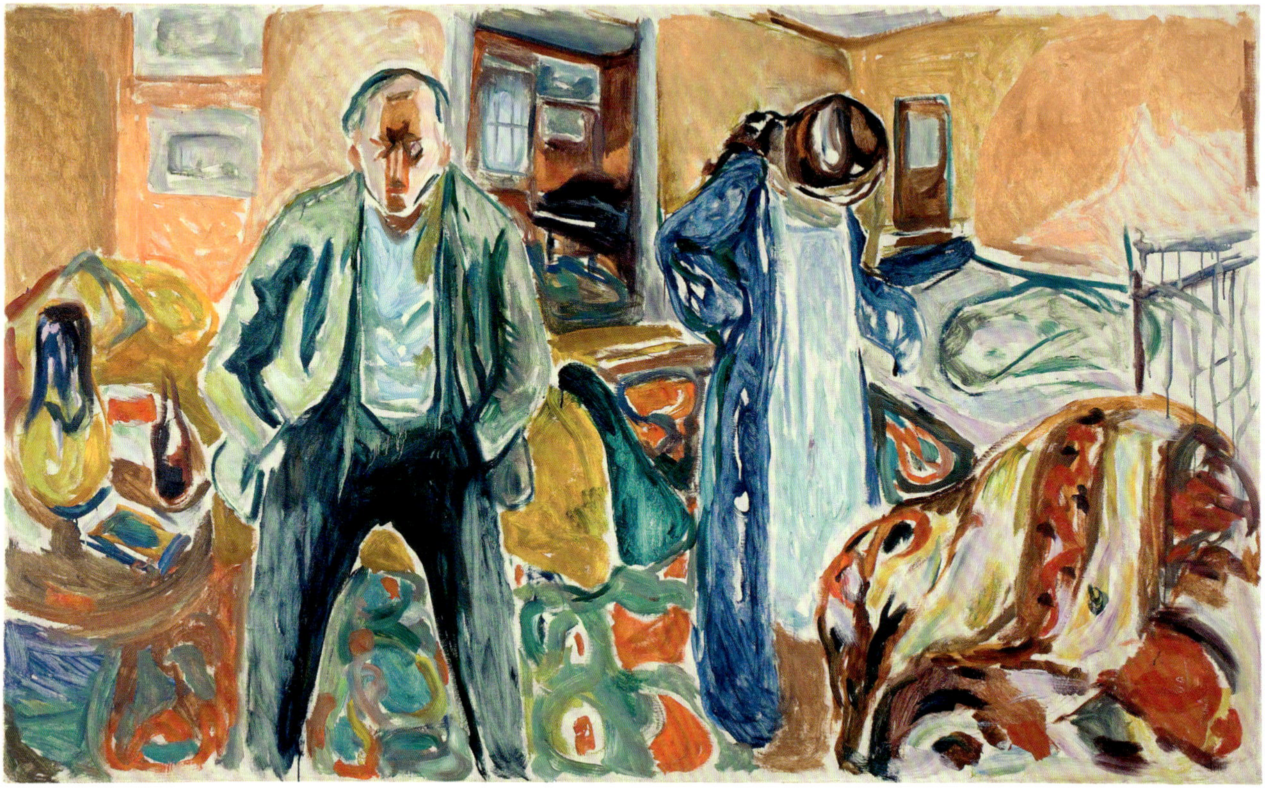

36

The Artist and His Model, 1919–21.
Munch Museum, Oslo

37

The Artist and His Model, 1919–21.
Munch Museum, Oslo

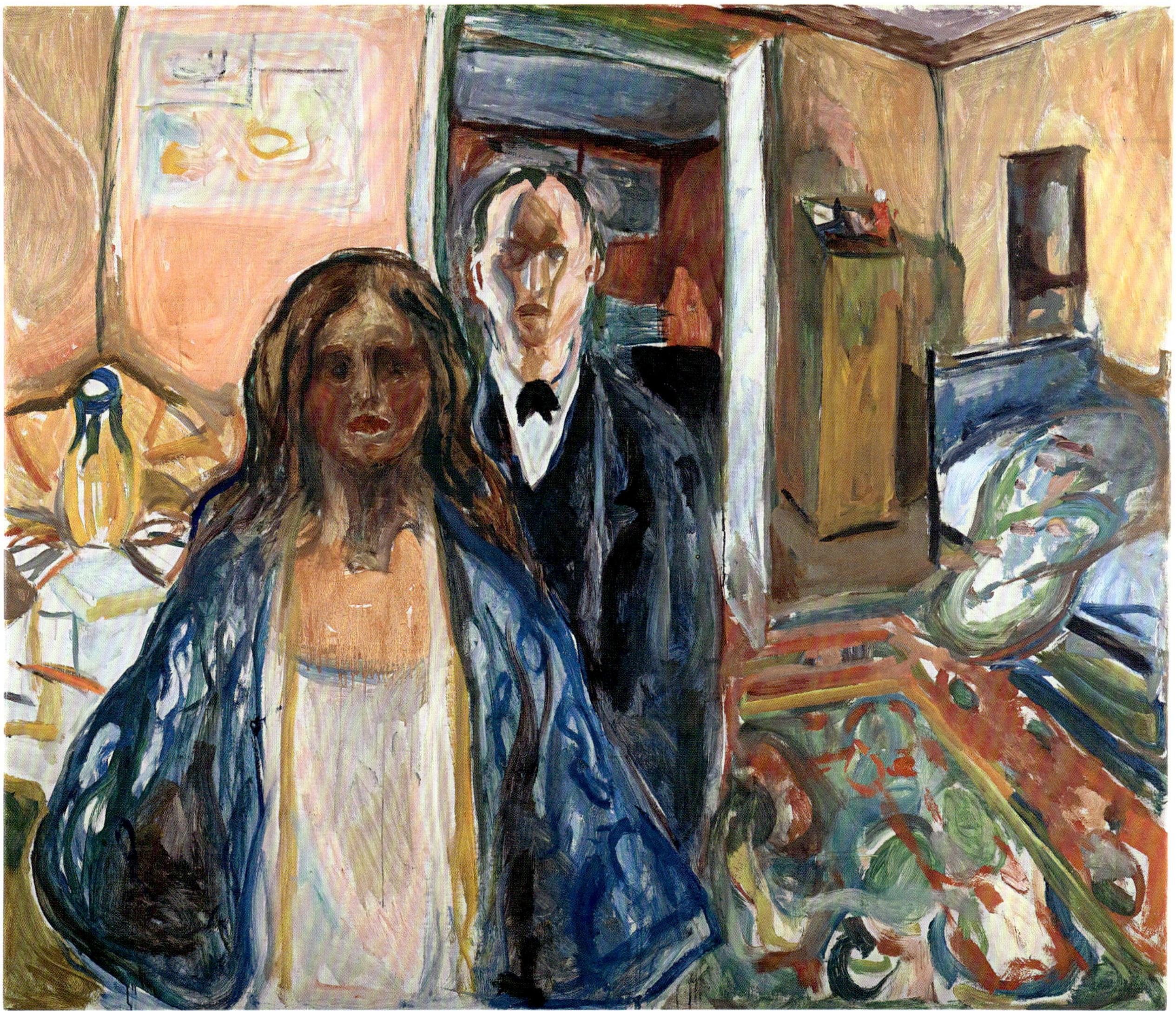

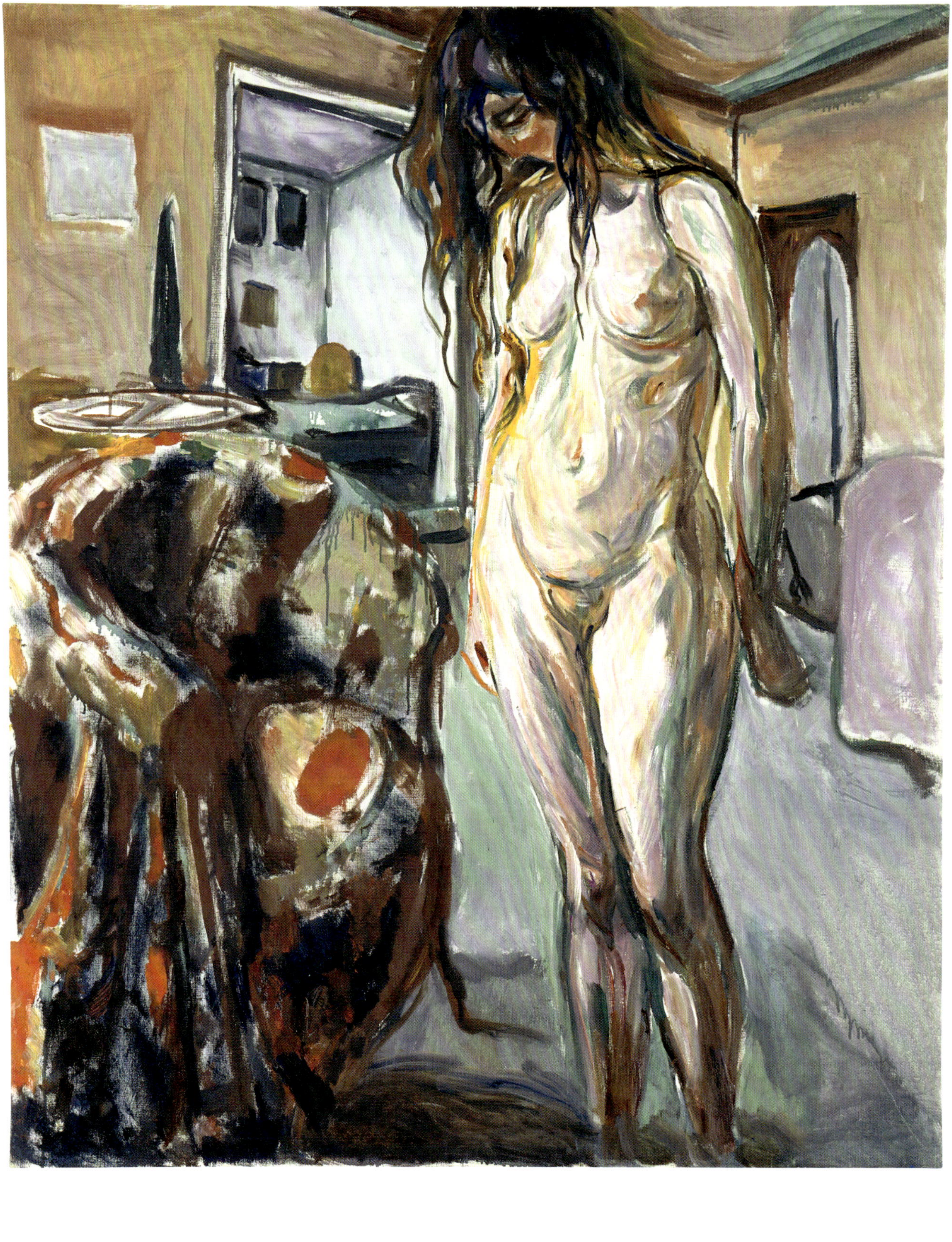

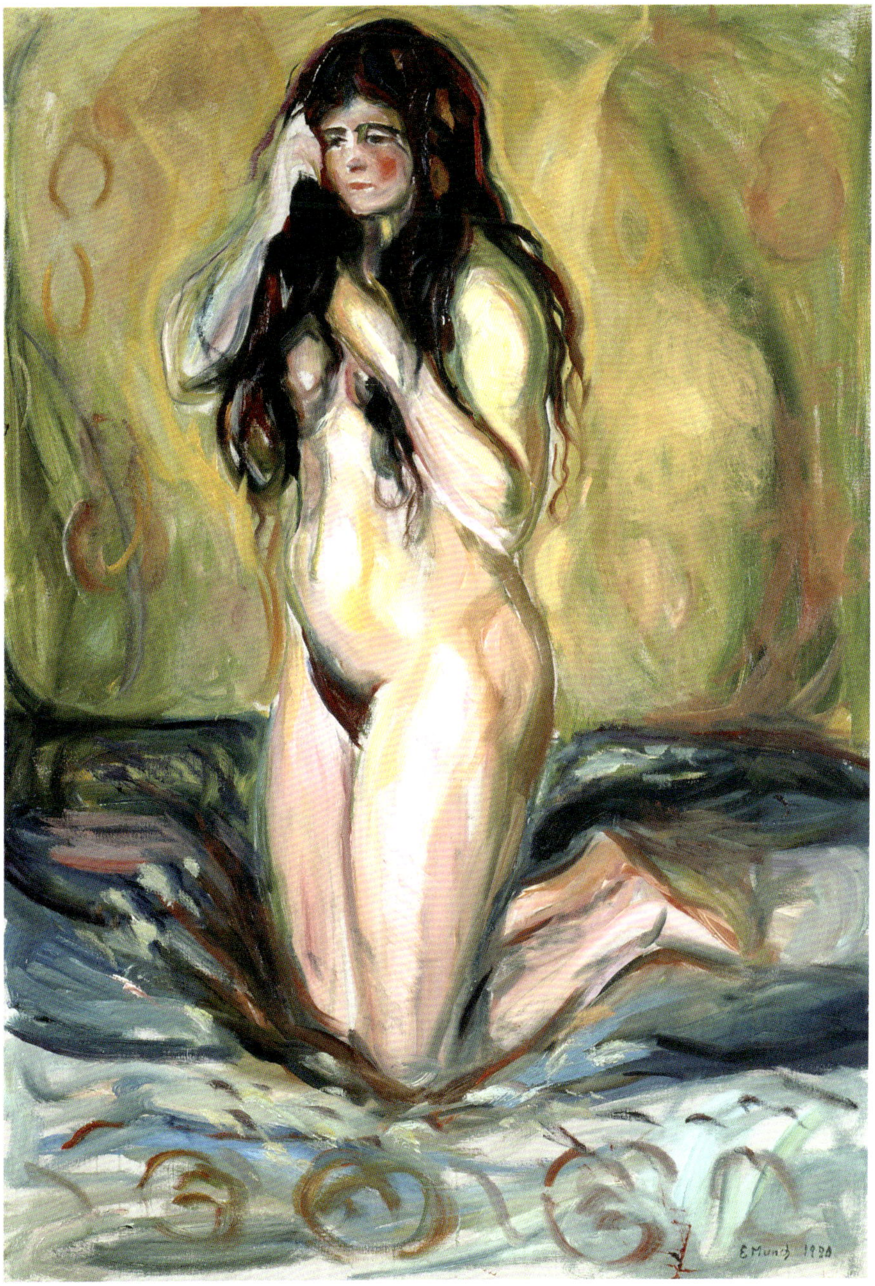

38

Model by the Wicker Chair, 1919–21. Munch Museum, Oslo

39

Female Nude (Anna), 1920. Sarah Campbell Blaffer Foundation, Houston

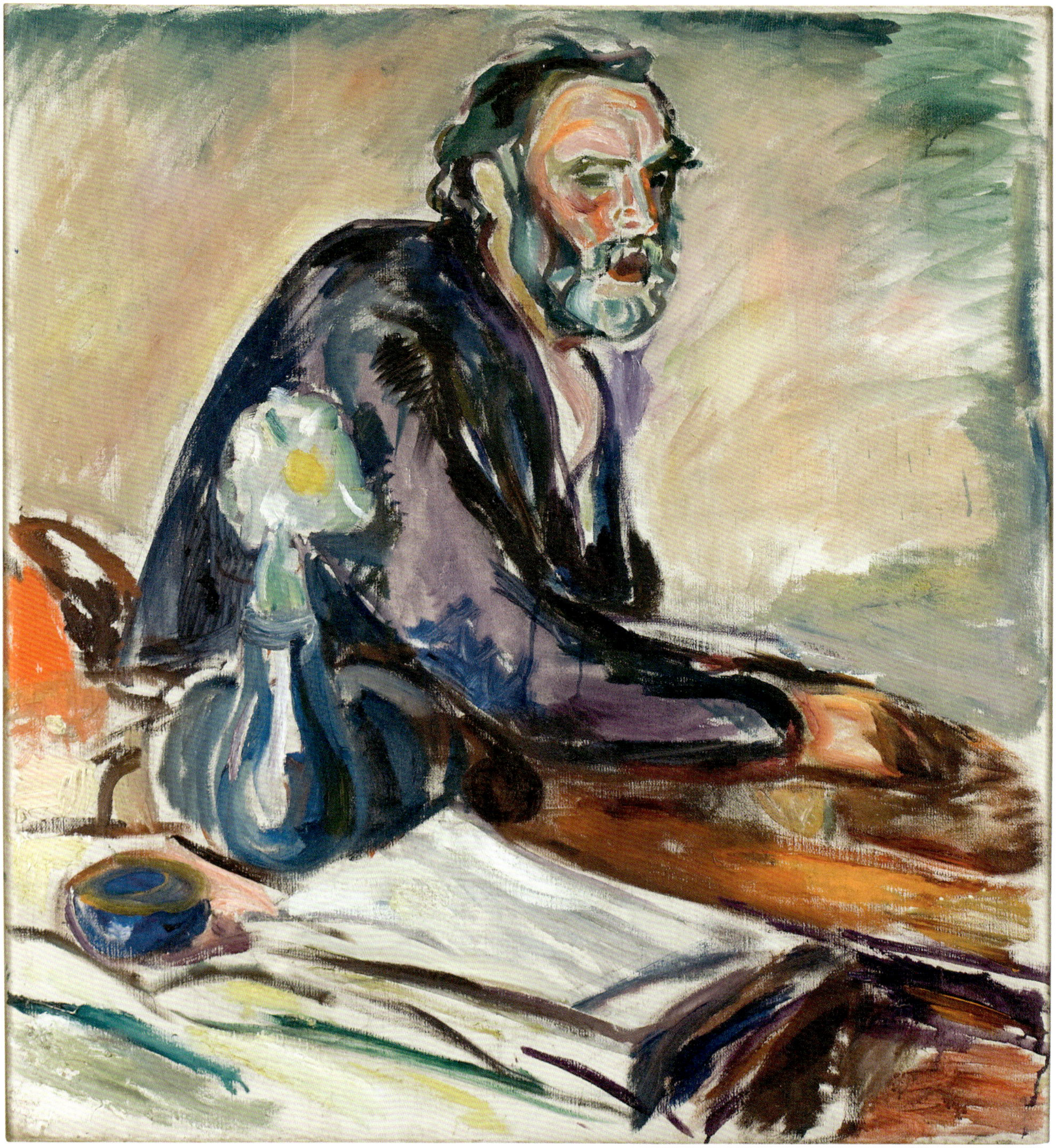

40

Man with Bronchitis, 1920.
Munch Museum, Oslo

41

Sleepless Night: Self-Portrait in Inner Turmoil,
1920. Munch Museum, Oslo

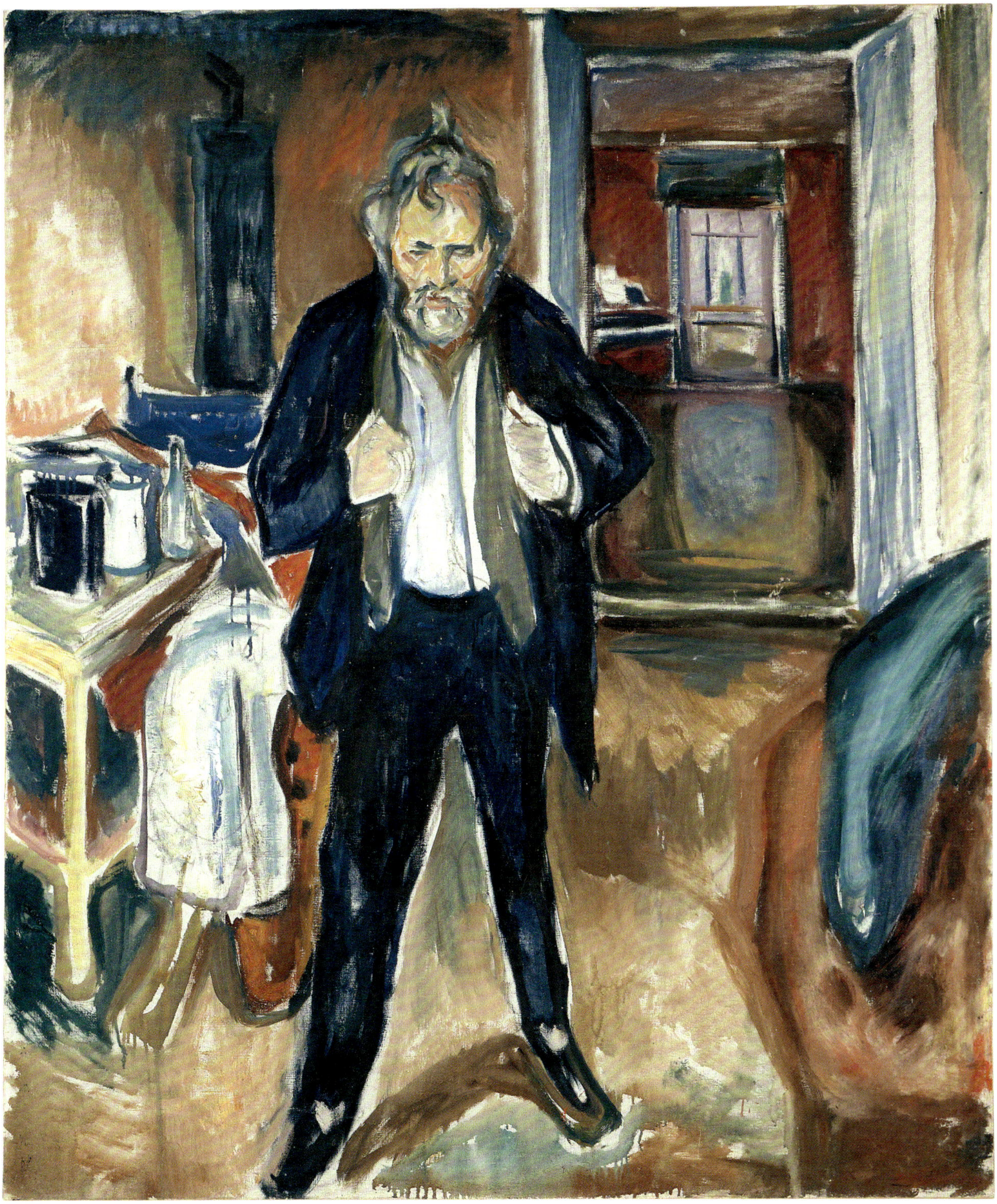

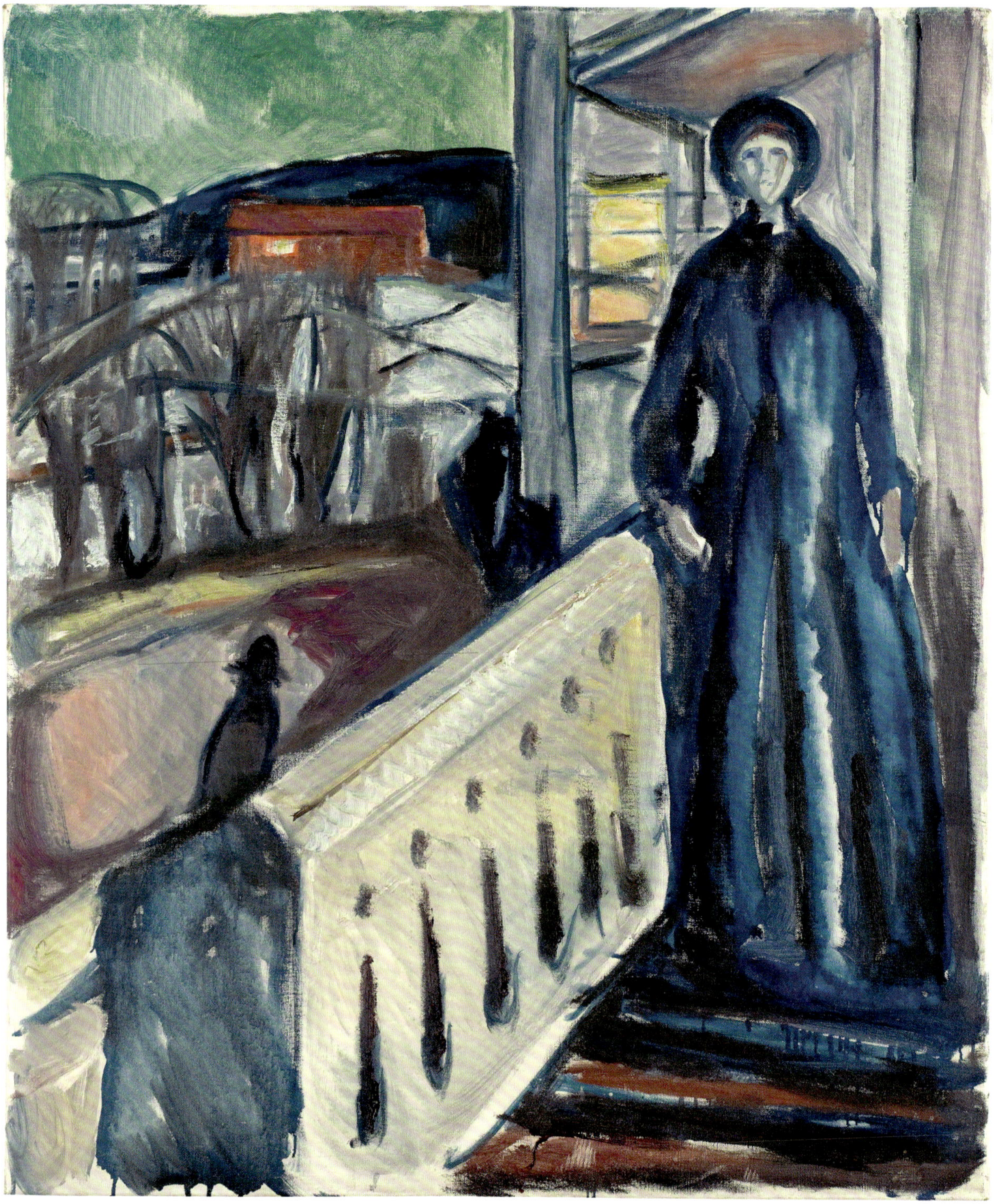

42
On the Veranda Stairs, 1922–24.
Munch Museum, Oslo

43
Starry Night, 1922–24.
Munch Museum, Oslo

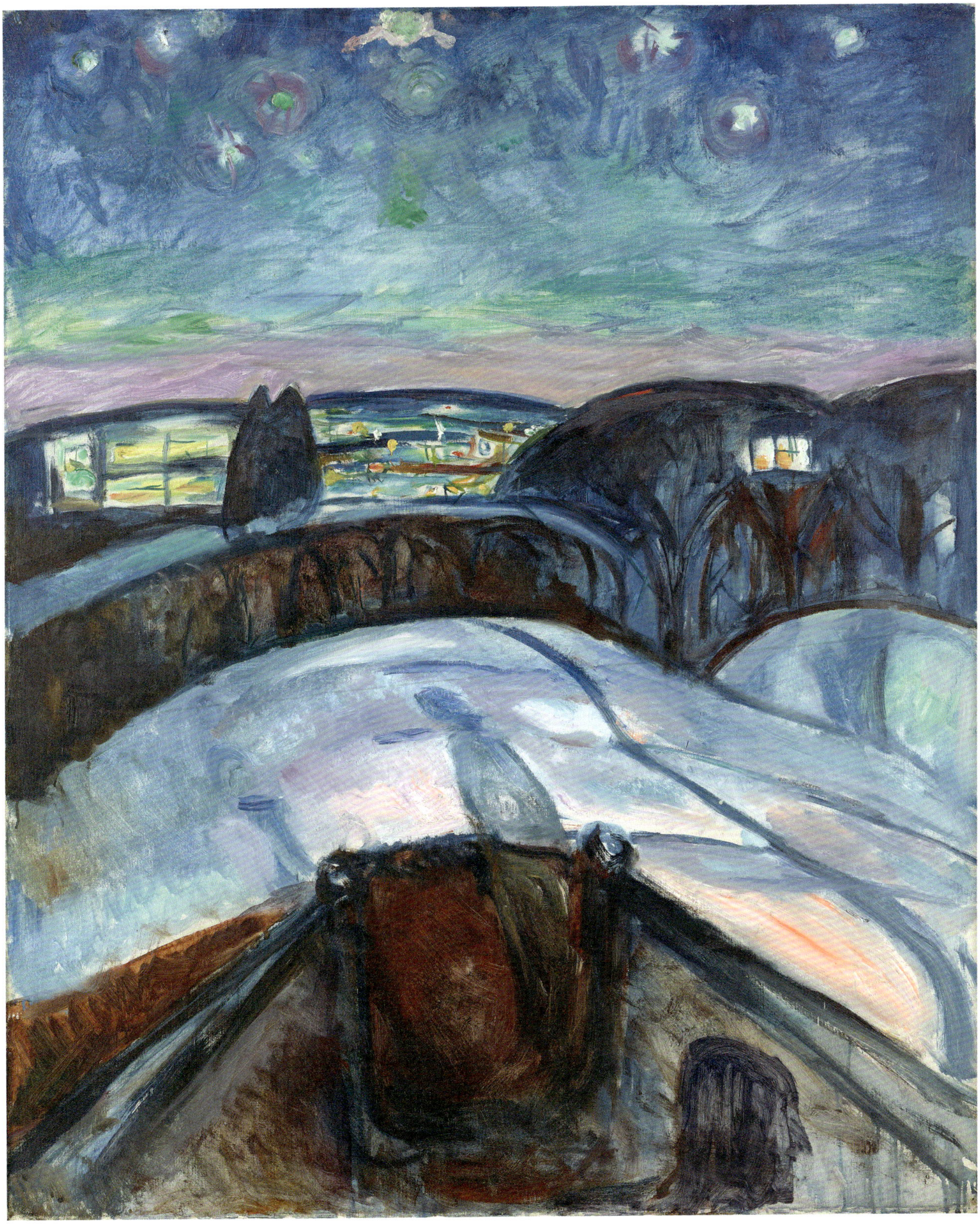

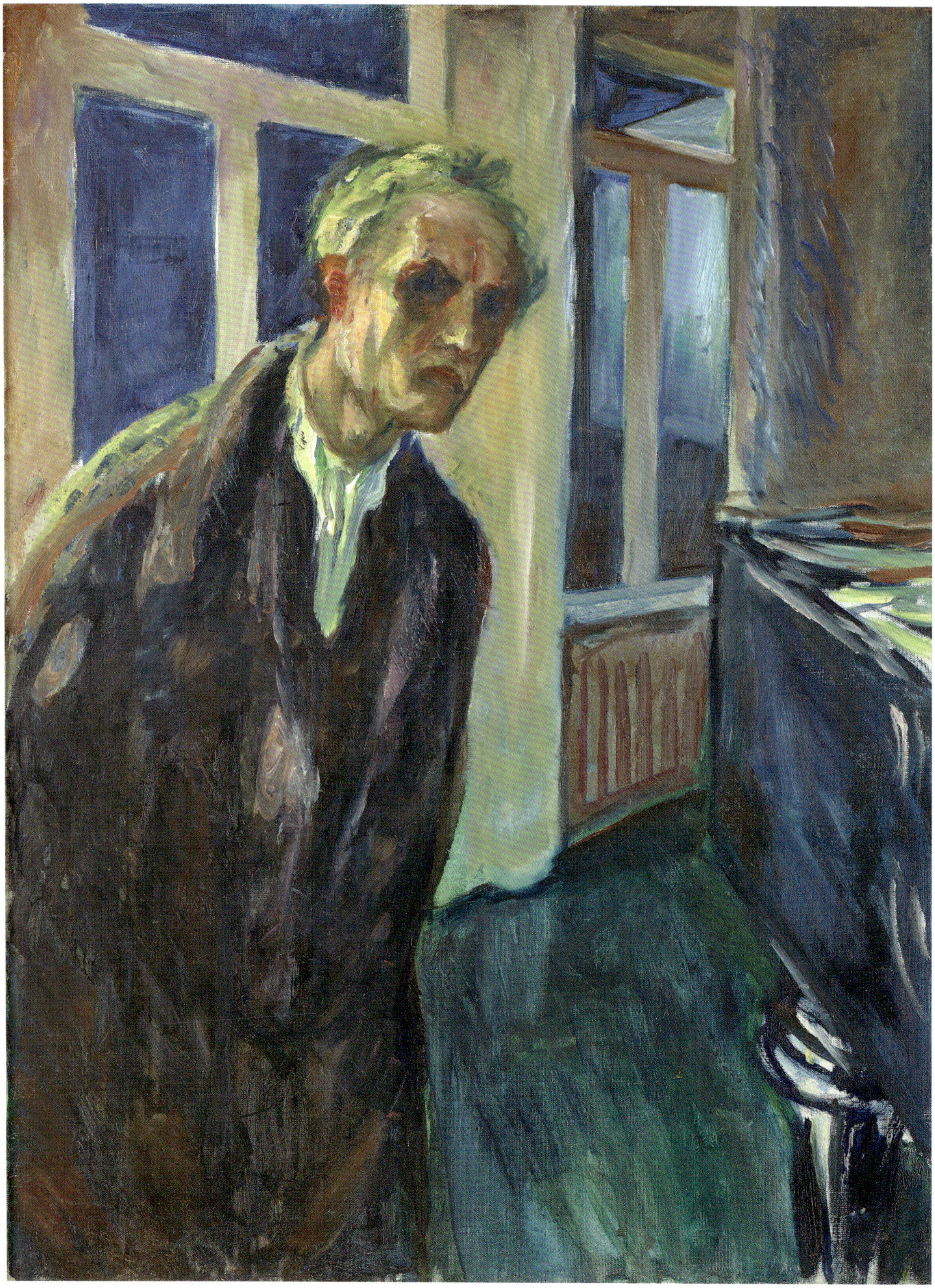

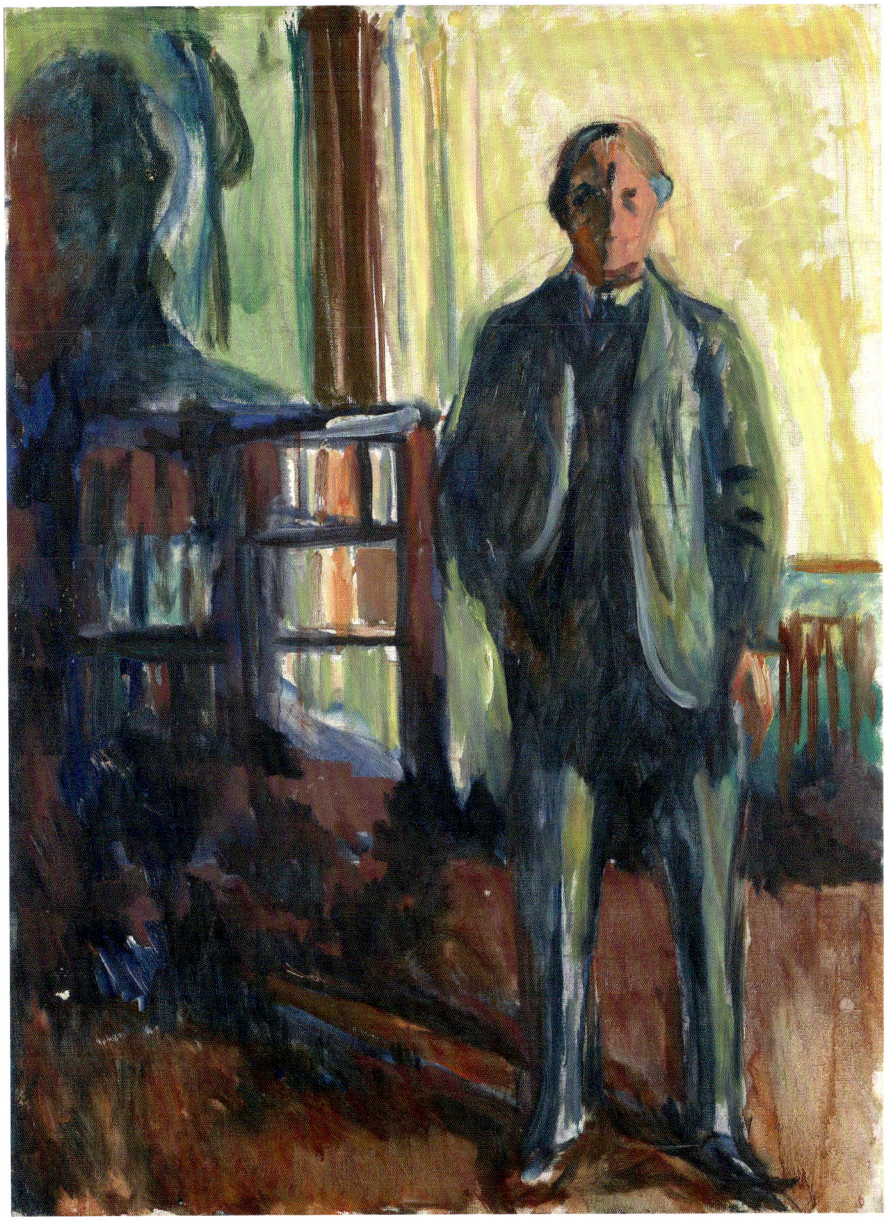

44

The Night Wanderer, 1923–24. Munch Museum, Oslo

45

Self-Portrait with Hands in Pockets, 1925–26. Munch Museum, Oslo

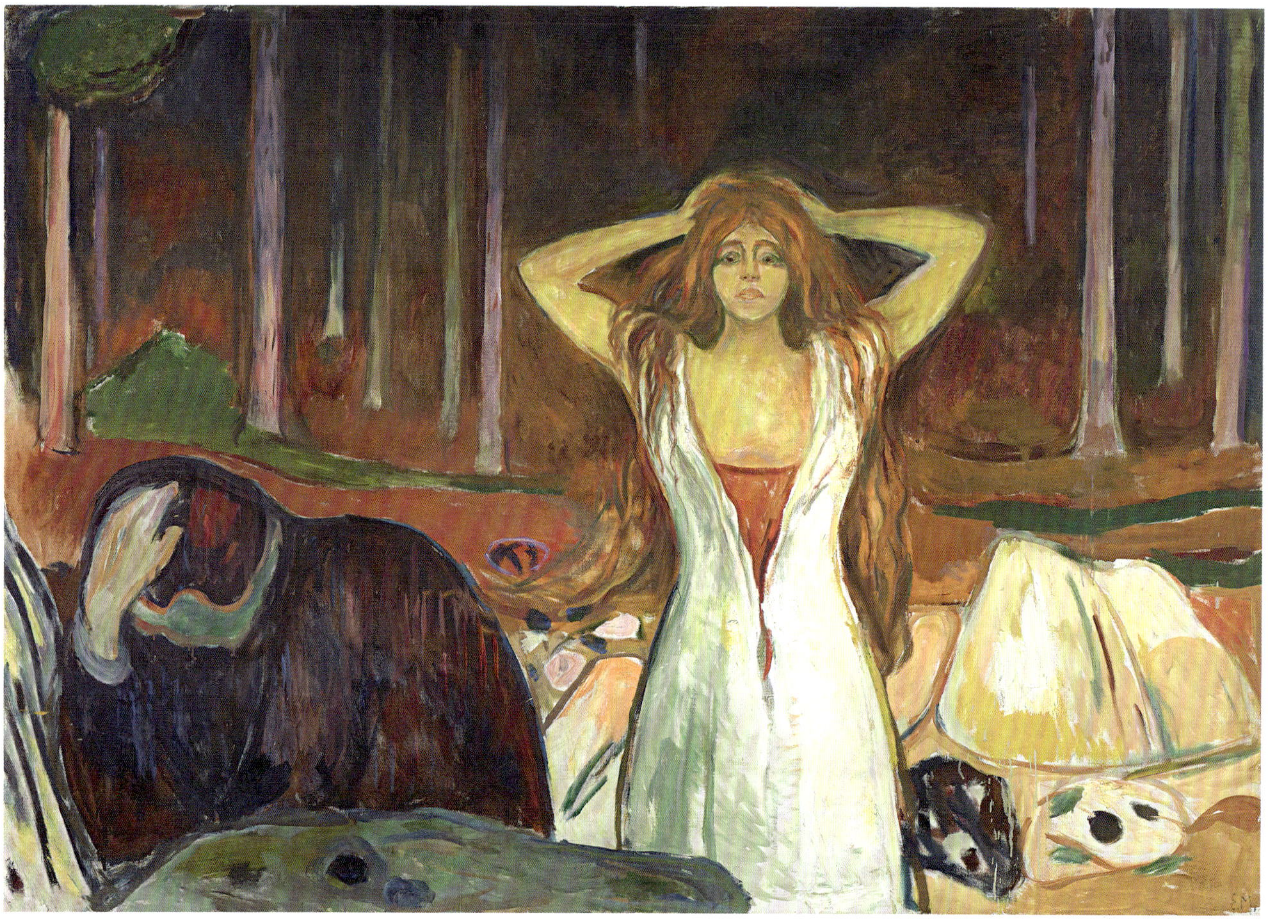

46

Ashes, 1925. Munch Museum, Oslo

47

The Dance of Life, 1925.
Munch Museum, Oslo

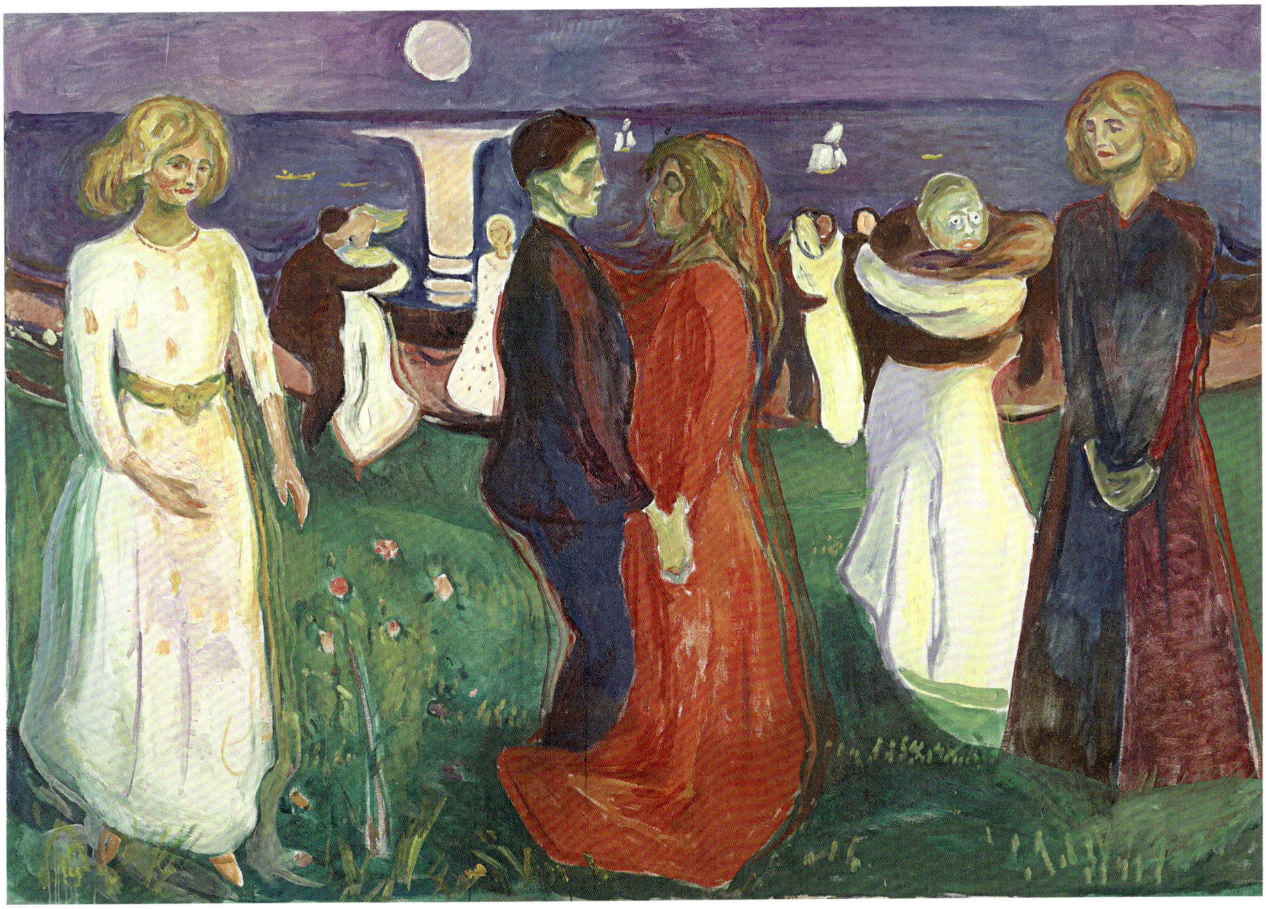

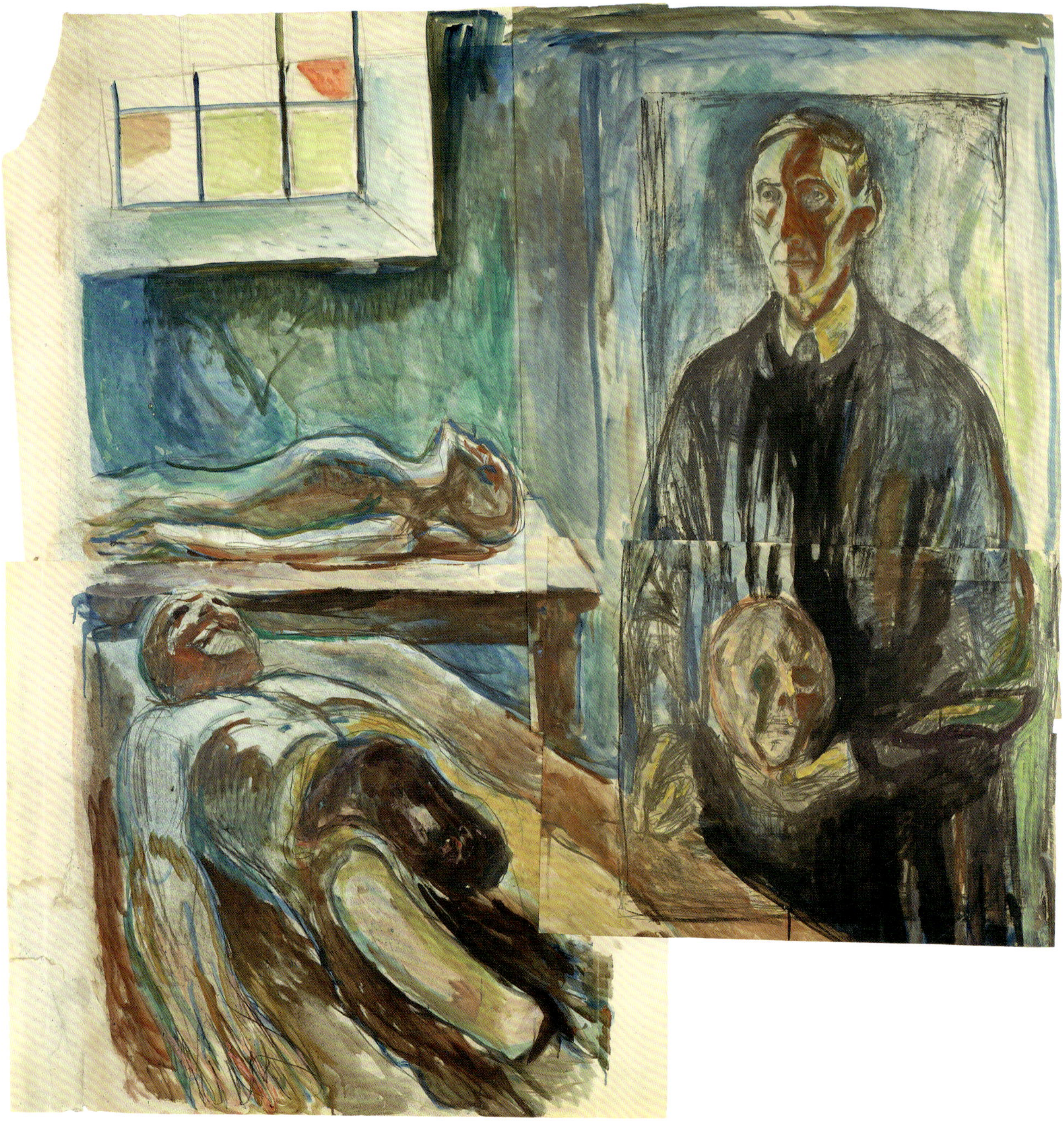

48

Anatomy Professor Kristian Schreiner, 1928–32. Munch Museum, Oslo

49

Self-Portrait with Bottles, ca. 1938. Munch Museum, Oslo

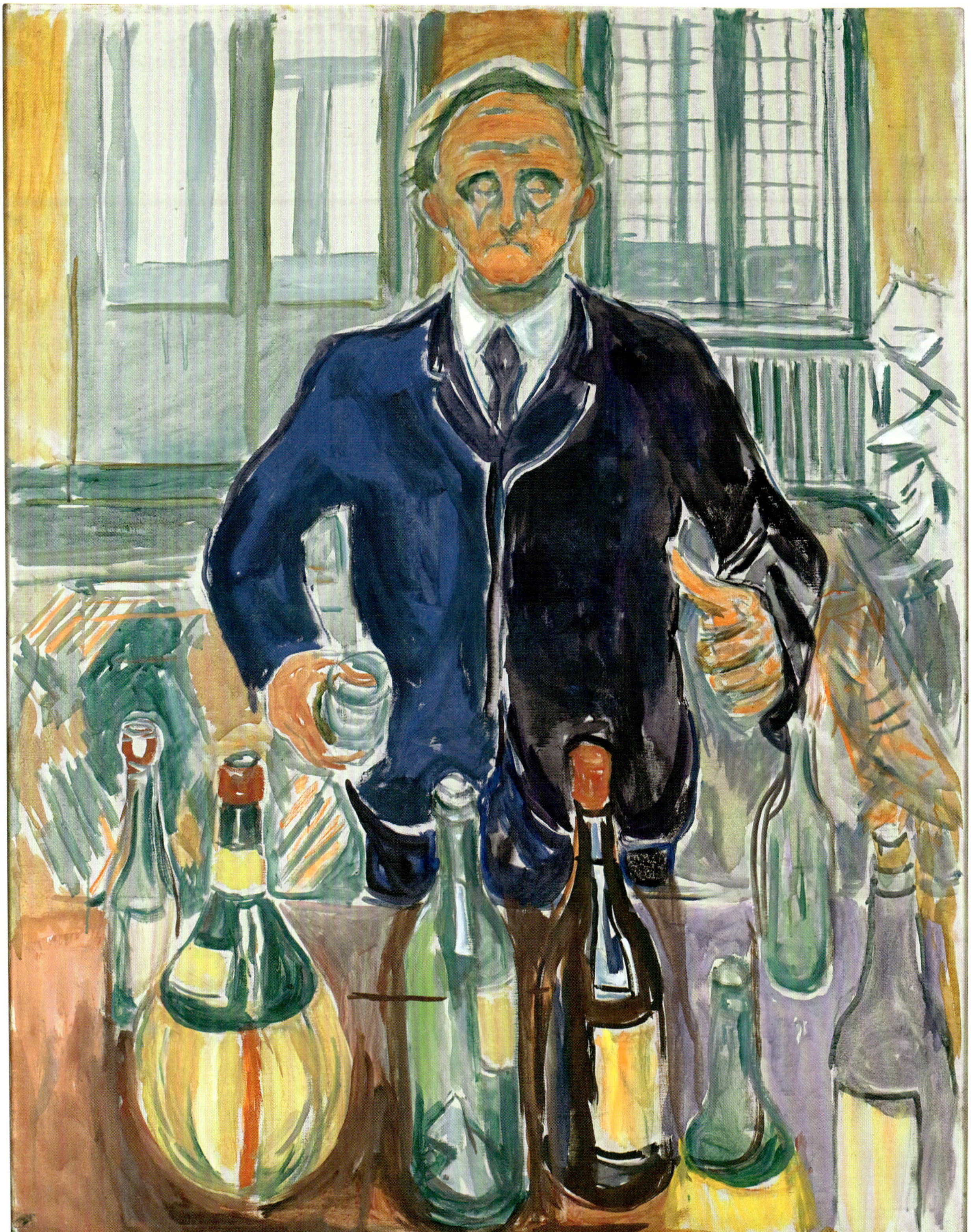

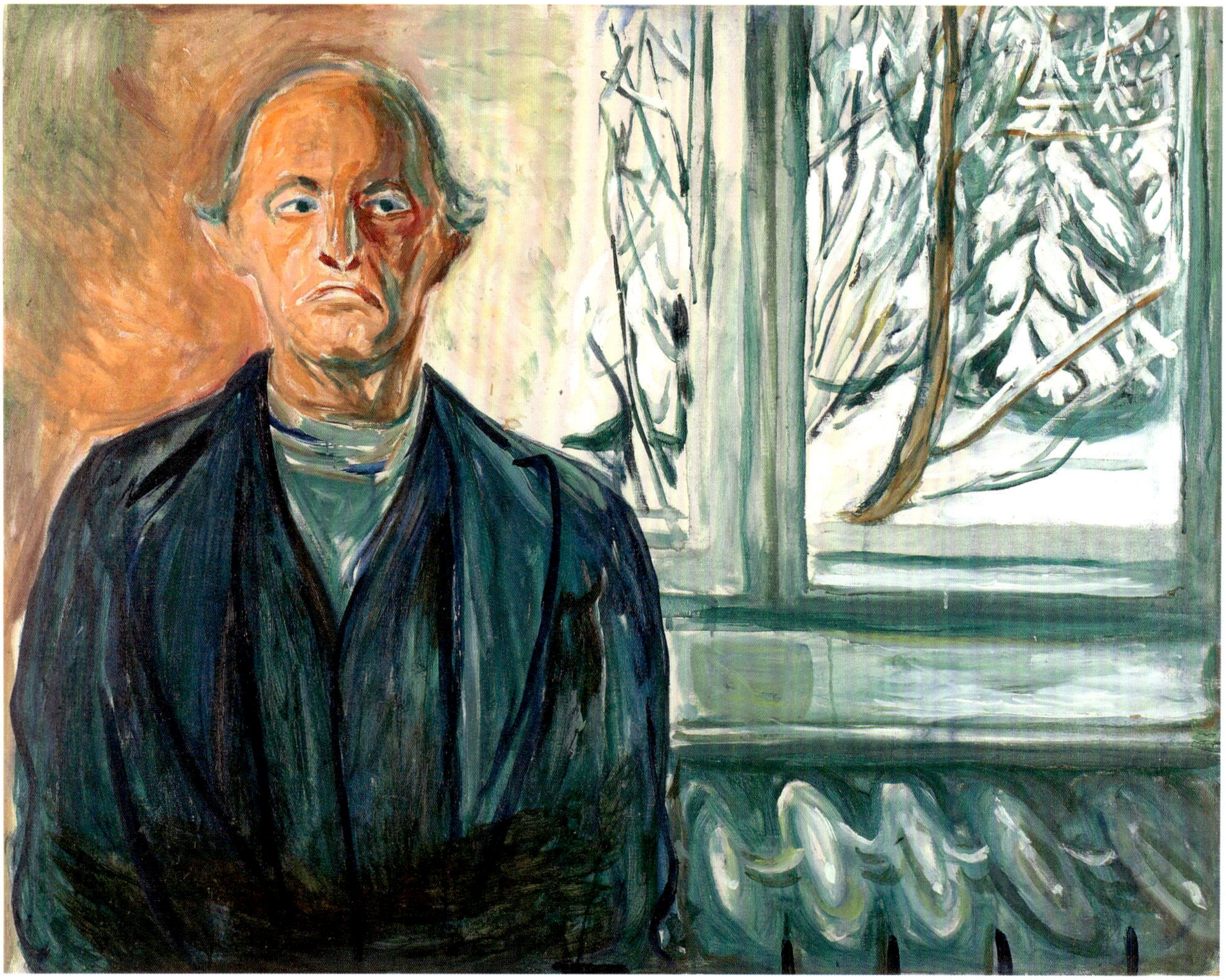

50

Self-Portrait by the Window, ca. 1940. Munch Museum, Oslo

51

Self-Portrait: Between the Clock and the Bed, 1940–43. Munch Museum, Oslo

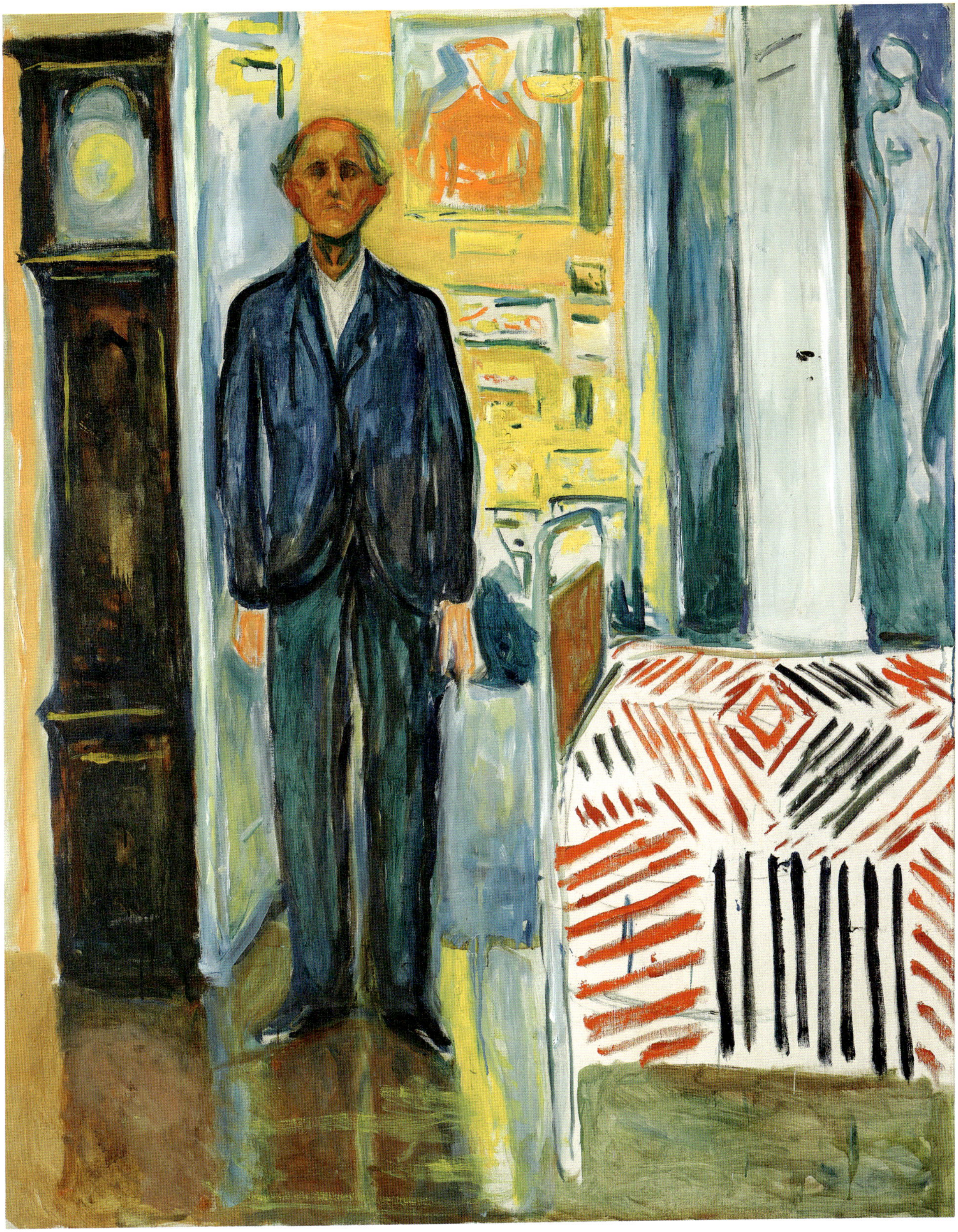

Chronology

Michèle Wijegoonaratna

1863
Born on December 12 at Engelhaug Farm in Løten, Norway, to Christian Munch, a surgeon in the army medical corps, and his wife, Laura Cathrine, neé Bjølstad.

1864
Moves to Kristiania (now Oslo) with his parents and his sister Johanne Sophie (1862–1877).

1868
His mother dies of tuberculosis at the age of thirty. Her sister, Karen Marie Bjølstad, takes over management of the household and care of the five children. An avid painter and draftswoman, she would promote the artistic talents of Edvard and his sisters.

1877
Sophie, Munch's favorite sister, dies of tuberculosis at the age of fifteen, an event that deeply affects the artist. His physical health is fragile, with frequent bouts of fever and asthmatic bronchitis.

1879
Begins engineering training at the Royal Technical College, Kristiania, but is frequently absent because of illness. Leaves the college after little more than a year. Decides to become a painter.

1880
Begins as a pupil at the Royal School of Design on December 18.

1882
Rents studio space in the Pultosten Building in Kristiania with six colleagues. Meets innovative and socially engaged naturalist artists Christian Krohg, Frits Thaulow, and Erik Werenskiold. The highly respected Krohg instructs and influences Munch.

1883
In June exhibits his work for the first time, showing one painting, *Study of a Head* (1883; Nasjonalmuseet for Kunst, Arkitektur og Design, Oslo) at the Norwegian Industry and Art Exhibition. Attends Thaulow's "open-air painting academy" at Modum.

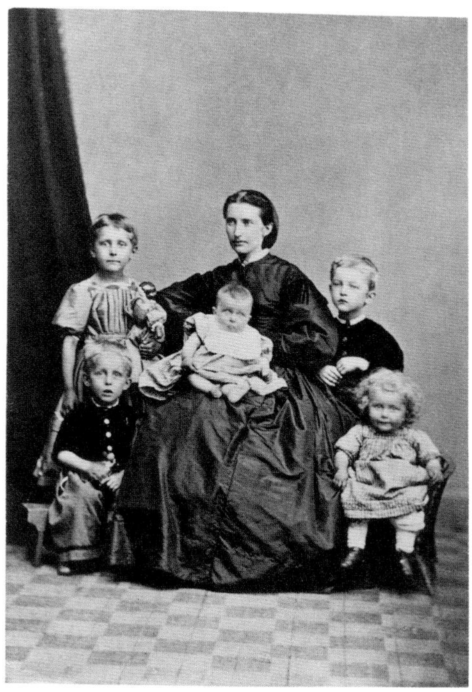

Munch's mother, Laura Cathrine, and her children, 1868. From left, Andreas (seated), Sophie (standing), Inger (in mother's lap), Edvard (standing), Laura (seated). Munch Museum Archives, Oslo

1884
Paints *Morning* (pl. 1) and exhibits it to great acclaim at the Autumn Exhibition in Kristiania; the painting is purchased by Thaulow. Meets the Kristiania Bohemians and the radical Hans Jaeger, who is the focal point for the avant-garde artists. Is awarded a grant of five hundred kroner from the Schäffer Endowment for study in Paris, but illness prevents him from going.

1885
Participates in the World's Fair in Antwerp with a painting of his younger sister, *Inger Munch in Black* (1884; Nasjonalmuseet), the first work he shows outside Norway. Travels on to Paris with financial support from Thaulow and then returns to Norway to participate in the Autumn Exhibition in Kristiania, where this painting is poorly received by critics. Begins illicit and tortured relationship with Milly Thaulow, the wife of Thaulow's brother, Carl.

1886
Exhibits *The Sick Child* (fig. 3) under the title *Study* at the Autumn Exhibition. The painting, which depicts his memory of Sophie's early death, provokes a storm of indignation among art critics and Munch's colleagues. He later states, "With *The Sick Child* I took a new direction — it was a breakthrough in my art."

1889
Has first solo exhibition at the University Students' Association, Kristiania, where he shows

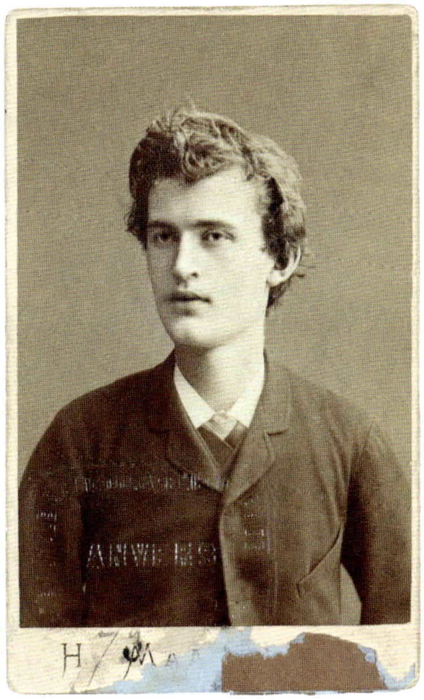

Edvard Munch, 1885. Entrance card to the Exposition Universelle des Beaux-Arts, Antwerp. Munch Museum Archives, Oslo

sixty-three paintings and forty-six drawings. Travels to Paris on government scholarship and enrolls in Léon Bonnat's art school. Represents Norway at the World's Fair in Paris with the painting *Morning*. Visits the Impressionist and Synthetist exhibition at Volpini's Café des Arts, where he sees work by Gauguin. Spends first of many summers at Åsgårdstrand. In November, his father dies, leaving the family destitute. Munch procures a loan from the wealthy Norwegian art collector Olaf Schou to assist with the family's finances. Sinks into a deep depression fueled by the effects of alcohol and nicotine; suffers from the flu, exhaustion, loneliness, and thoughts of death.

1890
Moves to Saint-Cloud on the Seine, near Paris. Writes the "Saint-Cloud Manifesto," an artistic statement that outlines his final break with naturalism. Receives second state scholarship and travels to Le Havre, where he is hospitalized with rheumatic fever.

1891
Begins sketches for paintings that will form the core of The Frieze of Life, a series of paintings on love, death, and the circle of life.

1892
Completes *Sick Mood at Sunset: Despair* (pl. 4), a motif that will develop the next year into *The Scream*. Exhibits by invitation at the Society of Artists in Berlin. Shows fifty-five paintings that evoke enormous indignation among society's members, general public, and press. Critical backlash results in exhibition's closing after one week. "Munch Affair" causes the society to split and eventually results in the formation of the Berlin Secession in 1898. Munch becomes an overnight celebrity and arranges for the exhibition to travel to Düsseldorf and Cologne before it returns to Berlin and goes on to Copenhagen, Breslau, Dresden, and Munich. Settles in Berlin.

1893
Frequents wine bar Zum Schwarzen Ferkel (The Black Piglet) and associates with literary circle that includes August Strindberg, Gustav Vigeland, Dagny Juel, and Stanisław Przybyszewski, who writes first

monograph on Munch in 1894. In December, exhibits fifty paintings in Berlin, including a series of six paintings he names Die Liebe (Love).

1894
Makes his first intaglio prints.

1895
Paints *Self-Portrait with Cigarette* (pl. 16) and sells it to the National Gallery in Kristiania following a successful exhibition at the Blomqvist gallery there. Shows fourteen paintings from The Frieze of Life. In Germany, Julius Meier-Graefe publishes portfolio containing eight of his intaglio prints. Munch family shaken by death of the artist's brother, Andreas, at the age of thirty.

Edvard Munch and Tulla Larsen, 1899. Munch Museum Archives, Oslo

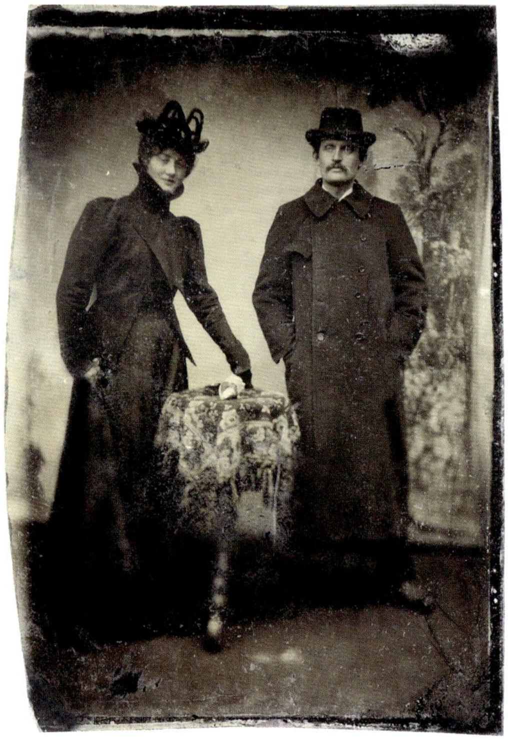

Edvard Munch, ca. 1894. Munch Museum Archives, Oslo

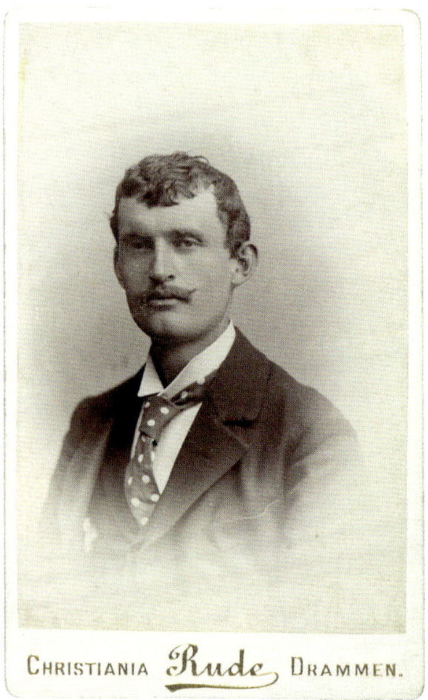

1896
Travels from Berlin to Paris and takes part in the Salon des Artistes Indépendants for the first time, exhibiting *The Sick Child* (pl. 20).

1897
Spends summer in Åsgårdstrand, where he buys small fisherman's house and works on scenes depicting the village, his garden, and the neighbor's children.

1898
Participates again at the Salon des Artistes Indépendants. In July, meets twenty-nine-year-old Tulla Larsen, the unmarried daughter of Kristiania's most prosperous wine merchant, with whom he embarks on a tempestuous relationship.

1899
Travels to Berlin, Paris, Nice, Florence, and Rome. Begins painting first version of *The Dance of Life* (fig. 18a). Convalesces from exhaustion at the Kornhaug Sanatorium, Fåberg, Norway.

1900
Has major exhibitions in Kristiania and Dresden. Travels to Berlin, Paris, Dresden, Italy, and Switzerland. Tries, but fails, to end relationship with Larsen.

1902
Exhibits The Frieze of Life, which now consists of twenty-two paintings, at the Berlin Secession. Meets the Lübeck ophthalmologist and art collector Max Linde, who purchases

graphic works from Munch and writes a book on the artist called *Edvard Munch and the Art of the Future*. Max Liebermann, the president of the Berlin Secession, invites him to exhibit The Frieze of Life. During a heated argument with Larsen, is shot in the hand. Period of intense psychological turmoil ensues.

1903
Joins the Société des Artistes Indépendants. Meets Eva Mudocci, an English violinist who becomes both a friend and a muse. Paints *Self-Portrait in Hell* (pl. 25) as well as portraits of Linde and his four sons. Sells eight hundred prints shown at an exhibition of graphic art organized by the Kunstfreunde (Friends of Art) in Hamburg.

1904
Berlin Secession honors Munch by electing him to full membership. Spends the winter in Berlin. Exhibits twenty paintings at the Vienna Secession.

1905
Stages successful exhibition in Prague that exerts considerable influence on Czech artists. Spends time in Denmark and Germany. Takes health cure at spa in Bad Elgersburg in Thuringia to overcome anxiety and dependence on alcohol.

1906
Resides in Weimar during spring and paints portraits of his friend and patron Harry Graf Kessler as well as a posthumous portrait of Friedrich Nietzsche (fig. 9). Designs stage sets for Henrik Ibsen's *Ghosts* and *Hedda Gabler* for Max Reinhardt's Deutsches Theater in Berlin. Paints *Self-Portrait with a Bottle of Wine* (pl. 27). Spends several periods in clinics to treat alcohol addiction.

1907
Travels to Warnemünde, on the Baltic Sea, and devotes time to intensive experimentation with painting and photography. Attempts to come to terms with failed love affair with Larsen in *The Death of Marat* (pl. 28).

1908
Receives Norway's Royal Order of Saint Olav. Jens Thiis, the director of the National Gallery, purchases Munch's work for the museum. Rasmus Meyer, an important collector from Bergen, also purchases works by the artist. Munch's paintings and graphic work are acclaimed. Travels to Copenhagen after a mental and physical collapse driven by alcohol abuse, hallucinations, and partial paralysis; admits himself to the psychiatric clinic of Dr. Daniel Jacobson, where he remains for eight months. Despite confinement, continues to organize exhibitions in Denmark, Germany, Norway, and Sweden.

1909
Remains at Dr. Jacobson's clinic until the spring, produces a series of lithographs entitled Alpha and Omega, and paints *Self-Portrait in the Clinic* (fig. 21). Returns to Norway in May and settles in Kragerø. Begins work on competition for murals for the University of Kristiania Festival Hall, known as the Aula.

Edvard Munch, Photographic self-portrait in Dr. Daniel Jacobson's clinic, Copenhagen, 1908. Munch Museum, Oslo (MM F 69)

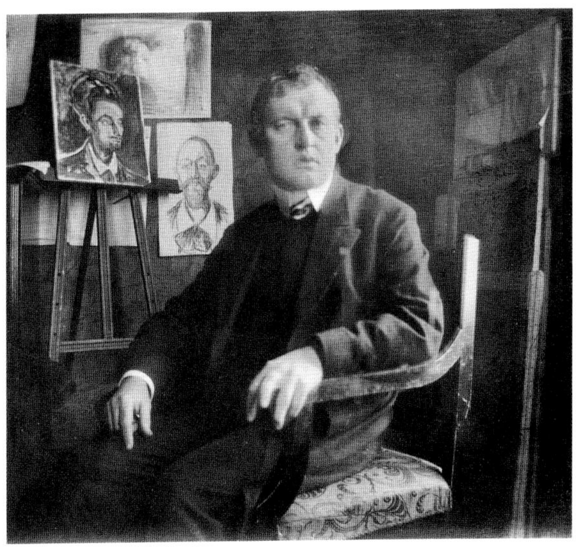

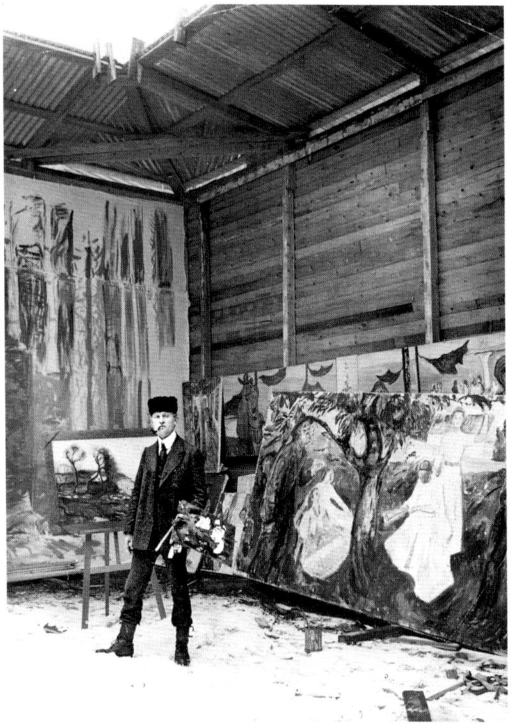

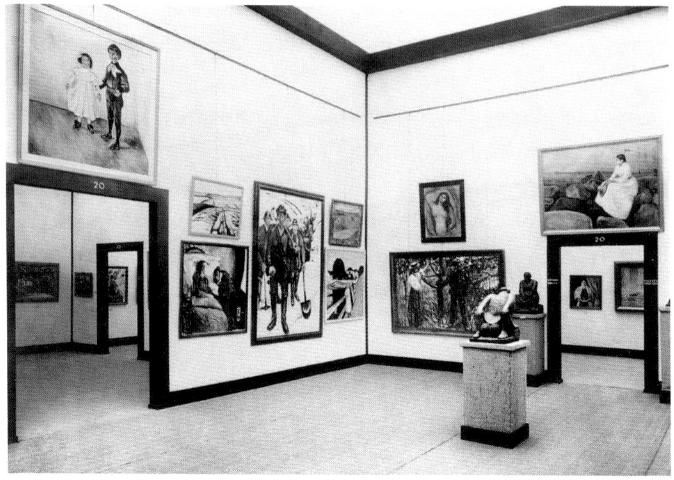

Left: Edvard Munch in his outdoor studio at Skrubben in Kragerø, 1911. Munch Museum Archives, Oslo

Above: View of the International Sonderbund Exhibition, Cologne, 1912. Munch Museum Archives, Oslo

1912
Is considered a significant exhibitor, alongside Cézanne, Gauguin, and Van Gogh, at the International Sonderbund Exhibition in Cologne, which focuses on Expressionists and their predecessors. Makes the acquaintance of the German art historian Curt Glaser, who dedicates a monograph to him in 1917.

1913
Presents eight etchings at the Armory Show in New York.

1914
University of Kristiania accepts his designs for the Festival Hall murals.

1915
Exhibits nine paintings and fifty-seven prints at the Panama-Pacific International Exposition in San Francisco

1916
Purchases the Ekely estate at Skøyen, on the outskirts of Oslo, where he spends most of his time until his death. The Festival Hall murals are finally revealed to the public.

1918
Holds a large exhibition at Blomqvist gallery, where he shows motifs from The Frieze of Life, which also becomes the title of the pamphlet he writes and publishes explaining and justifying the frieze.

1919
Purportedly contracts the Spanish flu. Paints *Self-Portrait with the Spanish Flu* (pl. 35); begins work on the series The Artist and His Model (pls. 36 and 37). Holds his first solo exhibition in America at the Bourgeois Gallery in New York.

1920–21
Visits Berlin, Wiesbaden, and Frankfurt. Has large exhibition at Cassirer's gallery in Berlin. Paints *Sleepless Night: Self-Portrait in Inner Turmoil* (pl. 41).

1922–24
At Kunsthaus Zürich, exhibits some five hundred works that subsequently travel to Bern and Basel. Purchases graphic works by German artists to provide them with financial support. Paints murals for the dining room at the Freia Chocolate factory in Kristiania. Becomes a member

of the Prussian Academy of Arts. Paints *The Night Wanderer* (pl. 44).

1925
Receives permission to paint in the National Gallery, where he makes late versions of *Ashes* and *The Dance of Life* (pls. 46 and 47).

1926
Sister Laura dies.

1927
Retrospective exhibitions held in Oslo and Berlin. His work is exhibited at the Carnegie International in Pittsburgh.

1928
Works on mural designs for Oslo City Hall.

1929
Builds a winter studio at Ekely.

Edvard Munch in his studio at Ekely, from *Der Querschnitt*, 1931. Munch Museum Archives, Oslo

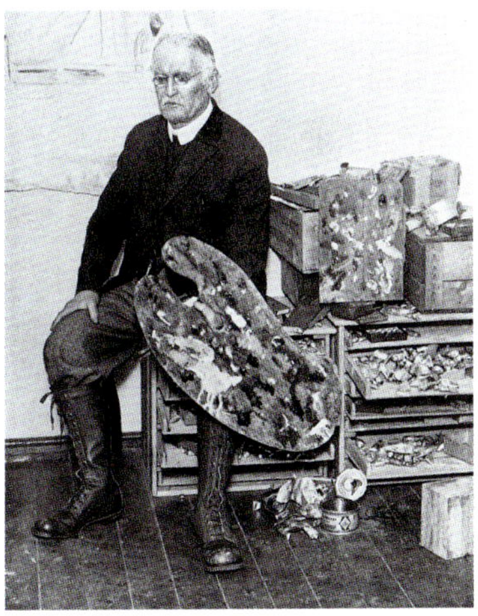

Edvard Munch in his winter studio at Ekely, 1938. Munch Museum Archives, Oslo

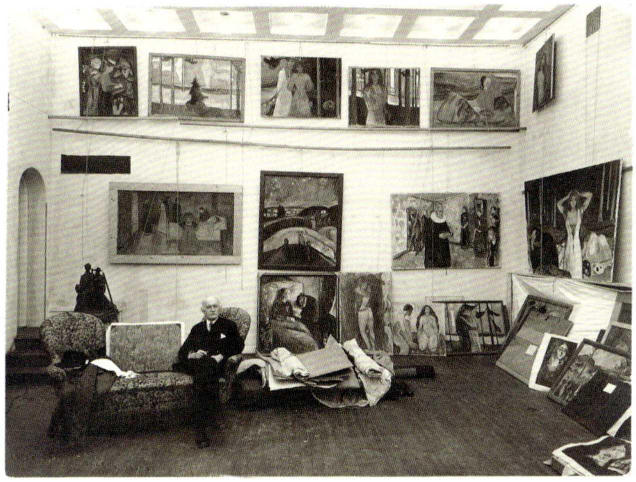

1930–31
Ruptured blood vessel in right eye causes temporary blindness. Focuses on photographic self-portraits.

1933
Receives numerous tributes on his seventieth birthday. Awarded the Grand Cross of the Order of Saint Olav. Jens Thiis and Pola Gauguin publish first biographies of Munch in Norwegian. Continues to complete several more variations on The Frieze of Life.

1934
Gives his painting *August Strindberg* (1892) to the Nationalmuseum, Stockholm. Named Commander in the French Legion of Honor.

1936
Exhibits in London for the first time, at the London Gallery.

1937
Represented at the 1937 World's Fair in Paris. The National Socialists declare eighty-two of his works in German museums "degenerate" and subsequently sell them.

1938–39
In 1938 Norwegian art dealer Holst Halvorsen buys fourteen of the works considered degenerate; sells them at auction in Oslo on January 23, 1939. War is declared in Europe.

1940
National Socialists invade Norway. Makes will bequeathing his estate to city of Oslo. Works on last self-portraits.

1942
First major presentation of his graphic works opens at the Brooklyn Museum in New York.

1943
Numerous celebrations are held to mark eightieth birthday. Munch contracts pneumonia.

1944
Dies on January 23 at his home in Ekely.

Notes

Manuscript materials prefaced with the designation *MM* corresponds to archival holdings in the Munch Museum, Oslo; those further identified by *N* are handwritten notes, those by *T* are writings included as elements of drawings or within sketchbooks.

Introduction
Gary Garrels, Jon-Ove Steihaug, and Sheena Wagstaff

1. See Elizabeth Prelinger, *After the Scream: The Late Paintings of Edvard Munch*, exh. cat. (Atlanta: High Museum of Art, 2001), p. 72.
2. Ibid., p. 156.
3. Quoted in *Edvard Munch: Complete Paintings; Catalogue Raisonné*, edited by Gerd Woll (London and New York: Thames and Hudson, 2009), vol. 2, *1898–1908*, p. 760.
4. See John B. Ravenal, *Jasper Johns and Edvard Munch: Inspiration and Transformation* (Richmond, Va.: Virginia Museum of Fine Arts and Yale University Press in Partnership with the Munch Museum, [2016]).

The Untimely Face of Munch
Allison Morehead

1. Hectography, which uses aniline dyes and gelatin, is a technique developed in the late nineteenth century for creating multiple images without a press. Munch made about a hundred hectographs in his lifetime. This particular one has been tentatively dated 1933, as have a number of similar hectographs in which he sports a full beard. The artist may have intended to reproduce it as a postcard, perhaps in relation to his seventieth birthday, for which he received numerous notes of congratulations, although no postcard with the image has been found. See Gerd Woll, *Edvard Munch: The Complete Graphic Works*, rev. ed. (London: Philip Wilson; Oslo: Orfeus Publishing, 2012), pp. 460, 472–73; email correspondence with Gerd Woll, June 13, 2016.
2. Reinhold Heller shared this observation with me. I am grateful to him, as well to Gemma Blackshaw and Sabine Wieber for their astute comments on an earlier version of this text.
3. The idea that Munch's self-portraiture offers privileged access to his psyche has been successfully critiqued in scholarship that emphasizes these works as fundamentally performative. See Patricia G. Berman, "Edvard Munch's *Self-Portrait with Cigarette*: Smoking and the Bohemian Persona," *The Art Bulletin* 75, no. 4 (December 1993), pp. 627–46; Jon-Ove Steihaug, "Edvard Munch's Performative Self-Portraits," in *Edvard Munch, 1863–1944*, edited by Mai Britt Guleng, Birgitte Sauge, and Jon-Ove Steihaug, exh. cat., Nasjonalgalleriet and Munch Museum, Oslo, 2013 (Milan: Skira, 2013), pp. 12–23; Patricia G. Berman, "Self-Portraits 'As': Expressionist Embodiments," in *Munch and Expressionism*, edited by Jill Lloyd and Reinhold Heller, exh. cat., Neue Galerie, New York, 2016 (Munich and New York: Prestel, [2016]), pp. 81–96.
4. On the use of mirrors and the complex viewing invoked by self-portraiture, see especially Joanna Woodall, "'Every Painter Paints Himself': Self-Portraiture and Creativity," in *Self-Portrait: Renaissance to Contemporary*, by Anthony Bond and Joanna Woodall, exh. cat., National Portrait Gallery, London; and Art Gallery of New South Wales, Sydney, 2005–6 (London: National Portrait Gallery, 2005), pp. 18–20.
5. Anthony Bond, "Performing the Self?" in Bond and Woodall, *Self-Portrait*, pp. 31–32.
6. Hans-Georg Gadamer, *Truth and Method*, 2nd rev. ed., translated by Joel Weinsheimer and Donald G. Marshall (London: Continuum, 2004), pp. 138–39.
7. In his brief comparison of these two paintings, Erik Mørstad argued that the frontality of the works made them especially liable to be read autobiographically. Erik Mørstad, "Edvard Munch under Medusas hode," *En Face: Kunsthistorisk Tidsskrift*, no. 1 (2003), p. 15. Dürer's self-portrait has been compared at greater length with Munch's 1895 *Self-Portrait with Cigarette* (pl. 16) and the lithograph *Self-Portrait with Skeleton Arm* (1895). See Gerd Woll, "Vita brevis ars longa: Munchs selvportretter som kunstnerisk overlevelses-prosjekt," in *Portrett i Norge*, edited by Anne Wichstrøm and Nils Messel (Oslo: Labyrinth Press, 2004), pp. 42–44; Steihaug, "Edvard Munch's Performative Self-Portraits," pp. 17, 23n19; Berman, "Self-Portraits 'As'," pp. 82–83. Max Linde concluded his study on Munch by pointing to Munch's and Dürer's work as an "art of eternal values that cannot be overlooked." Max Linde, *Edvard Munch und die Kunst der Zukunft* (Berlin: Friedrich Gottheiner, 1902), p. 16.

8. Laura Cumming, *A Face to the World: On Self-Portraits* (London: Harper, 2009), p. 156.
9. Biljana Topalova-Casadiego, "Technical Aspects of Edvard Munch's Paintings," in *Edvard Munch: Complete Paintings; Catalogue Raisonné*, vol. 2, *1898–1908*, edited by Gerd Woll (London and New York: Thames and Hudson, 2009), p. 437. Munch's panel (made up of three sections, joined together vertically) measures 70 × 44.3 cm, and Dürer's measures 67.1 × 48.9 cm.
10. Woll, "Vita brevis ars longa," pp. 40, 51n8.
11. Allison Morehead, *Nature's Experiments and the Search for Symbolist Form, Refiguring Modernism* (University Park, Pa.: Pennsylvania State University Press, [2017]), pp. 139–41.
12. There is no certainty about how the work was abraded or even who was responsible, but it would be neither the first nor the last time that Munch did violence to one of his paintings for effect, including *The Sick Child* (fig. 3) and the self-portrait dated 1886 (pl. 2). See Øystein Ustvedt and Trond E. Aslaksby, *Edvard Munch: Det syke barn; Historian om et mesterverk / The Sick Child: The Story of a Masterpiece*, exh. cat., (Oslo: Nasjonalmuseet, 2009); Dieter Buchhart, "Disappearance—Experiments with Material and Motif," in *Edvard Munch: Theme and Variation*, edited by Klaus Albrecht Schröder and Antonia Hoerschelmann, exh. cat., Albertina, Vienna, 2003 (Vienna: Albertina; Ostfildern-Ruit: Hatje Cantz, 2003), pp. 23–24.
13. The various arguments for the dating of this self-portrait are summarized in Mørstad, "Medusas hode." On some of the problems in dating Munch's work, see Gerd Woll, "Compiling a 'Catalogue Raisonné' of Edvard Munch's Paintings," in *Edvard Munch: An Anthology*, edited by Erik Mørstad (Oslo: Unipub, 2006), p. 146.
14. Arne Eggum, "Munch's Self-Portraits," in *Edvard Munch: Symbols and Images*, exh. cat. (Washington, D.C.: National Gallery of Art, 1978), p. 19.
15. Iris Müller-Westermann, *Munch by Himself*, exh. cat., Moderna Museet, Stockholm; Munch Museum, Oslo; and Royal Academy of Arts, London, 2005 (London: Royal Academy of Arts, 2005), p. 32. Müller-Westermann's argument in part relies on technical analyses of the work that have confirmed the presence of casein, which seems to point to a later date. See Jan Thurmann-Moe, *Munchs Rosskur: Experimente mit Technik und Material*, Hintergründe und Materialien, 20 (Hamburg: Dölling und Galitz, 1994), p. 16.
16. Reinhold Heller, *Munch: His Life and Work* (Chicago: University of Chicago Press, 1984), pp. 110, 232n48. The key date of 1892–93 in Munch's artistic development and the beginnings of his strategic deployment of an artistic persona are explored in Ingebjørg Ydstie and Mai Britt Guleng, eds., *Munch Becoming "Munch": Artistic Strategies, 1880–1892*, exh. cat. (Oslo: Munch Museum, 2008). See also Jay A. Clarke, *Becoming Edvard Munch: Influence, Anxiety, and Myth*, exh. cat. (Chicago: Art Institute, 2009).
17. For a helpful starting point for the literature on style, see Jaś Elsner, "Style," in *Critical Terms for Art History*, edited by Robert S. Nelson and Richard Shiff, 2nd ed. (Chicago: University of Chicago Press, 2003), pp. 98–109.
18. Eggum, "Munch's Self-Portraits," p. 19.
19. Joseph Koerner, "Self-Portraiture Direct and Oblique," in Bond and Woodall, *Self-Portrait*, p. 68.
20. Georges Didi-Huberman, "History and Image: Has the 'Epistemological Transformation' Taken Place?", in *The Art Historian: National Traditions and Institutional Practices*, edited by Michael F. Zimmermann, Clark Studies in the Visual Arts (Williamstown, Mass.: Sterling and Francine Clark Art Institute, 2003), p. 132. See also Georges Didi-Huberman, "Before the Image, Before Time: The Sovereignty of Anachronism," in *Compelling Visuality: The Work of Art in and out of Art History*, edited by Claire Farago and Robert Zwijnenberg (Minneapolis: University of Minnesota Press, 2003), pp. 31–44.
21. On anachronism as a way to emphasize presence rather than origins in an argument that draws substantially on the work of Didi-Huberman and Koerner, see Keith Moxey, *Visual Time: The Image in History* (Durham: Duke University Press, 2013), pp. 28–31, 156–58.
22. Michel Foucault, "Nietzsche, Genealogy, History," in *Language, Counter-Memory, Practice: Selected Essays and Interviews*, edited by Donald F. Bouchard (Ithaca: Cornell University Press, 1977), pp. 139–64. Ernest Thiel, a banker, avid art collector, and translator of Nietzsche into Swedish, commissioned Munch to paint an image of Nietzsche, an order the artist fulfilled in 1906 (Thielska Galleriet, Stockholm [fig. 9], and Munch Museum, Oslo). That same year, at the suggestion of Thiel, Munch completed two portraits of the philosopher's sister, Elisabeth Förster-Nietzsche, who headed up the Nietzsche Archive in Weimar (Thielska Galleriet and Munch Museum).
23. Patricia G. Berman, "The Invention of History: Julius Meier-Graefe, German Modernism, and the Genealogy of Genius," in *Imagining Modern German Culture, 1889–1919*, edited by Françoise Forster-Hahn, Studies in the History of Art, 53; Symposium Papers, 31 (Washington, D.C.: National Gallery of Art, 1996), p. 91.
24. The original German title of Meier-Graefe's book, first published in 1904, is *Entwicklungsgeschichte der modernen Kunst.*
25. Julius Meier-Graefe, *Modern Art: Being a Contribution to a New System of Aesthetics*, translated by Florence Simmonds and George W. Chrystal (New York: G. P. Putnam's Sons; London: W. Heinemann, 1908), vol. 2, pp. 279–80. Munch's stylistic inconsistency, stemming from his emphasis on meaning, has often been noted, most recently in Reinhold Heller, "Edvard Munch, Germany, and Expressionism," in Lloyd and Heller, *Munch and Expressionism*, pp. 41, 46.
26. Jay A. Clarke, "Meier-Graefe Sells Munch: The Critic as Dealer," in *Festschrift für Eberhard W. Kornfeld zum 80: Geburtstag*, edited by Christine E. Stauffer (Bern: Kornfeld, 2003), pp. 181–93.
27. Examples include many of Munch's portraits as well as the naturalistically rendered figure in the foreground of the painting *Women in Hospital* (1897; Munch Museum, Oslo [MM M 28]; see Woll, *Edvard Munch: Complete Paintings*, vol. 1, p. 395, no. 403), which contrasts strongly with the much more schematic background figures.
28. Repetition and return, especially of motif, have been the focus of a number of exhibitions. See especially Schröder and

Hoerschelmann, *Theme and Variation*; Paloma Alarcó, *Edvard Munch: Archetypes*, exh. cat., Museo Thyssen-Bornemisza, 2016 (Madrid: Fundación Colección Thyssen-Bornemisza, [2015]).

29. These debates are summed up in Woll, *Edvard Munch: Complete Paintings*, vol. 3, p. 908.

30. It is worthwhile remembering here what Heller has said about *The Scream*: first that, especially in its 1893 manifestation (fig. 8), it is stylistically alien to the rest of Munch's oeuvre, and second that Munch struggled to manage its visual impact once he decided to extend The Frieze of Life narrative beyond the theme of love, for which *The Scream*, initially titled *Despair*, had been conceived as the terminus. In other words, it is precisely the anachronistic iconicity of the painting that made it difficult for Munch to situate it in the midst of a larger series tracing a narrative from love to death. And indeed it is the same quality of *The Scream* that makes it, in all its versions, difficult to situate in the art-historical oeuvre. See Reinhold Heller, "'Could Only Have Been Painted by a Madman'—Or Could It?" in *Edvard Munch: The Modern Life of the Soul*, edited by Kynaston McShine, exh. cat. (New York: Museum of Modern Art, 2006), pp. 26, 28.

31. Jappe Nilssen, "Edvard Munchs store nye utstilling," *Dagbladet*, October 2, 1916, cited in Bessie Rainsford (Tina) Yarborough, "Exhibition Strategies and Wartime Politics in the Art and Career of Edvard Munch, 1914–1921" (PhD diss., University of Chicago, 1995), p. 164.

32. Jon-Ove Steihaug points out this art-historical fascination in "Edvard Munch's Performative Self-Portraits," pp. 16–17.

33. One criticism of the scholarship on Munch's self-portraiture, such as Müller-Westermann's (see note 15 above), is that it often treats the category of self-portraiture too broadly. See Patricia G. Berman, "The Many Lives of Edvard Munch," in Woll, *Edvard Munch: Complete Paintings*, vol. 4, p. 1287.

34. Jappe Nilssen, "Edvard Munch," *Dagbladet*, February 18, 1918, cited in Yarborough, "Exhibition Strategies," p. 224.

35. Friedrich Nietzsche, "On the Uses and Disadvantages of History for Life" (1874), in *Untimely Meditations*, edited by Daniel Breazeale and translated by R. J. Hollingdale (Cambridge: Cambridge University Press, 1997), pp. 64, 120–21.

36. On Munch's collaborations with biographers, see Jay A. Clarke, "Art Equals Life? Munch and the Problem of Biography," in Guleng, Sauge, and Steihaug, *Edvard Munch*, pp. 50–61. See also "The Business of Being Edvard Munch" by Patricia G. Berman in this volume.

37. Linde, *Edvard Munch*, p. 16.

38. Joseph Leo Koerner, *The Moment of Self-Portraiture in German Renaissance Art* (Chicago: University of Chicago Press, 1993), pp. 55–56, 59; Koerner, "Self-Portraiture Direct and Oblique," p. 68. See also Steihaug, "Edvard Munch's Performative Self-Portraits," p. 17.

39. Edvard Munch, note, 1890–92 (MM N 29, p. 3), in *Edvard Munch's Writings: English Edition*, published by the Munch Museum, Oslo; http://www.emunch.no/english.xhtml (accessed June 25, 2016).

40. There are many versions of this text. This is likely the earliest version, as translated in Reinhold Heller, *Edvard Munch: The Scream*, Art in Context ([New York: Viking Press, 1973]), p. 107.

41. Heller, "'Painted by a Madman'"; Morehead, *Nature's Experiments*, p. 161.

42. James G. Huneker, "Munich the Artistic," *The Musical Courier* 43, no. 13 (September 25, 1901), pp. 5–9.

43. Malcolm Bull, *Anti-Nietzsche* (London and New York: Verso, 2014).

44. Nietzsche, "Uses and Disadvantages," p. 94.

45. Ibid., p. 60. Nietzsche was referring here to the untimeliness of his classical studies, both their relevance for his own time and their enduring relevance.

46. Reinhold Heller, "Who Was / Is Edvard Munch?" (talk given at "Edvard Munch and / in Modernism," University of Oslo, September 18, 2013). I am grateful to Heller for providing me with a transcript of this talk. Loretta Würtenberg, founder of the Institute for Artists' Estates, Berlin, encourages artists to think in a similar way about their estates: "One of our main aims is to campaign for living artists to structure their legacies. . . . It may seem removed from the creative process, but we try to get artists to think of their estate as the last work of art they make." Cited in Anny Shaw, "How to Handle Fakes, Copyright and Catalogue Raisonnés: Berlin Institute Offers Tips for Artists' Estates," *The Art Newspaper* (March 4, 2016); http://theartnewspaper.com/news/how-to-handle-fakes-copyright-and-catalogues-raison-es-berlin-institute-offers-tips-for-artists-esta/ (accessed June 21, 2016).

47. This painting is central to the recent exhibition focused on the work of Munch and Jasper Johns. See John B. Ravenal, *Jasper Johns and Edvard Munch: Inspiration and Transformation* (Richmond, Va.: Virginia Museum of Fine Arts and Yale University Press in Partnership with the Munch Museum, [2016]).

48. Steihaug, "Edvard Munch's Performative Self-Portraits," p. 22.

Patterns in Munch's Painting Technique
Mille Stein

I am grateful to the conservation departments at the Nasjonalmuseet for Kunst, Arkitektur og Design and the Munch Museum for fruitful discussions and access to conservation reports. I am especially thankful to Inger Grimstad, paintings conservator at the Munch Museum, for her support throughout; to Thierry Ford, paintings conservator at the Nasjonalmuseet, for the X-radiograph of Munch's *Self-Portrait* of 1886; to Sigurd Nesse, the Norwegian Institute for Cultural Heritage Research (NIKU), for his work on the illustrations to my essay; to paintings conservator Charlotte Hale at The Metropolitan Museum of Art for her extremely useful comments on the technical aspects of Munch's way of painting; and last, but not least, to editor Margaret Donovan for her patience, her smoothing of my English, and her observant eye.

1. Edvard Munch, undated note (MM N 299, fol. 1r); http://www.emunch.no/HYBRIDNo

-MM_N0299.xhtml#ENo-MM_N0299-00-01r (accessed March 29, 2016). All translations by Francesca M. Nichols.
2. Munch, undated note (MM N 418, fol. 1r); http://emunch.no/HYBRIDNo-MM_N0418.xhtml#ENo-MM_N0418-00-01r (accessed November 28, 2016).
3. Munch, undated note (MM N 309); http://www.emunch.no/HYBRIDNo-MM_N0309.xhtml#.WJoSw5JWKT8 (accessed March 29, 2016).
4. The descriptions of the paintings in this essay are based mainly on my surface observations and studies of high-resolution photographs; the observations and analyses based on conservation reports and papers are specified. If otherwise not specified, factual information about the paintings derives from Gerd Woll, *Edvard Munch: Complete Paintings; Catalogue Raisonné*, 4 vols. (London and New York: Thames and Hudson, 2009).
5. The sketch (1940–43; pencil on paper, 18⅞ × 12⅝ in. [48 × 32 cm]) is in the Munch Museum, Oslo (MM T 2016).
6. In practice is it not possible to identify turpentine as a thinner in a dried oil paint. Elisabeth Reissner, "Ways of Making: Practice and Innovation in Cézanne's Paintings in the National Gallery," *National Gallery Technical Bulletin* 29 (2008), p. 10.
7. The painting was studied in raking light and using a stereo microscope. An ultraviolet photograph in the conservation archives at the Nasjonalmuseet documents a thick, uneven layer of a fluorescent medium on the painting. The paint was flattened during an undocumented lining process.
8. Especially in his early years as a painter, Munch often reused his supports, probably for economic reasons. The overpainted subject matter can sometimes be seen with the naked eye or on an X-radiograph, for instance, in *Norwegian Spring Landscape* (1890; Woll, *Edvard Munch: Complete Paintings*, vol. 1, p. 204).
9. Whether the painting was ever exhibited by Munch is uncertain (ibid., vol. 1, p. 150). But if had been, it might have been criticized for its formal aspects, as *The Sick Child* was. See Erik Mørstad, "The Improvisations of Edvard Munch," *Kunst og kultur* (2007), p. 140.
10. Mørstad, "Improvisations of Edvard Munch."
11. Munch, undated note (MM N 415, fol. 6v); http://www.emunch.no/TRANS_HYBRIDMM_N0415.xhtml#.WBc4by0rLs0 (accessed September 30, 2016).
12. An undated photograph by Ragnvald Væring of the 1886 self-portrait shows the work framed and unsigned and in a similar condition as today (MM V 0174). Munch could have signed the work either when it was sold or given away, but in 1890 at the latest. Woll, *Edvard Munch: Complete Paintings*, vol. 1, p. 150.
13. The paper is too thick for tracing, and there are no marks on the drawing indicating that Munch traced the composition from the drawing to the painting. Munch might have used a pantograph or similar device to transfer the composition from one medium to the other. Such an aid might also have been employed for the five reworkings of *The Sick Child*. See Unn Plahter and Leif Einar Plahter, "Munch's Paintings: Scientific Research in Retrospect," in *Public Paintings by Edvard Munch and His Contemporaries: Change and Conservation Challenges*, edited by Tine Frøysaker with Noëlle Streeton, Harmut Kutzke, Françoise Hanssen-Bauer, and Biljana Topalova-Casadiego (London: Archetype Publications, 2015), p. 10.
14. For more information about the infrared examination of *Puberty*, see Francesca Rosi, Laura Cartechini, Aldo Romani, Brunetto Giovanni Brunetti, Antonio Sgamellotti, Costanza Miliani, and Biljana Topalova-Casadiego, "Non-Invasive Investigation of the Materials and Painting Technique of *Puberty* (1894), *Anxiety* (1894) and *Vampire* (1895) by Edvard Munch," in Frøysaker, *Public Paintings*, pp. 96–99.
15. For binding and pigment analysis of *Puberty*, see Biljana Topalova-Casadiego, Claudia Daffara, Mattia Patti, Roberto Bellucci, Cecilia Frosinni, Raffaella Fontana, and Costanza Miliani, "Analysis of Munch's Paintings by Scanning Multispectral Infrared Reflectography: *Anxiety* (1894), *Puberty* (1894) and *Vampire* (1895)," in Frøysaker, *Public Paintings*, pp. 86–87.
16. Certain unfinished paintings, such as the portraits of Andreas Bjølstad (1888; Munch Museum), Ernest Thiel (1907; Thielska Galleriet, Stockholm), and Jens Thiis (1909; Munch Museum), support this theory of Munch's painting process.
17. The zinc white was identified by Unn Plahter; conservation department report, Munch Museum.
18. Plahter and Plahter, "Munch's Paintings," p. 26.
19. Thanks to paintings conservator Inger Grimstad, Munch Museum, for fruitful discussions on the original appearance of *Puberty*.
20. The color of the canvas might have been affected by the zinc white in the paste used to line the painting, the result being a less dark canvas than might be expected.
21. According to conservation reports at the Munch Museum, the painting was lined sometime between Munch's death in 1944 and 1951, and damages in the shadow and to the left of the girl's right ear were retouched in 1963. In 2011–12, during an examination of the painting, loose paint was consolidated. No documentation exists as to surface cleaning of the painting, which was placed under glass in 2012.
22. For a further description of the painting technique of *Puberty*, see Biljana Topalova-Casadiego, "Painterly Aspects of Puberty–The Results of Recent Studies," in *Edvard Munch: Pubertet / Puberty*, edited by Jay A. Clarke, Finn Skårderud, Biljana Topalova-Casadiego, and Ingebjørg Ydstie, exh. cat., Munch Museum, Oslo ([Oslo]: Orfeus Publishing, [2012]), pp. 66–84.
23. The work was acquired by the National Gallery in 1895. In the conservation archives of the museum, there is no information regarding the painting technique, except for the observation that the surface has an uneven gloss and seems never to have been varnished.
24. Erik Mørstad, "Responding to *Self-Portrait with Cigarette:* A Case History" in *Edvard Munch: An Anthology* (Oslo: Unipub, 2006), p. 90.
25. Max Linde, letter to Munch, April 24, 1906 (MM N K 2821).
26. For an introduction to this topic, see

Angela Lampe, "Reworkings: Dislocated Motifs; Munch's Tendency towards Repetition," in *Edvard Munch: The Modern Eye,* edited by Angela Lampe and Clément Chéroux, exh. cat., Centre Pompidou, Paris; Schirn Kunsthalle, Frankfurt; and Tate Modern, London, 2011–12 (London: Tate Pub., 2012), pp. 29–53.

27. Munch, diary entry, Saint-Cloud, February 5, 1890 (MM T 2771, fol. 03r); http://www.emunch.no/TRANS_HYBRIDMM_T2771.xhtml#.WBdF7S0rLs0 (accessed September 30, 2016).

28. The second version of *Death Struggle* (55 ⅛ × 71 ⅝ in. [140 × 182 cm]) is in the collection of the Statens Museum for Kunst, Copenhagen.

29. Janine Wardius, "Edvard Munch's *Evening on Karl Johan* and Its Changes of Appearance" in Frøysaker, *Public Paintings*, p. 43.

30. The underdrawing was executed with a fine brush and a liquid medium on a white preprimed canvas. Kamila Korbela, "Edvard Munch's Painting Technique and/or Environmental Influences: Creation of a Foundation for Conservation Interventions," in Frøysaker, *Public Paintings*, pp. 249–50.

31. There have been no technical examinations of the painting, but a black underdrawing would most probably be visible with the naked eye because of the large areas of exposed ground. A preliminary sketch, executed in either oil or crayon, has not yet been found.

32. Some scholars believe the paintings in the last category—those with bird droppings, water stains, weathered paint surfaces, and major paint losses—are artifacts resulting from Munch's practice of exposing them to the elements to change their appearance. See Jan Thurmann-Moe, "Edvard Munchs 'Rosskur' als Vorläufer informeller Techniken," in *Informel: Material und Technik*, edited by Heinz Althöfer and Iris Benner, Schriftenreihe des Museums am Ostwall, 4 (Dortmund: Museum am Ostwall, 2004), pp. 27–34; Dieter Buchhart, "Edvard Munch: Signs of Modern Art; The Duality of a Material-Based Modernity," translated by Paul Aston, in *Edvard Munch: Signs of Modern Art*, edited by Dieter Buchhart, exh. cat., Fondation Beyeler, Riehen/Basel; and Kunsthalle Würth, Schwäbisch Hall, 2007 (Riehen/Basel: Fondation Beyeler; Ostfildern: Hatje Cantz, 2007), pp. 11–23; Mille Stein, "Edvard Munch and the 'Kill-or-Cure' Remedy: Analysis of the Ekely Collection at the Munch Museum," *Zeitschrift für Konsttechnologie und Konservierung* 28, no. 2 (2014), pp. 279–97; Mille Stein, "Edvard Munch og 'hestekuren': En revurdering," *Kunst og Kultur* 100, no. 1 (2017).

33. Oil has been found in a recent study of these two works. See Brian Singer, Trond E. Aslaksby, Biljana Topalova-Casadiego, and Eva Storevik Tveit, "Investigations of Materials Used by Edvard Munch," *Studies in Conservation* 55, no. 4 (2010), pp. 274–92.

34. Most of the paintings from Munch's estate are unvarnished. See M[ille] Stein and J[ohannes] Rød, "A Contribution to the Varnish History of the Paintings by Edvard Munch at the National Museum and Munch Museum, Oslo," in Frøysaker, *Public Paintings*, pp. 257–70.

35. Munch, undated note (MM N 415, fol. 7r); http://www.emunch.no/TRANS_HYBRIDMM_N0415.xhtml#.WBc4by0rLs0 (accessed September 30, 2016).

36. Most of the pigment analyses of Munch paintings were performed on his early paintings; see Plahter and Plahter, "Munch's Paintings," pp. 10–26. The Munch Museum is currently working on a study of paint tubes from his estate; http://munchmuseet.no/en/conservation-munchs-paint-tubes-and-working-materials (accessed September 30, 2016). For Munch's palettes from Åsgårdstrand, https://digitaltmuseum.no/search/?aq=owner%3A%22MUH%22+descname%3A%22Kunst%22. (accessed September 30, 2016); for those from his estate: https://www.google.no/search?q=Munchs+palett&safe=active&rlz=1C1SFXN_enNO499NO500&espv=2&biw=1440&bih=804&source=lnms&tbm=isch&sa=X&ved=0ahUKEwiMhoi1isvQAhWlFZoKHZiFA5cQ_AUIBigB#imgrc=CDKdcybFxKB2JM%3A.

37. Reissner, "Ways of Making," pp. 15, 19.

38. For more information on Munch's painting technique, see Biljana Topalova-Casadiego, "Technical Aspects of Edvard Munch's Paintings" in Woll, *Edvard Munch: Complete Paintings*, vol. 2, pp. 425–58.

The Business of Being Edvard Munch
Patricia G. Berman

Research for this article was generously supported by the Theodora L. and Stanley H. Feldberg Chair at Wellesley College. I would like to thank Sheena Wagstaff and Sabine Rewald for inviting me to write this article, and Gerd Woll, Frank Høifødt, Lasse Jacobsen, Allison Morehead, Reinhold Heller, Sam Engelstad, and Jeanne Hablanian for their assistance. This research is deeply indebted to the groundbreaking work of Tina Yarborough, whose untimely death in 2016 left a hole in our scholarly community.

1. Edvard Munch, "Art and Money" (MM T 2601), translated in *Munch in His Own Words*, by Poul Erik Tøjner (Munich and New York: Prestel, 2001), p. 141.

2. Munch, letter to Sigurd Høst, December 12, 1913, quoted in Bessie Rainsford (Tina) Yarborough, "Exhibition Strategies and Wartime Politics in the Art and Career of Edvard Munch, 1914–1921" (PhD diss., University of Chicago, 1994), p. 50.

3. Jappe Nilssen, "Edvard Munch: 1863–12. Desember–1913," *Kunst og Kultur* 4 (1913–1914), pp. 81, 82.

4. In 1909 the painting was sold to Rasmus Meyer in Bergen; it is now in the collection of KODE Kunstmuseene i Bergen.

5. Nilssen, "Edvard Munch," p. 87.

6. Erik Werenskiold, letter to painter Henrik Sørensen, February 1934, published in Erik Werenskiold, "Tidligere upubliserte brev fra Erik Werenskiold," *Kunst og Kultur* (1989), p. 234. Unless otherwise noted, all translations are my own, in collaboration with Sam Engelstad. The painting was exhibited twelve times between 1891 and 1894 and then six more times in Munch's lifetime, including the Sonderbund exhibition, Cologne, in 1912, and Munch's two major retrospectives in Oslo and Berlin in 1927. See *Edvard Munch: Complete Paintings; Catalogue Raisonné*, vol. 1, *1880–1897*, edited by Gerd Woll (London and New York: Thames and Hudson, 2009), p. 188, n. 182.

7. Werenskiold, "Tidligere upubliserte," p. 235. Werenskiold also recalled speaking with Eilif Peterssen, like himself an ardent early advocate of Munch, about the purchase: "Eilif Peterssen also voted against the purchase, and when I asked him why he did so, he gave the same reason. . . . 'I willingly admit that was stupid. I should have placed the gallery's and Munch's interests above my own irritation, but I believed at the time that the entire affair was unsavory. I spoke with Munch about it once, but he shrugged it off; he would not discuss it.'" (Werenskiold, "Tidligere upubliserte," p. 235). On the press battle over Munch's works in 1909, see Tone Skedsmo, "To norske kunstsamlere ved århundreskiftet Olaf Schou og Rasmus Meyer" (Magistergrad diss., University of Oslo, 1976), and summarized in her article, "The National Gallery Munch Collection: Historical Background," in *Edvard Munch i Nasjonalgalleriet* (Oslo: Nasjonalgalleriet, 1998), pp. 21–22. The steering committee went straight to the press to report that Thiis had worked behind its back; Thiis responded in a letter to the newspaper *Aftenposten* on April 2, 1909. After consultation, the museum acquired *The Day After* (1894), *Puberty* (1894), *Ashes* (1894), *The Frenchman (Marcel Archinard)* (1904), and *On the Veranda* (1902), all of which continue to be a part of the museum's permanent collection.

The National Gallery (Nasjonalgalleriet) was founded in 1842; in 2003 it became a part of the National Museum of Art, Architecture and Design (Nasjonalmuseet for Kunst, Arkitektur og Design).

8. Julius Meier-Graefe, "Edvard Munch: Eight Intaglio Prints" (1895), translated in *Edvard Munch 1895: Første år som grafiker / First Year as a Graphic Artist*, exh. cat. (Oslo: Munch Museum, 1995), unpag.

9. The scholarship examining Munch in relation to the marketplace includes the following: numerous publications by Gerd Woll, especially "Edvard Munchs grafikk i tre nordiske samlinger: Privatsamlinger som ledd i kunstnerens markesdføring av sine arbeider," *Konsthistorisk Tidskrift* 57, no. 3–4 (1988), pp. 76–82; and "Fifty Years of Printmaking," in *Edvard Munch: The Complete Graphic Works*, rev. ed. (London: Philip Wilson; Oslo: Orfeus Publishing, 2012), pp. 8–28; Yarborough, "Exhibition Strategies"; Jay A. Clarke, "Meier-Graefe Sells Munch: The Critic as Dealer," in *Festschrift für Eberhard W. Kornfeld zum 80: Geburtstag*, edited by Christien E. Stauffer (Bern: Kornfeld, 2003), pp. 181–93; Jay. A. Clarke, "Munch's Critical Reception in the 1890s and His 'Place' in History," in *Seeing and Beyond: Essays on Eighteenth- to Twenty-first-Century Art in Honor of Kermit S. Champa*, edited by Deborah J. Johnson and David Ogawa (New York: Peter Lang, 2005), pp. 185–209; and especially her *Becoming Edvard Munch: Influence, Anxiety, and Myth*, exh. cat. (Chicago: Art Institute, 2009); Atle Næss, *Munch: En Biografi* ([Oslo]: Gyldendal, 2004); and Reinhold Heller, "'Could Only Have Been Painted by a Madman'– Or Could It?" in *Edvard Munch: The Modern Life of the Soul*, edited by Kynaston McShine, exh. cat. (New York: Museum of Modern Art, 2006), pp. 16–31; Patricia G. Berman and Pari Stave, *Munch / Warhol and the Multiple Image*, exh. cat., Scandinavia House, Nordic Center, New York, 2013 (New York: American-Scandinavian Foundation, [2013]). On the notion of "Munch" the persona vs. Munch the practicing artist, see Patricia G. Berman, "(Re-)Reading Edvard Munch: Trends in the Current Literature," *Scandinavian Studies* 66, no. 1 (Winter 1994), pp. 45–67; "The Many Lives of Edvard Munch," in Woll, *Edvard Munch: Complete Paintings*, vol. 4, pp. 1277–93.

10. Robert Jensen, "The Avant-Garde and the Trade in Art," *Art Journal* 47, no. 4 (Winter 1988), p. 360.

11. Woll, *Edvard Munch: The Complete Graphic Works*, p. 8.

12. Woll, "Edvard Munchs grafikk," p. 76; and Gerd Woll, *Edvard Munch: A Genius of Printmaking*, exh. cat., Kunsthaus, Zurich, 2013–14 (Ostfildern: Hatje Cantz, [2013]), p. 38.

13. Arne Eggum, ed., *Edvard Munch / Gustav Schiefler Briefwechsel*, Veröffentlichungen des Vereins für Hamburgische Geschichte (Hamburg: Verlag Verein für Hamburgische Geschichte, 1987), p. 242.

14. Michael C. FitzGerald, *Making Modernism: Picasso and the Creation of the Market for Twentieth-Century Art* (New York: Farrar, Straus, and Giroux, 1995), pp. 3–4.

15. Munch's friend Christian Gierløff humorously portrayed the artist's business practices in the 1913/14 volume of *Kunst og Kultur*. He relates how, on his daily tour, Munch first goes to the train station in Moss, "where he buys the whole assortment of newspapers and magazines and stacks them in his coat pocket," and then proceeds to the post office, where "like the other large companies in town, he has his own commodious mailbox overflowing with letters, magazines, and foreign newspapers, which he also places in his coat pockets." The artist next walks to the steamship pier, where he has a "prodigious number of things to fix and expedite and dispatch every day," but so specific are his tasks that no one can help him. Gierløff goes on to say that Munch has no domestic spaces in any of the forty-three rooms in his many houses in Kragerø, Nedre Ramme, Åsgårdstrand, Grimsrød, and Jeløy because each one is a workplace stuffed with paintings, easels, packing cases, lithograph presses, etching supplies, "in a chaos" that is intelligible only to him. He describes year-old telegrams, unread, and correspondence from all over the world, some unopened, that threatened to overtake him. "No," he concludes, "Munch is no businessman; yet circumstances have forced him to put his native intelligence to use in an effort to become one." Christian Gierløff, "Munch Selv," *Kunst og Kultur* (1913–14), pp. 102–3.

16. Woll, *Genius of Printmaking*, pp. 35–36.

17. By this time, the artist had already placed his works in nine exhibitions in Kristiania, Antwerp, and Copenhagen— an indication of both his ambitions and his connections. See Ingebjørg Ydstie, "Introduction," in *Munch Becoming "Munch": Artistic Strategies, 1880–1892*, edited by Ingebjørg Ydstie and Mai Britt Guleng, exh. cat. (Oslo: Munch Museum, 2008). On Munch's early exhibition strategies and his assertion of his singularity, see Mai Britt Guleng, "Exhibition Strategy and Artistic Individuality: Edvard Munch's Critics in 1892," in ibid., pp. 211–29. A summary of Munch's exhibitions in Oslo may be found in Nina Sørlie, "Edvard Munch Møter publikum i Kristiania," in *Edvard Munchs Livsfrise: En rekonstruksjon av utstillingen hos*

Blomqvist 1918, edited by Karen Lerheim and Gunnar Sørensen, exh. cat., Munch Museum, Oslo ([Oslo]: Munch Museum and Labyrinth Press, 2002), pp. 50–61; and a full chronology in Woll, *Edvard Munch: Complete Paintings*, vol. 4, pp. 1615–34.

18. Woll, *Genius of Printmaking*, p. 36. See also Reinhold Heller, *Munch: His Life and Work* (Chicago: University of Chicago Press, 1984), pp. 44–45. This was Munch's fourth attempt to secure the fellowship. A letter of recommendation for the 1889 application, which was begun in Munch's handwriting, continued in another's (possibly dictated by Munch himself), and signed by six of Norway's leading artists, cites his solo exhibition as evidence of his eligibility: "it has opened our eyes to his great natural talent." It is discussed and reproduced in Lasse Jacobsen, "Edvard Munch's Applications for Endowment Grants and the Government Stipend for Artists," in *Edvard Munch's Writings, English Edition;* "http://emunch.no /ENGART_applications_eng.xhtml #.V9RkiZN97R0 (accessed October 6, 2016).

19. For the admission to the exhibition, see Woll, *Genius of Printmaking*, p. 36; for the lighting, see Poul Erik Tøjner and Bjarne Riiser Gundersen, *Skrik: Historien om et bilde* (Oslo: Forlaget Press, [2013]), p. 33.

20. Mai Britt Guleng, "Edvard Munch and the Source of Creativity," in *The Shore of Love: Edvard Munch and Åsgårdstrand*, edited by Jan Åke Pettersson, exh. cat., ([Tønsberg]: Haugar Art Museum; [Lillehammer]: Lillehammer Art Museum, [2010]), p. 32; Nina Sørlie, "Kunsten møter publikum: De private kunstformidlerne og det modeerne kunstmarkedets fremversk I Kristiania, 1870–1914" (MA thesis, University of Oslo, 1998), pp. 67–70.

21. Andreas Aubert, "I anledning af Edvard Munchs Udstillling," *Dagbladet*, May 19, 1889, as translated in Heller, *Munch*, p. 43. Nonetheless, Aubert, who had previously championed Munch's work, praised the artist's sense of color and indicated in the review that he had been misguided in his training. He later acted as middleman on sales of Munch's work to the Bergen collector Rasmus Meyer and supported the National Gallery purchase of Munch's works in 1908. See Skedsmo, *To norske kunstsamlere*, p. 34.

22. Jorunn Veiteberg, *Den Norske plakaten* (Oslo: Pax, 1998), p. 14.

23. Ute Kuhlemann Falck, "The Mirror–Munch's *Frieze of Life* on paper," in *Edvard Munch: Works on Paper,* edited by Magne Bruteig and Ute Kuhlemann Falck, exh. cat., Munch Museum, Oslo, 2013–14 ([Oslo]: Munch Museum; [Brussels]: Mercatorfonds, [2013]), pp. 145–47. See also Bente Torjusen, "The Mirror," in *Edvard Munch: Symbols and Images*, exh. cat. (Washington, D.C.: National Gallery of Art, 1978), pp.185–87.

24. Munch also created such poster self-advertisements in 1901, 1910, 1916, and 1927. He used the poster from 1910 as a polemical statement about the mural competition at the University of Kristiania. A wounded eagle rises high, while down below a group of tiny police fire upon him from the familiar buildings of the university complex. The allegorical eagle, with a bleeding wing and a broken chain attached to its leg, clearly points to Munch's self-image as a martyr to the institution as well as a kind of reversed Prometheus, the eagle and not the man, unchained. See Patricia G. Berman, "Strategisk modernitet: Munch og Universitetet" in *Edvard Munchs Aulamalerier: Fra kontroversielt prosjekt til nasjonalskatt,* edited by Peder Anker and Patricia G. Berman (Oslo: Messel, 2011), pp. 47ff. I would like to thank Dag Rustad, Master's Candidate at the University of Oslo, for his research in "Edvard Munch's Posters: Between Fine Art and Mass Communication," for the seminar "Collisions and Collusions: Modernity and Public Art," at the Munch Museum in 2013.

25. On the closure and repercussions of Munch's 1892 Berlin exhibition, see Reinhold Heller, "'Affæren Munch,' Berlin 1892–1893," *Kunst og Kultur* 52 (1969), pp. 175–91; Indina Kampf, "'Ein enormes Ärgernis' oder: Die Anarchie in der Malerei; Edvard Munch und die deutsche Kritik, 1892–1902," in *Munch und Deutschland*, edited by Uwe M. Schneede and Dorothee Hansen, exh. cat., Kunsthalle der Hypo-Kulturstiftung, Munich; Hamburger Kunsthalle; and Nationalgalerie, Berlin, 1994–95 (Stuttgart: G. Hatje, 1994), pp. 82–90; Guleng, "Exhibition Strategy," pp. 211–29; and Clarke, "Munch's Critical Reception."

26. Munch, letter to Karen Bjølstad, November 17, 1892, letter no. 129, in *Edvard Munchs Brev Familien*, edited by Inger Munch, Oslo Kommunes Kunstsamlinger; Munch-Museets skrifter, 1 (Oslo: Johan Grundt Tanum, 1949), p. 122.

27. Karen Bjølstad, letter to Munch, dated "Sunday evening," letter no. 131, in ibid., p. 124.

28. "Kunst og Vitenskap," *Aftenposten*, December 4, 1892, a translation of G[eorg] V[oss], "Kunst, Wissenschaft und Literatur," *National Zeitung* (November 6, 1892). In the article, Voss identifies the "Scandinavian" school as nascent, and he criticizes Munch both for being outside the bounds of that school, which he sees as naive and bound up in nature, and for being distinctive. He ends the article by stating that this artist should be interesting to German art circles. On Voss and the shaping of Munch's reputation in Berlin, see Monika Krisch, *Die Munch-Affäre: Rehabilitierung der Zeitungskritik; Eine Analyse äesthetischer und kulturpolitischer Beurteilungskriterien in der Kunstberichterstattung der Berliner Tagespresse zu Munchs Ausstellung 1892* (Mahlow bei Berlin: TENEA, 1997), p. 49; Yarborough, "Exhibition Strategies," p. 214; and Clarke, "Munch's Critical Reception," pp. 188–89.

29. Munch, letter to Karen Bjølstad, undated, letter no. 132, in Munch, *Edvard Munchs Brev Familien*, p. 124.

30. Martha Ward makes the observation that such services, in concert with the proliferation and marketing of newspapers, had the effect of homogenizing and depoliticizing art criticism. See Martha Ward, "From Art Criticism to Art News: Journalistic Reviewing in Late-Nineteenth-Century Paris," in *Art Criticism and Its Institutions in Nineteenth-Century France*, edited by Michael R. Orwicz (Manchester and New York: Manchester University Press, 1994), p. 163.

31. Nils Messel, "Edvard Munch and His Critics in the 1880s," in Ydstie and Guleng, *Munch Becoming "Munch,"* p. 160.

32. Anonymous [signed "r"], "Vi gjør Strike!"

Aftenposten, October 2, 1902. Clipping in Munch Museum Archives.

33. O.D.A., "Edv. Munchs Kunst," *Aftenposten*, October 7, 1902. Clipping in Munch Museum Archives.

34. Munch and many of his later supporters claimed that his work had been met consistently by negative, and even hostile, criticism. However, as art historian Nils Messel observed, "No other Norwegian artist has been received, from the very first time he exhibited, with greater enthusiasm and acclamations by those who, at heart, had not the faintest idea of what he was all about.... In an astonishingly short time, and with a little help from his most ardent supporters, he entered the realm of fiction depicting his own tragic universe, which was unlike anyone else's, and consequently unobtainable for the critics of his time." Messel, "Edvard Munch," p. 159. In other words, Munch's positive criticism was underplayed in order to secure his identity as an outsider.

35. On Munch's stock books, see Woll, *Genius of Printmaking*, p. 28. On the stock book as a marketing tool, see Nicholas Green, "Circuits of Production, Circuits of Consumption: The Case of Mid-Nineteenth-Century French Art Dealing," *Art Journal* 48, no. 1 (Spring 1989), p. 31.

36. The stock book entitled "Edvard Munch" and identified as the "Nordisk Katalogue" ("Nordic" Catalogue) consists of 188 graphic works, all numbered, as well as the suite Alpha and Omega and pages of animal representations. It corresponds to a printed catalogue entitled *Katalog over Grafisk Kunst Edvard Munch* that includes titles and prices (no. 188, *Syg Pige*, is listed on p. 10). The checklist is identical to *Katalog öfver målninger och Grafisk Konst af Edvard Munch*, dated "1913, Salon Joël, Stockholm."

37. See Yarborough, "Exhibition Strategies," and "Public Confrontations and Shifting Allegiances: Edvard Munch and the Art of Exhibition," in McShine, *Modern Life of the Soul*, pp. 65–77.

38. Munch created approximately two hundred self-portraits throughout his career. For a recounting of these, see Iris Müller-Westermann, *Munch by Himself*, exh. cat., Moderna Museet, Stockholm; Munch Museum, Oslo; and Royal Academy of Arts, London, 2005 (London: Royal Academy of Arts, 2005), p. 15.

39. See Patricia G. Berman, "Edvard Munch's *Self-Portrait with Cigarette*: Smoking and the Bohemian Persona," *The Art Bulletin* 75, no. 4 (December 1993), pp. 627–46.

40. Gemma Blackshaw, "Klimt, Schiele, and Schönberg: Self Portraits," in *Facing the Modern: The Portrait in Vienna 1900*, edited by Gemma Blackshaw, exh. cat. (London: National Gallery, 2013), p. 115. See also John E. Toews, "Refashioning the Masculine Subject in Early Modernism: Narratives of Self-Dissolution and Self-Construction in Psychoanalysis and Literature, 1900–1914," in *The Mind of Modernism: Medicine, Psychology, and the Cultural Arts in Europe and America, 1880–1940*, edited by Mark S. Micale (Stanford: Stanford University Press, 2004), pp. 298–335.

41. On site identification, see Patricia G. Berman, "Edvard Munch's Maladie du Siècle," in *Edvard Munch*, edited by Nozomi Endo, exh. cat. (Tokyo: Setagaya Art Museum, 1997), pp. 211–15, 222–23; and "Self-Portraits 'As': Expressionist Embodiments," in *Munch and Expressionism*, edited by Jill Lloyd and Reinhold Heller, exh. cat., Neue Galerie, New York, 2016 (Munich and New York: Prestel, [2016]), pp. 81–96.

42. Hans Dedikem, "Edvard Munch," *Morgenbladet*, March 27, 1909. Clipping in Munch Museum Archives.

43. See Beatrice von Bismarck, "Harry Graf Kessler und die französische Kunst um die Jahrhundertwende," *Zeitschrift des Deutschen Vereins für Kunstwissenschaft* 42, no. 3 (1988), pp. 47–62.

44. A.S., "Edvard Munch," *Verdens Gang*, March 14, 1912. Clipping in Munch Museum Archives; see also Müller-Westermann, *Munch by Himself*, p. 123.

45. One bill for framing (undated) in Munch's possession cites forty-three hours of work for a total of 32.10 kroner, the equivalent of a month's wages for a domestic worker (MM K 5400). Several bills for transport and travel insurance, archived at the Munch Museum, suggest the great volume of material traveling by train and steamship as well as how quickly the relatively small sums mounted up. One shipment from Warnemünde, Germany, to Copenhagen in February 1909 cost 27.50 kroner (MM K 5417). (The annual compensation for an urban domestic servant at the time was somewhere around two hundred kroner a year or 1.46 kroner per day, according to Ola H. Grytten, "Nominal Wages in Norway, 1726–1940 by Occupation," in *Historical Monetary Statistics for Norway*, pt. 2 [Oslo: Norges Bank, 2007], pp. 259, 335; http://www.norges-bank.no/pages/64940/Nominal_wages_in_Norway.pdf [accessed October 6, 2016]).

46. See Woll, *Genius of Printmaking*, p. 22.

47. Munch, letters to Kollmann, nos. 86 (MM N 3196-1/2, November 11, 1912), 87 (MM N 3201, November 27, 1912), and 92 (MM N 3214-1/2, December 20[?], 1912).

48. Eberhard Grisebach, letter to Munch, November 17, 1912, translated in Woll, *Genius of Printmaking*, p. 37, original in Munch Museum Archives.

49. Munch, Kragerø, letter to Albert Kollmann, 1912 (MM N 3812). He reports exhibitions under way in Vienna, Munich, Paris, Amsterdam, Kristiania, and Cologne.

50. See Stephen Kern, *The Culture of Time and Space, 1880–1918: With a New Preface* (Cambridge, Mass.: Harvard University Press, [1983], 2003), especially Chapter 8: "Distance." See also Wolfgang Schivelbusch, *The Railway Journey: The Industrialization of Time and Space in the Nineteenth Century* (Berkeley: University of California Press, 2014).

51. In the early 1890s, Munch conceived of the idea that arranging his paintings in a particular sequence helped his audience to understand their content relationally—a process resulting in what he later termed "The Frieze of Life." Because the relational installation of his works required a deep knowledge of his ideas and because each iteration of the sequences relied on the architecture and environment of the specific gallery, it was incumbent upon Munch or one of his trusted allies to oversee the work. On The Frieze of Life, see Reinhold Heller, "Edvard Munch's 'Life Frieze': Its Beginnings and Origins" (PhD diss., Indiana University, 1969); Mara-Helen Wood, ed.,

Edvard Munch: The Frieze of Life, exh. cat. (London: National Gallery, 1992); and Lerheim and Sørensen, *Edvard Munchs Livsfrise*. On Munch's consideration of architecture as an affective environment, see Wenche Volle, "Munchs rom" (PhD diss., Oslo School of Architecture and Design, 2012).

52. Munch, Prague, letter to Albert Kollmann, February 2, 1905 (MM N 3161).

53. Emil Filla, "Tsjekkerne og Edvard Munch," *Kunst og Kultur* 25 (1939), pp. 66–68.

54. Nicholas Green, "Dealing in Temperaments: Economic Transformation of the Artistic Field in France during the Second Half of the Nineteenth Century," *Art History* 10, no. 1 (March 1987), p. 59.

55. On the many chains of Munch's partners and middlemen, see Næss, *Munch*, pp. 258–67.

56. On Zum Schwarzen Ferkel, see Carla Lathe, "The Group Zum Schwarzen Ferkel: A Study in Early Modernism" (PhD diss., University of East Anglia, Norwich, 1972). An excellent summary may be found in Lasse Jacobsen, "Zum schwarzen Ferkel," in *Edvard Munch's Writings, English Edition*; emunch.no /ENGART_ferkel_eng.xhtml (accessed October 6, 2016).

57. Stanisław Przybyszewski, ed., *Das Werk des Edvard Munch: Vier Beiträge* (Berlin: S. Fischer, 1894). Przybyszewski had already published an important article entitled "Psychic Naturalism," one of the first to interpret Munch's work as a fusion of form and psychology. Stanisław Przybyszewski, "Psychischer Naturalismus," *Neue Deutsche Rundschau: Freie Bühne* 5, no. 1 (1894), pp. 150–56. For an analysis, see Carla Lathe, "Edvard Munch and the Concept of 'Psychic Naturalism,'" *Gazette des Beaux-Arts* 93 (March 1979), pp. 135–46.

58. See Lidia Głuchowska, "Stanisław Przybyszewski, Edvard Munch und Gustav Vigeland: Transmedial Cultural Exchange from Scandinavia to the Balcans [*sic*] at the Turn of the 19th and 20th Centuries," conference paper delivered in "Between Art and Mass Communication: Edvard Munch and Print Cultures," Munch Museum, Oslo, 2013.

59. Dagny Przybyszewska, letter to Munch, undated (MM K 1933); http://emunch.no /HYBRIDNo-MM_K1933.xhtml#ENo-MM _K1933-01-03 (accessed October 6, 2016). Munch's exhibition took place at Alexander Krywułt's gallery in 1903, two years after Dagny's death.

60. Dagny Przybyszewska, letter to Munch, undated (MM K 1934); http://emunch.no /HYBRIDNo-MM_K1934.xhtml#ENo-MM _K1934-01 (accessed October 6, 2016). Stanisław Przybyszewski also helped to realize the exhibitions in Warsaw as well as one in Prague in 1905.

61. Meier-Graefe's text accompanying this portfolio is published and translated in Gerd Woll, *Edvard Munch 1895: Første år som grafiker/ First Year as a Graphic Artist*, exh. cat. (Oslo: Munch Museum, 1995), unpag.

62. Clarke, "Meier-Graefe Sells Munch," p. 186.

63. See Patricia G. Berman, "The Invention of History: Julius Meier-Graefe, German Modernism, and the Genealogy of Genius," in *Imagining Modern German Culture, 1889–1919*, edited by Françoise Forster-Hahn, Studies in the History of Art, 53; Symposium Papers, 31 (Washington, D.C.: National Gallery of Art, 1996), pp. 90–105. Jenny Anger examines the ideological underpinnings of Meier-Graefe's approach to canon formation in "Courbet, the Decorative, and the Canon: Rewriting and Rereading Meier-Graefe's 'Modern Art,'" in *Partisan Canons*, edited by Anna Brzyski (Durham: Duke University Press, 2007).

64. Robert Jensen, *Marketing Modernism in Fin-de-Siècle Europe* (Princeton: Princeton University Press, 1994).

65. Meier-Graefe, letter to Munch, December 12, 1895, as published in Catherine Krahmer and Ingrid Grüninger, eds., *Kunst ist nicht für Kunstgeschichte da: Briefe und Dokumente*, Veröffentlichungen der Deutschen Akademie für Sprache und Dichtung Darmstadt, 77 (Gottingen: Wallstein, 2001), p. 19; cited in Clarke, "Meier-Graefe Sells Munch," p. 189.

66. Woll, *Edvard Munch 1895*, p. 12. The commissioning and marketing of the Meier-Graefe portfolio are examined in Clarke, "Meier-Graefe Sells Munch," pp. 181–94.

67. See Hilde M. J. Rognerud, "'Zarathustra-Nietzsche med vinger': Edvard Munch maler samtidens motefilosof," *Kunst og Kultur* 94, no. 3 (2011), pp. 146–60.

68. Munch, letter to Kollmann, April 29, 1904 (MM N 3195).

69. Munch, letter to Kollmann, January 8, 1909 (MM N 3142-1/2).

70. Munch, letter to Kollmann, August 26, 1911 (MM N 3167).

71. Kollmann, postcard to Munch, September 1, 1911 (MM K 2674).

72. Munch, postcard to Kollmann, dated "September 1911"[?] (MM N 3171).

73. Munch, letter to Kollmann, August 26, 1912 (MM N 3187).

74. On Munch's German patrons, see Stefan Pucks, "'Und die Deutschen begannen mich kräftig zu unterstützen': Edvard Munchs Förderer in Deutschland 1902–1912," in Schneede and Hansen, *Munch und Deutschland*, pp. 91–99. Correspondence between Linde and Munch is published in Max Linde, *Edvard Munchs brev*, Munch-museets skrifter (Oslo: Dreyer, 1954).

75. See Ingrid Mössinger and Katharina Metz, eds., *Henry van de Velde und Edvard Munch in Chemnitz*, exh. cat., Kunstsammlungen Chemnitz-Museum, Theaterplatz (Bielefeld: Kerber, 2013), p. 11; Reinhold Heller, "Strømpefabrikanten, Van de Velde og Munch," *Kunst og Kultur* 51, no. 2 (1968), pp. 80–104.

76. Max Linde, *Edvard Munch und die Kunst der Zukunft* (Berlin: Friedrich Gottheimer, 1902), p. 9. On this rhetoric, see Anita Brookner, *The Genius of the Future: Studies in French Art Criticism; Diderot, Stendhal, Baudelaire, Zola, the Brothers Goncourt, Huysmans* (London and New York: Phaidon, 1971). Robert Jensen notes that such status as a vanguardist helped to "naturalize" and familiarize an otherwise difficult artist (Jensen, *Marketing Modernism*, p. 4).

77. Woll, *Genius of Printmaking*, p. 23. For the catalogue, see Eggum, *Briefwechsel*, p. 109. Schiefler published a second volume of Munch's graphics in 1928, *Edvard Munch: Das graphische Werk; 1906–1926* (Berlin: Euphorion, 1928), the preparation of which the artist found onerous.

78. Woll, *Genius of Printmaking*, p. 39.

79. Kollmann, letter to Munch, August 30, 1912 (MM K 2608).
80. Glaser, letter to Munch, December 1, 1913, translated in Yarborough, "Exhibition Strategies," p. 50. The biography appeared in 1922: Curt Glaser, *Edvard Munch* (Berlin: Bruno Cassirer, 1922).
81. Christian Gierløff described the circle: "We were comrades-in-arms and plainspoken. I never heard Munch or any of his colleagues being called 'master,' much less 'genius,' among his friends. In their writings, Thiis and Jappe were not always shy about using such adjectives, but never among friends." Christian Gierløff, *Edvard Munch selv* (Oslo: Gyldendal, 1953), p. 13.
82. National Library, Oslo, letter collection (NBO letter no. 604), quoted in Helle C. Aaneland, "Kunstkritikken Jappe Nilssen og hans kamp for anerkjennelse av Edvard Munchs kunst, belyst gjennom hans anmedelse av Munchs utstilling i Kunstforeningen 1913" (Master's thesis, University of Oslo, 2009), p. 24.
83. Edvard Munch, letter to Jappe Nilssen, April 8, 1909; National Library, Oslo, letter collection (NBO letter no 604 [PN 727]); available in *Edvard Munchs Tekster, Digitalt Arkiv,* http://www.emunch.no/HYBRIDPN0727.xhtml#ENB_PN0727_1_57256A00001 (accessed October 7, 2016).
84. Jappe Nilssen, "Edvard Munch," *Dagbladet,* April 1, 1911. Clipping in Munch Museum Archives.
85. Jappe Nilssen, "Edv. Munchs utstilling," *Dagbladet,* April 22, 1911. Clipping in Munch Museum Archives.
86. Margrethe Lømo, "Din hengivne Jens Thiis. Hvordan Jens Thiis fremmet Edvard Munch gjennom tekst, samling og kuratering i perioden 1900–1913" (Master's thesis, Univerity of Oslo, 2014), pp. 58–60.
87. Thiis, letter to Munch, October 15, 1902 (MM K 1131).
88. See, for example, Jens Thiis, "Edvard Munch," *Kunst og Kultur* 4 (1913–14), pp. 67–80.
89. Munch, draft of letter to Jens Thiis, undated (MM N 3112).
90. Munch, letter to Thiis [1933?] (MM N 3112).
91. Munch, draft of letter to Thiis, [1933?] (MM N 3117).
92. Glaser, *Edvard Munch*, pp. 2–3, translated in Yarborough, "Exhibition Strategies," p. 331.
93. Glaser, *Edvard Munch*, p. 7.
94. Ludvig Ravensberg, diary entry, May 8, 1909 (LOR number 537), Munch Museum Archives.
95. Munch, undated notation (MM N 143), translated in Tøjner, *Munch*, p. 162.
96. Reinhold Heller, "Who Was / Is Edvard Munch?" Talk given in Oslo, September 18, 2013, and "Edvard Munch as Photographed for His 75th Birthday, 1938: Strategies in Defense of a Legacy," *Kunst og Kultur* 100, no. 1 (2017).

Munch on the Periphery
Richard Shiff

For essential aid in research, I thank Jon-Ove Steihaug and his colleagues at the Munch Museum, Sindre Stemshaug Bornstein, Per Kirkeby, Erik Steffensen, Jeanette Lindholdt Madsen, Georg Baselitz, Detlev Gretenkort, Katharina Grosse, Natalija Martinovic, Bridget Riley, Caitlin Haskell, Gabriella Moreno, Michael Sittenfeld, and, especially, Jeannie McKetta.

1. Heinrich von Kleist, "Von der Überlegung: Eine Paradoxe" (1810), in *Werke und Briefe: In vier Bänden*, edited by Siegfried Streller, Bibliothek Deutscher Klassiker, 186 (Frankfurt: Deutscher Klassiker, 1978), vol. 3, p. 471. Unless otherwise noted, translations from French and German are the author's.
2. Paul Gauguin, letter to Charles Morice, July 1901, in *Lettres de Gauguin à sa femme et à ses amis, recueillies et préfacées par Maurice Malingue, et illus. de 32 reproductions et fac-similés*, edited by Maurice Malingue (Paris: B. Grasset, [1946]), p. 301.
3. Guillaume Apollinaire, "Du sujet dans la peinture moderne," *Les soirées de Paris*, no. 1 (February 1912), p. 2. On the history of "pure painting," see Richard Shiff, "Dream of Abstraction," in *Abstraction: Paths to Abstraction, 1867–1917*, edited by Terence Maloon (Sydney: Art Gallery of New South Wales, 2010), pp. 52–69 (esp. 61–63).
4. Emile Bernard, "Paul Cézanne," *L'Occident* 6 (July 1904), p. 21.
5. Clement Greenberg, "Complaints of an Art Critic" (1967), *The Collected Essays and Criticism*, edited by John O'Brian, vol. 4, *Modernism with a Vengeance, 1957–1969* (Chicago: University of Chicago Press, 1993), p. 271.
6. Charles Sanders Peirce argues for the objectivity of all isolated visual sensations, even those that prove inconsistent and misleading with respect to actual physical conditions: Charles Sanders Peirce, "Perception" (1903), in *Collected Papers of Charles Sanders Peirce*, 8 vols., edited by Charles Hartshorne, Paul Weiss, and Arthur W. Burks (Cambridge, Mass.: Belknap Press of Harvard University Press, 1960–66), vol. 7, pp. 368–76.
7. Henri Bergson, *Matière et mémoire: Essai sur la relation du corps à l'esprit* (1896), Bibliothèque de philosophie contemporaine; Histoire de la philosophie générale (Paris: Presses Universitaires de France, 1968), p. 245.
8. This quotation and the one immediately above are from Edvard Munch, MM N 29, *eMunch: Edvard Munch's Writings, English Edition*, trans. Francesca M. Nichols, at http://emunch.no/TRANS_HYBRIDMM_N0029.xhtml#.WANhEPkrLIU (accessed October 16, 2016).
9. Munch, MM T 2785, in *Munch in His Own Words*, edited by Poul Erik Tøjner (Munich and New York: Prestel, 2001), p. 96. I would prefer *The Cry* to *The Scream* as the English title for Munch's paintings on this theme because the range of connotations is broader. A cry is a sound, perhaps loud, perhaps piercing, perhaps emotionally charged with personal anxiety, but it can also be the vocalization associated with a form of life—the cry of the gull, the cry of the wolf, the cry of the human infant. The majority of scholars seem to prefer "scream" to "cry," so I follow this established practice. Numerous sources can be invoked with respect to Munch's notions of a universal life-force, a pantheistic spiritualism, and the organicity of all physical matter (which he associated with an origin in crystallization): "Nature is one though

we see it in different stages of development. We call one of them the crystal, another the cell ... another the plant, another the animal.... Not only does the living approach the inorganic, but the inorganic approaches the living"; Wilhelm Bölsche, *Haeckel, His Life and Work* ([Charleston, S.C.]: Nabu Press, 2010), quoted in Shelley Wood Cordulack, *Edvard Munch and the Physiology of Symbolism* (Madison, N.J.: Fairleigh Dickinson University Press; London: Associated University Presses, 2002), pp. 95–96. Cordulack states that Munch owned a copy of this book, from an edition of 1906. Her research articulates several lines of correspondence between the thinking of Munch and Ernst Haeckel (remembered today for the dictum "ontogeny recapitulates phylogeny"). Speculation of this kind, linking organic and inorganic matter, was common among nineteenth-century thinkers: "Man lives by pulses; our organic movements are such; and the chemical and ethereal agents are undulatory and alternate"; Ralph Waldo Emerson, "Experience" (1844), in *Essays* (London: G. Richards, 1901), p. 250. "What we call matter is not completely dead, but is merely mind hidebound with habits. It still retains the element of diversification; and in that diversification there is life": Charles Sanders Peirce, "The Law of Mind" (1892), in Hartshorne, Weiss, and Burks, *Collected Papers*, vol. 6, p. 111.

10. Munch, "April 15, 1929," in Tøjner, *Munch in His Own Words*, p. 110.

11. Munch, "February 1930," in Tøjner, *Munch in His Own Words*, p. 110.

12. See note 8 above.

13. Munch, MM N 43, *eMunch: Edvard Munch's Writings, English Edition*, at http://emunch.no/TRANS_HYBRIDMM_N0043.xhtml#.WANjx_krLIU (accessed October 16, 2016).

14. At a later date, Munch attempted to capture a moment of intense focus by painting the portrait of a friend from the memory of a glimpse at extremely close range, which, even more than in *The Scream*, exaggerated the perspective differential. See his *Caricature Portrait of Henrik Lund* (1905; Munch Museum, Oslo) and the associated commentary (MM T 157), in Tøjner, *Munch in His Own Words*, p. 137: "[The image of Lund] was unnaturally large—as he had been so close to me—and his wife in a flaming red dress, who had sat further away, was quite small."

15. Munch, MM T 2785, in Tøjner, *Munch in His Own Words*, p. 131.

16. Paul Mantz, *Salon de 1847* (Paris: F. Sartorius, 1847), pp. 102–3.

17. Edvard Munch, *Livsfrisens tilblivelse* (Oslo, [1929?]), p. 9, quoted and translated in Dieter Buchhart, "1880–1892: Munch, the Radical Innovator and His Experimentation with Naturalism, Impressionism, and Symbolism," translated by Paul Aston, in *Edvard Munch: Signs of Modern Art*, edited by Dieter Buchhart (Riehen / Basel: Fondation Beyeler; Ostfildern: Hatje Cantz, 2007), p. 43.

18. Mantz, *Salon de 1847*, p. 97.

19. The version of *Death in the Sickroom* in the Nasjonalmuseet for Kunst, Arkitektur og Design, Oslo, develops a different set of lateral rhythms and includes indications of parallel floorboards in recession.

20. Munch, MM T 2730, in Tøjner, *Munch in His Own Words*, p. 95.

21. Munch, MM T 2800, in ibid., p. 186.

22. Christian Krohg, review, November 27, 1891, quoted and translated in Reinhold Heller, *Munch: His Life and Work* (Chicago: University of Chicago Press, 1984), p. 82.

23. Julius Meier-Graefe, *Entwicklungsgeschichte der modernen Kunst*, 3 vols. (Stuttgart: Hoffmann, 1904), vol. 1, p. 394.

24. Haro von Wedderkop, *Sonderbund Ausstellung, 1912: Führer nebst Vorwort* (Bonn: A. Ahn, 1912), p. 45.

25. T[hadée] N[atanson], "Correspondance de Kristiania: M. Edvard Munch," *La revue blanche* 9, no. 59 (November 15, 1895), p. 478.

26. Thadée Natanson, "Paul Cézanne," *La revue blanche* 9, no. 60 (December 1, 1895), p. 499.

27. Paul Sérusier, quoted in Maurice Denis, "Cézanne" (1907), in *Théories, 1890–1910: Du symbolisme et de Gauguin vers un nouvel ordre classique*, 4th ed. (Paris: L. Rouart et J. Watelin, 1920), p. 252. On the phenomenon of "loss of subject" and its social significance, see Richard Shiff, "He Painted," in *Cézanne's Card Players*, edited by Nancy Ireson and Barnaby Wright, exh. cat., Courtauld Gallery, London; and The Metropolitan Museum of Art, New York, 2010–11 (London: Courtauld Gallery, 2010), pp. 72–91; Richard Shiff, "Morality, Materiality, Apples," in *The World Is an Apple: The Still Lifes of Paul Cézanne*, edited by Benedict Leca, exh. cat., Barnes Foundation, Philadelphia; and Art Gallery of Hamilton, Ontario, 2014–15 (Hamilton, Ont., and London: Art Gallery of Hamilton in association with D Giles Limited, 2014), pp. 145–95.

28. Thadée Natanson, "Salon des Indépendants," *La revue blanche* 10, no. 69 (April 15, 1896), p. 379.

29. Thadée Natanson, "Petite gazette d'art," *La revue blanche* 12, no. 88 (February 1, 1897), pp. 140–43.

30. See the inset that refers to Munch's *Madonna* in a set of caricatures from 1895, reproduced in Antonia Hoerschelmann, "Crossover: Munch and Modernism," in *Edvard Munch: Theme and Variation*, edited by Klaus Albrecht Schröder and Antonia Hoerschelmann (Vienna: Albertina; Ostfildern-Ruit: Hatje Cantz, 2003), p. 15.

31. "Strange seductiveness": see discussion in text at note 16.

32. Maurice Denis, reporting Gauguin's words according to Paul Sérusier; Maurice Denis, "L'influence de Paul Gauguin" (1903), in Denis, *Théories, 1890–1910*, p. 167.

33. Paul Gauguin, letter to Emile Schuffenecker, August 14, 1888, in *Correspondance de Paul Gauguin: Documents, témoignages*, vol. 1, *1873–1888*, edited by Victor Merlhès (Paris: Fondation Singer-Polignac, 1984), p. 210.

34. Charles Morice, "Paul Cézanne," *Mercure de France* 65 (February 15, 1907), p. 593.

35. Meyer Schapiro, "The Liberating Quality of Avant-Garde Art," *Art News* 56 (Summer 1957), pp. 36–42.

36. Greenberg, "Cézanne and the Unity of Modern Art" (1951), in *Collected Essays*, vol. 3, p. 87.

37. Greenberg, "Henri Rousseau and Modern Art" (1946), in *Collected Essays*, vol. 2, pp. 93–95.

38. Hans Sedlmayr, *Art in Crisis: The Lost Centre*, translated by Brian Battershaw (Chicago: H. Regnary, 1958), p. 235.

39. Ibid., pp. 133–34.

40. Ibid., pp. 139–41. The characterization is unfair to Munch, though Sedlmayr would not have recognized his pantheism as a valid spiritual element. "Nothing is dead, and matter is alive. There is life in all things, 'God' in all things, and we are 'God'": Edvard Munch, "June 1939: Producing Life," in Tøjner, *Munch in His Own Words*, p. 110.

41. Greenberg, "Religion and the Intellectuals" (1950), in *Collected Essays*, vol. 3, p. 42.

42. Sedlmayr, *Art in Crisis*, p. 138.

43. Greenberg, "Religion and the Intellectuals," p. 42.

44. On the weathering process, see Dieter Buchhart, "Edvard Munch: Signs of Modern Art; The Duality of a Material-Based Modernity," translated by Paul Aston, in Buchhart, *Edvard Munch*, pp. 11–23.

45. The assumption, Munch's and others', is that sensation precedes conceptualization and interpretation. This position accords with "common sense." As an alternative, one can argue that a person's cultural indoctrination restricts sensitivity, so that only those sensory phenomena subject to interpretation register on consciousness. Exceptions may be traumatic. Hence our experience of unaccountable, unexplainable sensations wavers between delight and anxiety.

46. During the late 1940s, Barnett Newman eliminated representational imagery, but, retaining the emotion without the organization, resisted being identified as an "abstract artist": "I was particularly unwilling to get involved in the fundamentals of painting composition which had been the alternative developed by abstract artists who were professional abstractionists"—in other words, Newman's forms were reduced beyond what an abstractionist would regard as suited to compositional analysis (Barnett Newman, unpublished interview by Allene Talmey for *Vogue* magazine, audiotape, 1966, Barnett Newman Foundation Archives, New York; courtesy Barnett Newman Foundation).

47. Bridget Riley, email to the author, October 2, 2016.

48. Per Kirkeby, unpublished interview by Erik Steffensen, September 8, 2016, translation courtesy Jeanette Lindholdt Madsen (slightly modified by author). In recognition of the emotional connection to Munch, Poul Erik Tøjner dedicated *Munch in His Own Words* to Kirkeby.

49. Many of Kirkeby's paintings and sculptures appear at first to be abstractions; a viewer gradually discovers figural and geological motifs. He published a number of short books on various artists, devoting one to Munch. During the 1980s, Baselitz included an image of Munch in a series of paintings on the Der Brücke artists. During the 2000s, he painted images of feet, imagining that they corresponded to those left out of the frame of a well-known photograph of Munch at Ekely.

50. Georg Baselitz, email to the author, August 26, 2016, translation courtesy Detlev Gretenkort (slightly modified by author). See also Georg Baselitz, "Outcomes, Prospects, Bounces: Georg Baselitz Talks to Rainer Michael Mason" (2006), in *Georg Baselitz*, edited by Rainer Michael Mason, exh. cat., Museo d'Arte Moderna, Lugano 2007 (Milan: Silvana; Lugano: Museo d'Arte Moderna, 2007), p. 163.

51. Katharina Grosse, unpublished statement, 2005, for an art competition in Norway (courtesy Katharina Grosse and Natalija Martinovic).

52. Katharina Grosse, interviewed in Melissa Ragona, "Katharina Grosse: Lush Irreverence," *Art Papers* 32, no. 5 (September-October 2008), p. 43.

Works in the Exhibition

All works are by Edvard Munch (Norwegian, Løten 1863–1944 Ekely). Unless otherwise stated, all were exhibited in San Francisco, New York, and Oslo.

1. *Morning*
1884
Oil on canvas
38 × 40¾ in. (96.5 × 103.5 cm)
KODE Kunstmuseene i Bergen, Rasmus Meyers Samlinger (RMS.M.236)
New York only

2. *Self-Portrait*
1886
Oil on canvas
13 × 9⅝ in. (33 × 24.5 cm)
Nasjonalmuseet for Kunst, Arkitektur og Design, Oslo (NG.M.01915)

3. *Lady in Black (Olga Buhre)*
1891
Oil on canvas
28¾ × 23¼ in. (73 × 59 cm)
Statens Museum for Kunst, Copenhagen (KMS2096)

4. *Sick Mood at Sunset: Despair*
1892
Oil on canvas
36¼ × 26⅜ in. (92 × 67 cm)
Thielska Galleriet, Stockholm
San Francisco and New York only

5. *Death in the Sick Room*
1893
Oil on canvas
53 × 63 in. (134.5 × 160 cm)
Munch Museum, Oslo
(MM M 418)

6. *Moonlight*
1893
Oil on canvas
55⅜ × 53⅛ in. (140.5 × 135 cm)
Nasjonalmuseet for Kunst, Arkitektur og Design, Oslo (NG.M.0194)

7. *Night in Saint-Cloud*
1893
Oil on canvas
27½ × 22¼ in. (70 × 56.5 cm)
Private collection
New York and San Francisco only

8. *Self-Portrait under the Mask of a Woman*
1893
Tempera on unprimed wood panel
27½ × 17½ in. (70 × 44.3 cm)
Munch Museum, Oslo
(MM M 229)

9. *Starry Night*
1893
Oil on canvas
42¾ × 47½ in. (108.5 × 120.5 cm)
Von der Heydt-Museum, Wuppertal, Germany (G. 1179)
New York only

10. *The Storm*
1893
Oil on canvas
36¼ × 51⅝ in. (92 × 131 cm)
The Museum of Modern Art, New York. Gift of Mr. and Mrs. H. Irgens Larsen and acquired through the Lillie P. Bliss and Abby Aldrich Rockefeller Funds, 1974
San Francisco and New York only

11. *Despair*
1894
Oil on canvas
36¼ × 28½ in. (92 × 72.5 cm)
Munch Museum, Oslo
(MM M 513)

12. *Madonna*
1894
Oil on canvas
35½ × 27 in. (90 × 68.5 cm)
Munch Museum, Oslo
(MM M 68)
Oslo only

13. *Puberty*
1894
Oil on unprimed canvas
58⅝ × 44⅛ in. (149 × 112 cm)
Munch Museum, Oslo
(MM M 281)

14. *At the Deathbed*
1895
Oil and tempera on unprimed canvas
35⅜ × 47½ in. (90 × 120.5 cm)
KODE Kunstmuseene i Bergen, Rasmus Meyers Samlinger (RMS.M.251)
San Francisco and Oslo only

15. *The Scream*
1895
Pastel on cardboard
31⅛ × 23¼ in. (79 × 59 cm)
Private collection
Not in exhibition

16. *Self-Portrait with Cigarette*
1895
Oil on canvas
43½ × 33⅝ in. (110.5 × 85.5 cm)
Nasjonalmuseet for Kunst, Arkitektur og Design, Oslo (NG.M.00470)
San Francisco and New York only

17. *The Smell of Death*
1895
Tempera and oil on unprimed canvas
39⅜ × 43¼ in. (100 × 110 cm)
Munch Museum, Oslo
(MM M 34)
San Francisco and Oslo only

18. *Madonna*
1895–97
Oil on canvas
36⅝ × 29½ in. (93 × 75 cm)
Private collection
New York only

19. *Madonna*
1895–97(?)
Oil on canvas
39¾ × 27¾ in. (101 × 70.5 cm)
Collection of Catherine Woodard and Nelson Blitz, Jr.
San Francisco and New York only

20. *The Sick Child*
1896
Oil on canvas
47⅞ × 46⅝ in. (121.5 × 118.5 cm)
Göteborgs Konstmuseum
(GKM 0975)
San Francisco and New York only

21. *The Kiss*
1897
Oil on canvas
39 × 31⅞ in. (99 × 81 cm)
Munch Museum, Oslo
(MM M 59)

22. *Inheritance*
1897–99
Oil on canvas
55½ × 47¼ in. (141 × 120 cm)
Munch Museum, Oslo
(MM M 11)

23. *Red Virginia Creeper*
1898–1900
Oil on canvas
47 × 47⅝ in. (119.5 × 121 cm)
Munch Museum, Oslo
(MM M 503)

24. *Eye in Eye*
1899–1900
Oil on canvas
53½ × 43¼ in. (136 × 110 cm)
Munch Museum, Oslo
(MM M 502)

25. *Self-Portrait in Hell*
1903
Oil on canvas
32¼ × 26 in. (82 × 66 cm)
Munch Museum, Oslo
(MM M 591)

26. *Self-Portrait with Brushes*
1904
Oil on canvas
77½ × 35⅞ in. (197 × 91 cm)
Munch Museum, Oslo
(MM M 751)

27. *Self-Portrait with a Bottle of Wine*
1906
Oil on canvas
43½ × 47½ in. (110.5 × 120.5 cm)
Munch Museum, Oslo
(MM M 543)

28. *The Death of Marat*
1907
Oil on canvas
60¼ × 58⅝ in. (153 × 149 cm)
Munch Museum, Oslo
(MM M 4)

29. *The Sick Child*
1907
Oil on canvas
46¾ × 47⅝ in. (118.7 × 121 cm)
Tate Modern, London
San Francisco and New York only

30. *Jealousy*
Ca. 1907
Oil on canvas
22⅝ × 33¼ in. (57.5 × 84.5 cm)
Munch Museum, Oslo
(MM M 614)

31. *The Scream*
Ca. 1910
Tempera and oil on unprimed cardboard
32⅞ × 26 in. (83.5 × 66 cm)
Munch Museum, Oslo
(MM M 514)
Oslo only

32. *Self-Portrait with Hand under Cheek*
1911
Oil on canvas
32⅝ × 27⅜ in. (83 × 69.5 cm)
Munch Museum, Oslo
(MM M 117)
San Francisco and Oslo only

33. *Weeping Nude*
1913–14
Oil on canvas
43½ × 53⅛ in. (110.5 × 135 cm)
Munch Museum, Oslo
(MM M 540)

34. *Death Struggle*
1915
Oil on canvas
68½ × 90½ in. (174 × 230 cm)
Munch Museum, Oslo
(MM M 2)

35. *Self-Portrait with the Spanish Flu*
1919
Oil on canvas
59 × 51⅝ in. (150 × 131 cm)
Nasjonalmuseet for Kunst, Arkitektur og Design, Oslo
(NG.M.01867)

36. *The Artist and His Model*
1919–21
Oil on canvas
47½ × 78¾ in. (120.5 × 200 cm)
Munch Museum, Oslo
(MM M 723)

37. *The Artist and His Model*
1919–21
Oil on canvas
50⅜ × 60¼ in. (128 × 153 cm)
Munch Museum, Oslo
(MM M 75)

38. *Model by the Wicker Chair*
1919–21
Oil on canvas
48¼ × 39⅜ in. (122.5 × 100 cm)
Munch Museum, Oslo
(MM M 499)

39. *Female Nude (Anna)*
1920
Oil on canvas
59 × 41¾ in. (150 × 106 cm)
Sarah Campbell Blaffer Foundation, Houston
(BF.1974.4)
San Francisco and Oslo only

40. *Man with Bronchitis*
1920
Oil on canvas
39⅝ × 37⅜ in. (100.5 × 95 cm)
Munch Museum, Oslo
(MM M 449)

41. *Sleepless Night: Self-Portrait in Inner Turmoil*
1920
Oil on canvas
59 × 50¾ in. (150 × 129 cm)
Munch Museum, Oslo
(MM M 76)

42. *On the Veranda Stairs*
1922–24
Oil on canvas
35 × 29⅞ in. (89 × 76 cm)
Munch Museum, Oslo
(MM M 454)

43. *Starry Night*
1922–24
Oil on canvas
47½ × 39⅜ in. (120.5 × 100 cm)
Munch Museum, Oslo
(MM M 32)

44. *The Night Wanderer*
1923–24
Oil on canvas
35⅜ × 26¾ in. (90 × 68 cm)
Munch Museum, Oslo
(MM M 589)

45. *Self-Portrait with Hands in Pockets*
1925–26
Oil on canvas
31½ × 23⅝ in. (80 × 60 cm)
Munch Museum, Oslo
(MM M 112)

46. *Ashes*
1925
Oil on canvas
54⅞ × 78¾ in. (139.5 × 200 cm)
Munch Museum, Oslo
(MM M 417)

47. *The Dance of Life*
1925
Oil on canvas
56¼ × 81⅞ in. (143 × 208 cm)
Munch Museum, Oslo
(MM M 777)

48. *Anatomy Professor Kristian Schreiner*
1928–32
Collage, lithograph, and watercolor
54⅞ × 54 in. (139.5 × 137.2 cm)
Munch Museum, Oslo
(MM T 2909)
New York and Oslo only

49. *Self-Portrait with Bottles*
Ca. 1938
Oil on canvas
46½ × 36⅝ in. (118 × 93 cm)
Munch Museum, Oslo
(MM M 43)

50. *Self-Portrait by the Window*
Ca. 1940
Oil on canvas
33⅛ × 42½ in. (84 × 108 cm)
Munch Museum, Oslo
(MM M 446)

51. *Self-Portrait: Between the Clock and the Bed*
1940–43
Oil on canvas
58⅞ × 47½ in. (149.5 × 120.5 cm)
Munch Museum, Oslo
(MM M 23)

For Further Reading

Berman, Patricia G. "Edvard Munch's *Self-Portrait with Cigarette*: Smoking and the Bohemian Persona." *The Art Bulletin* 75, no. 4 (December 1993), pp. 627–46.

———. "(Re-)Reading Edvard Munch: Trends in the Current Literature." *Scandinavian Studies* 66, no. 1 (Winter 1994), pp. 45–67.

———. "The Invention of History: Julius Meier-Graefe, German Modernism, and the Genealogy of Genius." In *Imagining Modern German Culture, 1889–1919*, edited by Françoise Forster-Hahn, pp. 90–105. Studies in the History of Art 53; Symposium Papers, 31. Washington, D.C.: National Gallery of Art, 1996.

Bond, Anthony, and Joanna Woodall. *Self Portrait: Renaissance to Contemporary*. Exh. cat. National Portrait Gallery, London; and Art Gallery of New South Wales, Sydney, 2005–6. London: National Portrait Gallery, 2005.

Buchhart, Dieter. "Disappearance—Experiments with Material and Motif." In *Edvard Munch: Theme and Variation*, edited by Klaus Albrecht Schröder and Antonia Hoerschelmann, pp. 23–39. Vienna: Albertina; Ostfildern-Ruit: Hatje Cantz, 2003.

Buchhart, Dieter, ed. *Edvard Munch: Signs of Modern Art*. Exh. cat., Fondation Beyeler, Riehen / Basel; and Kunsthalle Würth, Schwäbisch Hall, 2007. Riehen / Basel: Fondation Beyeler; Ostfildern: Hatje Cantz, 2007.

Clarke, Jay A. *Becoming Edvard Munch: Influence, Anxiety, and Myth*. Exh. cat. Chicago: Art Institute, 2009.

Clarke, Jay A., Finn Skårderud, Biljana Topalova-Casadiego, and Ingebjørg Ydstie. *Edvard Munch: Pubertet / Puberty*. Exh. cat, Munch Museum, Oslo, 2012. [Oslo]: Orfeus Publishing, [2012].

Cordulack, Shelley Wood. *Edvard Munch and the Physiology of Symbolism*. Madison, N.J.: Fairleigh Dickinson University Press; London: Associated University Presses, 2002.

Frøysaker, Tine, ed. With Noëlle Streeton, Harmut Kutzke, Françoise Hanssen-Bauer, and Biljana Topalova-Casadiego. *Public Paintings by Edvard Munch and His Contemporaries: Change and Conservation Challenges*. London: Archetype Publications, 2015.

Greenberg, Clement. "Complaints of an Art Critic" (1967). In *The Collected Essays and Criticism*, edited by John O'Brian. vol. 4, pp. 265–71. 4 vols. Chicago: University of Chicago Press, 1986–93.

Guleng, Mai Britt. *eMunch.no: Text and Image*. Oslo: Munch Museum, 2011.

Guleng, Mai Britt, Birgitte Sauge, and Jon-Ove Steihaug. *Edvard Munch, 1863–1944*. Exh. cat., Nasjonalgalleriet and Munch Museum, Oslo, 2013. Milan: Skira, 2013.

Heller, Reinhold. *Edvard Munch: The Scream*. Art in Context. [New York: Viking Press, 1973].

———. *Munch: His Life and Work*. Chicago: University of Chicago Press, 1984.

Lampe, Angela, and Clément Chéroux, eds. *Edvard Munch: The Modern Eye*. Exh. cat. Centre Pompidou, Paris; Schirn Kunsthalle, Frankfurt; and Tate Modern, London, 2011–12. London: Tate Pub., 2012.

Lloyd, Jill, and Reinhold Heller, eds. *Munch and Expressionism*. Exh. cat., Neue Galerie, New York, 2016. Munich and New York: Prestel, [2016].

McShine, Kynaston, ed. *Edvard Munch: The Modern Life of the Soul*. Exh. cat. New York: Museum of Modern Art, 2006.

Morehead, Allison. *Nature's Experiments and the Search for Symbolist Form*. Refiguring Modernism. University Park, Penn.: Pennsylvania State University Press, [2017].

Mørstad, Erik, ed. *Edvard Munch: An Anthology*. Oslo: Unipub, 2006.

Müller-Westermann, Iris. *Munch by Himself*. Exh. cat. Moderna Museet, Stockholm; Munch Museum, Oslo; and Royal Academy of Arts, London, 2005. London: Royal Academy of Arts, 2005.

Plahter, Leif Einar. "Beneath the Surface of Edvard Munch: Technical Examinations of Four Paintings by Edvard Munch." In *Conservare necesse est: Festkrift til Leif Einar Plahter på hans 70-årsdag / For Leif Plahter on His 70ieth Birthday*, edited by Erling Skaug, pp. 111–27. Oslo: Nordisk Konservatorforbund, Den norske seksjon, 1999.

Plahter, Unn, and Leif Einar Plahter. "Munch's Paintings: Scientific Research in Retrospect." In *Public Paintings by Edvard Munch and His Contemporaries: Change and Conservation Challenges*, edited by Tine Frøysaker with Noëlle Streeton, Harmut Kutzke, Françoise Hanssen-Bauer, and Biljana Topalova-Casadiego, pp. 3–36. London: Archetype Publications, 2015.

Prelinger, Elizabeth. *After the Scream: The Late Paintings of Edvard Munch*. Exh. cat. Atlanta: High Museum of Art, 2002.

Rosenblum, Robert, et al. *Edvard Munch: Symbols and Images*. Exh. cat. Washington, D.C.: National Gallery of Art, 1978.

Schröder, Klaus Albrecht, and Antonia Hoerschelmann, eds. *Edvard Munch: Theme and Variation*. Exh. cat. Albertina, Vienna, 2003. Vienna: Albertina; Ostfildern-Ruit: Hatje Cantz, 2003.

Shiff, Richard. "Dream of Abstraction." In *Abstraction: Paths to Abstraction, 1867–1917*, edited by Terence Maloon, pp. 52–69. Exh. cat. Sydney: Art Gallery of New South Wales, 2010.

———. "Golf [Wave]." Translated by Els Kuijpers. In *Edvard Munch*, edited by Øivind Storm Bjerke et al., pp. 160–73. Exh. cat. Paris: Pinacothèque de Paris; Rotterdam: Kunsthal, 2010.

Stang, Ragna. *Edvard Munch: The Man and His Art.* Translated by Geoffrey Culverwell. New York: Abbeville Press, 1979.

Stein, Mille. "Edvard Munch Paintings with Bird Droppings: Analysis of the Ekely Collection at the Munch Museum." *Zeitschrift für Kunsttechnologie und Konservierung* 25, no. 1 (2011), pp. 93–102.

———"Edvard Munch's Paintings with Water Stains: Analysis of the Ekely Collection at the Munch Museum." *Zeitschrift für Kunsttechnologie und Konservierung* 25, no. 2 (2011), pp. 273–84.

———"Edvard Munch Paintings with Weathered Paint Surface: Analysis of the Ekely Collection at the Munch Museum." *Zeitschrift für Kunsttechnologie und Konservierung* 26, no. 2 (2012), pp. 435–47.

———"Edvard Munch and the 'Kill-or-Cure' Remedy: Analysis of the Ekely Collection at the Munch Museum." *Zeitschrift für Kunsttechnologie und Konservierung* 28, no. 2 (2014), pp. 279–97.

Tøjner, Poul Erik, ed. *Munch in His Own Words.* Munich and New York: Prestel, 2001.

Topalova-Casadiego, Biljana. "Technical Aspects of Edvard Munch's Paintings." In *Edvard Munch: Complete Paintings; Catalogue Raisonné.* Vol. 2, *1898–1908*, edited by Gerd Woll, pp. 425–53. London: Thames and Hudson, 2009.

Ustvedt, Øystein, and Trond E. Aslaksby. *Edvard Munch: Det syke barn; Historian om et mesterverk / The Sick Child: The Story of a Masterpiece.* Exh. cat. Oslo: Nasjonalmuseet, 2009.

Van Dijk, Maite, Magne Bruteig, and Leo Jansen, eds. *Munch, Van Gogh.* Exh. cat. Munch Museum, Oslo, 2015; and Van Gogh Museum, Amsterdam, 2015–16. Brussels: Mercatorfonds, 2015.

Woll, Gerd. *Edvard Munch: Complete Paintings; Catalogue Raisonné.* 4 vols. London and New York: Thames and Hudson, 2009.

———. *Edvard Munch: The Complete Graphic Works.* Rev. ed. London: Philip Wilson; Oslo: Orfeus Publishing, 2012.

Yarborough, Bessie Rainsford (Tina). "Exhibition Strategies and Wartime Politics in the Art and Career of Edvard Munch, 1914–1921." PhD diss., University of Chicago, 1994.

Ydstie, Ingebjørg, ed. *Madonna.* Translated by Francesca M. Nichols. Exh. cat. Munch Museum, Oslo, 2008. Bergen: Vigmostad and Bjørke, 2008.

——— *The Scream.* Translated by Francesca M. Nichols. Exh. cat. Munch Museum, Oslo, 2008. Bergen: Vigmostad and Bjørke, 2008.

———. *Munch's Laboratory: The Path to the Aula.* Exh. cat. Oslo: Munch Museum, [2011].

Ydstie, Ingebjørg, and Mai Britt Guleng, eds. *Munch Becoming "Munch": Artistic Strategies, 1880–1892.* Exh. cat. Oslo: Munch Museum, 2008.

Index

Italic numbers refer to pages with illustrations.

Photograph Credits

© 2017 Artists Rights Society (ARS), New York: fig. 27, pls. 15, 19, 39
© 2017 Artists Rights Society (ARS), New York. © Thielska Galleriet, photo by Tord Lund: fig. 9, pl. 4
© 2017 Artists Rights Society (ARS), New York, photo courtesy of Gothenburg Museum of Art, Sweden: fig. 33
© 2017 Artists Rights Society (ARS), New York, photo courtesy of Gothenburg Museum of Art, Sweden, photo by Hossein Sehatlou: pl. 20
© 2017 Artists Rights Society (ARS), New York. KODE–Art Museums of Bergen, Rasmus Meyer Collection, photo by Dag Fosse: figs. 17b, 19, 21, pls. 1, 14
© 2017 Artists Rights Society (ARS), New York. © Sotheby's 2016–Ars Longa, Vita Brevis Collection, Tor Petter Mygland: fig. 2
© 2017 Artists Rights Society (ARS), New York, photo by MOLAB © Munch Museum: fig. 15b
© 2017 Artists Rights Society (ARS), New York, photo © Munch Museum: p. 2, figs. 4, 5, 7, 11, 12, 13, 14b, 14c, 15a, 15c, 17a, 17c, 18b, 18d, 20, 22, 25, 26, 29, 30, 32, pls. 5, 8, 11, 12, 13, 17, 21, 22, 23, 24, 25, 26, 27, 28, 30, 31, 32, 33, 34, 36, 37, 38, 40, 41, 42, 43, 44, 45, 46, 47, 48, 49, 50, 51
© 2017 Artists Rights Society (ARS), New York, digital image © The Museum of Modern Art / Licensed by SCALA / Art Resource, NY: pl. 10
© 2017 Artists Rights Society (ARS), New York. Nasjonalmuseet, Oslo, photo by Børre Høstland: figs. 3, 8, 14a, 16, 18a, 18c, pls. 2, 16
© 2017 Artists Rights Society (ARS), New York. Nasjonalmuseet, Oslo, photo by Jacques Lathion: pls. 6, 35
© 2017 Artists Rights Society (ARS), New York. Private Collection, image © The Metropolitan Museum of Art: pl. 7
© 2017 Artists Rights Society (ARS), New York. Private Collection, photo © Christie's Images / Bridgeman Images: pl. 18
© 2017 Artists Rights Society (ARS), New York. © SMK photo: pl. 3
© 2017 Artists Rights Society (ARS), New York. © Tate, London 2015: pl. 29
© 2017 Artists Rights Society (ARS), New York. From Gerd Woll, *Edvard Munch: Complete Paintings; Catalogue Raisonné*, London, Thames and Hudson, 2009, vol. 1, p. 47: fig. 1
© 2017 Artists Rights Society (ARS), New York / VG Bild-Kunst, Bonn. Nasjonalmuseet, Oslo, photo by Frode Larsen: fig. 28
© 2017 Artists Rights Society (ARS), New York. Von der Heydt-Museum, Wuppertal, photo by Antje Zeis-Loi: pl. 9
© Blauel Gnamm-Artothek: fig. 6
Image courtesy of Katharina Grosse and MoMA PS1, photo by Pablo Enriquez: fig. 34
Courtesy of Harvard Map Collection, Harvard Library: fig. 24
Digital image © The Museum of Modern Art / Licensed by SCALA / Art Resource, NY: fig. 31
Photo © Munch Museum. Munch Museum Archives, Oslo: pp. 129, 130 (top right), 131, 132 (top right)
Photo © Munch Museum. Munch Museum Archives, Oslo, photo by A. F. Johansen: p. 132 (top left)
Photo © Munch Museum. Munch Museum Archives, Oslo, photo by J. Lindegaard: p. 128
Photo © Munch Museum. Munch Museum Archives, Oslo, photo by Martin Munkacsi: p. 133 (bottom left)
Photo © Munch Museum. Munch Museum Archives, Oslo, photo by Rude: p. 130 (bottom left)
Photo © Munch Museum. Munch Museum Archives, Oslo, photo by Ragnvald Væring: fig. 10, p. 133 (top right)
Courtesy of Private Collection / Bridgeman Images: fig. 23